Stephen Channing

THE MARGATE TALES

Published by Ōzaru Books, an imprint of BJ Translations Ltd
Street Acre, Shuart Lane, St Nicholas-at-Wade,
BIRCHINGTON, CT7 0NG, U.K.
www.ozaru.net

First edition published 1 April 2011
Printed by Lightning Source
ISBN: 978-0-9559219-5-7

CONTENTS

1

List of Illustrations

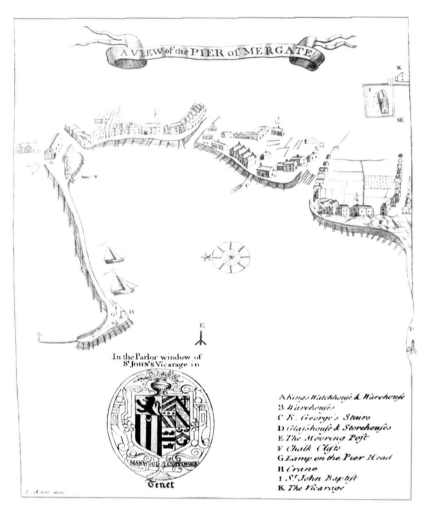

An Early Eighteenth Century map of Margate and its harbour

Custom House Corner in 1779

This is a depiction of Custom House Corner taken from the old pier in 1779. Notice the rough wooden fences that were supposed to protect this area, later known as Cold Harbour or Bankside, some locals called it Little Beach. Today the new Turner Contemporary sits smugly on this spot.

Introduction

Having always had an interest in history, especially local history, I have built up quite a large collection of books, magazines and other articles associated with the past. In 1997 I graduated with a degree in social and economic history from the University of Kent, during which I studied, among other subjects, local history. I found the subject most interesting, and I believe there will always be plenty of hidden material waiting to be uncovered. This became evident while I was researching for information for a dissertation. During the course of my research, I was often distracted by interesting articles unrelated to the pertinent subject.

It was while researching Thanet's farming that a detailed description of early Margate appeared in front of me. What I had stumbled across was a letter sent to an early newspaper recounting the memories of a gentleman called Stewart Viney, who lived and worked in Margate nearly two hundred years ago. His reminiscences of Margate and its many characters were really vibrant, being told in a way that brought old Margate alive to me, with descriptions of people, places and occurrences recounted in a very humorous but highly intelligent manner.

Having no time to pursue these articles, I copied and kept all the interesting stories I stumbled across, including more letters on the subject of Margate by Viney. Then, when time permitted, I set to work researching the archive material at Margate library more methodically, to see whether any more such gems existed. A large proportion of the archive material consists of guides, directories, newspapers, magazines, etc, detailing information not related specifically to Margate. However, every now and then something special would surface and I found many articles, several of which related to people and places I had never previously heard mentioned.

After many months of intermittent searching I had a collection of material that I thought would be of interest to others. Most were small extracts from various sources that pertained specifically to Margate. Having been granted permission to use this material in a book on Margate's history, I set to work gathering further material from newspapers, web sites, my own large collection of antique books and various other sources. Eventually I had enough material for a book of articles, anecdotes, etc offering an insight into how Margate initially developed as a genteel health resort, ultimately catering for countless thousands of people, some less genteel than others. I decided to arrange everything I had found in chronological order so that I could see if a pattern would emerge that would give me some indication of when and why Margate became such a hot spot. I could see many indications of Margate's rise from being a small fishing village with a dilapidated pier, to a resort attracting young and old, rich and poor, the famous and not so famous, the aristocratic and the lowly, many of whom apparently enjoyed the attractions under the guise of a pseudonym.

I could see a combination of factors, both national and local, that whet the appetites of locally based entrepreneurs, encouraging them to capitalise on an opportunity that may never come their way again. Many people believe the catalyst for Margate's rise was Benjamin Beale's invention of the bathing machine in 1753, but the development appears to have started at least twenty-five years prior to his invention. Beale appears to have been one of many entrepreneurs who invested in Margate during a time when Londoners in particular were becoming aware of the health benefits and pleasures to be associated with the sea.

This book is about the people who came to Margate and what they saw. It will give an insight into the type of person who came and what it was that lured them to Margate. It offers the general public access to previously hidden, dispersed or archived material from various sources, which I hope will educate, inform and, primarily, entertain.

The book gives a brief account of Margate in the days before sea bathing fame followed by three main sections, each of which represents a period of significant change within Margate's history. Each section contains collated contemporary material, most of which has been reproduced as originally printed or recorded. I trust the modern reader will appreciate that the terminology used in some of the extracts, which would not today be considered politically correct, was indicative of attitudes at the time, and may be reflected upon to consider how attitudes have changed in today's society.

Profound thanks to Margate Library for allowing me access to their materials, and to Shirley for her great patience in correcting my script.

S.M. Channing

A brief account of Margate in the days before sea bathing fame (1586-1724)

What was Margate like before its rise in popularity as a sea side resort? Up to the early 18th century, the small fishing village of Margate's ideal sheltered location offered a safe harbour for shipping, allowing the harbour to be used for transporting local produce such as grain and fish for the London market, as well as for the exportation of goods to the continent. The malt industry was also significant for the area at this time

The village was also ideally placed for travel to and from Holland, particularly useful after the 'Glorious Revolution' when the Dutch King, later William III, won the English, Scottish, and Irish crowns from his uncle and father-in-law, James II, who was deposed in 1688.

Margate was also a military post, protecting the Channel in times of war and merchant ships from the enemy's privateers. Supplies of ordnance, arms and ammunition were stored here, the military fleet took on supplies of food and water here when the need arose, and the Duke of Marlborough chose Margate for going abroad and landing from his several campaigns.

As time passed, the effects caused by natural changes to Margate's coastline led to the consequent decline in its usefulness as a port, mainly due to the lack of funding that was desperately needed to address the state of the silted-up harbour and dilapidated pier. Margate's harbour could no longer accommodate the larger ships that were needed to keep up with the demand of an ever increasing London populace and the foreign export trade. Diminishing fish harvests, due to the practice of seaweed being harvested for fertiliser destroying the habitats and feeding grounds of the local sea life, had also caused Margate's economy to wane. Fishing and shipping and their related industries, such as the repair of nets, sails, boats, rope making, etc, were all affected by the decline. The traditional way of life, that had lasted for centuries up to the early eighteenth century, a system where families rotated their employment throughout the year by becoming ploughmen, fishermen and then harvesters, had all but disappeared.

However, it could be surmised that, owing to the previous level of activity outlined above, the number of inns, pubs etc would have far exceeded that required by the local population, thus rendering the town particularly prepared for the initial influx of visitors which were to form the basis of its new economy.

Eighteenth century bathing scene

This early depiction of a bathing scene at Margate clearly shows the expression of anticipation on the face of a young lady who is just about to be dunked by the two burly 'Dippers.'

One of the earliest accounts of Margate can be found in Camden's[1] great work Britannia, a topographical and historical survey of all of Great Britain and Ireland. Camden's survey started in 1577, with the first edition appearing in 1586, and included this account of the people of Thanet:

William Camden (1551-1623)

...Neither must I passe over heere in silence that which maketh for the singular praise of the inhabitants of Tenet, those especially which dwell by the roads or harboroughs of Margat, Ramsgat and Broadstear. For they are passing industrious, and as if they were *amphibii*, that is, both land-creatures and sea-creatures, get their living both by sea and land, as one would say, with both these elements: they be fisher-men and plough men, as well husband-men as mariners, and they that hold the plough-taile in earing [tilling] the ground, the same hold the helme in steering the ship. According to the season of the yeare, they knit nets, they fish for cods, herrings, mackarels, &, they saile, and carry foorth merchandise. The same againe dung and mannure their grounds, plough, sow, harrow, reape their corne, and they inne [store] it, men most ready and well apointed both for sea and land, and thus goe they round and keepe a circle in these their labours. Furthermore, whereas that otherwhiles there happen shipwrackes here (for they lie full against the shore those most dangerous flats, shallowes, shelves, and sands so much feared of sailers, which they use to call The Goodwin Sands, The Brakes, The Four-Foots, The Whitdick &., these men are wont to bestir themselves lustily in recovering both ships, men, and marchandise endangered...

(Britannia, William Camden, 1586)

Some 137 years later in 1723, closer to Margate's rise in popularity, John Lewis[2] offers a much more detailed account of Margate:

---

[1] William Camden (1551-1623) was an English antiquarian, historian, and officer of arms, who wrote the first detailed historical account of the reign of Elizabeth I of England.

[2] Rev. John Lewis (1675-1747), Vicar of Margate in Thanet, was an active local antiquarian, and he provides a full account of the Isle of Thanet in his History of Thanet in 1723.

John Lewis (1675-1747)

…It is a small fishing town, irregularly built, and the houses very low, and has formerly been of good repute for the fishing and coasting trade. In 1631, I find a market was kept here, of which a return was made to Dover every month, but this seems not to have continued long, nor does it appear by what authority it was kept at all. On that part of the town which lays next the sea is a pier of timber built east and west in the form of a half moon to defend the bay from the main sea, and make a small harbour for ships of no great burden and for fishing craft. By the present appearance of the chalky rocks on each side of this pier at low water, it would seem as if anciently nature itself had formed a creek or harbour there, the mouth of which was just broad enough to let small vessels go in at. But, as the land on each side of this creek was, in process of time, washed away by the sea, the inhabitants were obliged to build this pier to keep their town from being over flown by the ocean; and to defend that part of it which lays next the water by jetties or piles of timber. This pier was at first but small and went but a little way out into the sea; but the land still continuing to wash away, so that the sea lay more heavily on the back of it than usual, it has been, by degrees, enlarged. At what time this pier was built at first, is now unknown but it is certain that in Queen Elizabeth's reign this pier was maintained by certain rates paid for corn and other merchandise shipped, and landed in it. These rates were confirmed by the Lord Warden of the Cinque Ports, who from time to time has renewed and altered the decrees made by him for the ordering and management of this little harbour…

…As the passage from England to Holland is reckoned the shortest from this place, it has had the honour of being often visited, of late years, by great personages who have gone over thither. Thus, in particular that noble asserter and defender of the rights and liberties of mankind, and particularly of those of Great Britain, King William III of glorious memory often came hither in his way to and from Holland. His present Most Excellent Majesty has twice landed here. Her Royal Highness the Princess of Wales came first on shore at this place and that successful and victorious general the late Duke of Marlborough used to choose this for his place of going abroad, and landing when he went and came to and from the several campaigns he made…

…The trade of this poor town is now very small, and would be considerably less, was it not for its being the market of the whole island, where the inhabitants bring their corn to send it to London by Hoys which go from hence every week. By this trade is the pier and harbour chiefly maintained, according to the rites. The shipping trade (which once was pretty considerable before the harbour was so much washed away by the sea and the ships built too large to lay up here), is now all removed to London, where the few

14

masters who live here lay up victual, and refit their vessels. Malting is another branch of the trade of this place, which was formerly so large that there were about 40 malt-houses in this parish. But this trade is now gone much to decay; though certainly here might be made the best malt in England, the barley which grows here being so very good, and the land naturally so kind for it. The malt, it seems, having formerly been made here had been very coarse for the use of the distillers has now so much lost its credit, that the present masters find little encouragement to make their malt fine for a London market where they are almost sure to be out sold by the Hertfordshire and north-country malt-men, whose malt bears a better name.

About 40 years ago one Mr Prince of this place drove a great trade here in brewing a particular sort of ale, which from its being first brewed at a place called Northdown in this parish went by the name of Northdown ale, and afterwards was called Margate ale. But whether it's owing to the art of brewing this liquor or the dying of the inventor of it, or the humour of the gentry and people altering to the liking the pale north-country ale better, the present brewers vend little or none of what they call by the name of Margate ale, which is a great disadvantage to their trade. The hanging and drying of herrings is of great use to the poor of this town, a great many of whom are employed in the season for them, to wash, salt, spit, and hang them. But this is a trade that would be still more beneficial to the place were these herrings caught by the inhabitants, because there would then be more employment for the poor, many of which here have little to do in spinning and twisting of twine to make nets with, and knitting the nets, &c. But about 40 years ago, the fishery here went so much to decay, that they who depended on it were forced to sell their large boats, or let them run out, so that now the boats in which they fish are so small, that they dare not go far off to sea in them, nor venture out of the pier in a fresh gale of wind.

The fish generally caught here, are whiting (which are often no bigger than smelts[3]), whelks red and white, lobsters, pungers[4], oysters and eels. Of these last I've been told by the old fisher-men such plenty has been caught here formerly, that they used to measure them by the bushel, but for these many years past they have been very scarce. The reason of this, perhaps, may be the

---

[3] The smelt is a sea fish that lives in the coastal waters of Europe, typically 15 to 18 cm long.

[4] A large edible locally caught crab.

15

great use that has of late been made of the sea woore[5] or waure hereabouts, not only in raking up such of it as is cast up by the sea to mix with the dung and lay on the land, but stripping the rocks of it to burn and make kelp, thereby taking away both the harbour and food of these fish, and others of like nature which lay near the shore. Of this I find complaint made to the Lord Warden, 35 year of Elizabeth's reign that by the burning and taking up the sea woore the inhabitants of the island were annoyed in their health and greatly hindered in their fishing. Accordingly a warrant was granted to the deputies of the mayors of Dover and Sandwich to forbid or restrain the burning or taking up of any sea woore within the Isle of Thanet, either by any inhabitant of the said island, or stranger, notwithstanding any licence, grant, &c. granted heretofore by the Lord Warden. It seems owing a good deal to this decay of the fishing here, with the falling off of the foreign trade and the removal of so many of the substantial inhabitants, on that account, from this place to London that the charge of the poor is so much increased within these 80 years past...

...A little above this town of Margate to the northward on the cliff is a small piece of ground called the Fort, which has been a long time put to that use, and was formerly maintained by the deputies here, at the charge of the parish. A large and deep ditch is on the land side of it next the town, which used to be scoured and kept clean of weeds and rubbish. At the entrance into it towards the east was a strong gate which was kept locked to preserve the ordnance, arms, and ammunition here, for here were two brass guns which the parish bought and repaired at their own charge. Here was likewise a watch-house in which men watched with the parishes arms provided for that purpose. In war time this place is still made use of; a gunner is appointed by the government with a salary of £20 per annum and a flag staff erected to hoist a flag upon occasion. There are likewise sent hither from the tower 10 or 12 pieces of ordnance, carriages, &c. with ammunition for them. This provision is not only a safeguard to the town, but a great means of preserving merchants ships, going round the North Foreland into the Downs, from the enemies privateers which often lurk thereabouts to snap up ships sailing that way, which cannot see them behind the land. But as these lurking thieves lay open to the places on the other side of the Foreland, particularly Broadstairs, an account of them is sent to the gunner of this fort or platform who gives notice to the ships sailing that way of their danger, by hoisting a flag and firing a gun...

("The history and antiquities ecclesiastical and civil of the Isle of Tenet in Kent," By John Lewis, 1723)

---

[5] Seaweed.

Daniel Defoe[6], following one of his tours of Great Britain, published the following very brief mention of Margate in 1724:

Daniel Defoe (1659/61-1731)

…till we come to Margate and the North Foreland. The town of Margate is eminent for nothing that I know of, but for King William frequently landing here in his returns from Holland, and for shipping a vast quantity of corn for the London market, most, if not all of it, the product of the Isle of Thanet, in which it stands…

("A tour thro' the whole island of Great Britain," Daniel Defoe, 1724)

Apart from an evident decline in Margate's economy, the above accounts of Margate, by Lewis in 1723 and Defoe in 1724, do not indicate any significant changes to Margate's age old trades since Camden's account 138 years previous. There is no mention of anything to do with sea bathing or any other activity that may have drawn visitors to Margate other than the buying and selling of merchandise, the presence of the military or the odd aristocrat setting off for the continent. It appears that we have to move forward a few more years to see evidence of any marked change in what Margate had to offer that may explain the beginnings of Margate's increase in economic prosperity.

---

[6] Daniel Defoe (ca. 1659-1661 – 1731), born Daniel Foe, was an English writer, journalist, and pamphleteer, who gained fame for his novel 'Robinson Crusoe'. Defoe is also notable for 'A tour thro' the Whole Island of Great Britain' (1724-27), which provided a panoramic survey of British trade on the eve of the Industrial Revolution.

A Time of Opportunity (1724-1735)

By the end of the seventeenth century the perceived health benefits of mineral springs, such as those at Spa in Belgium (1326) and Aachen in Germany (used since Roman times) had led to the opening of many inland Spas around England offering, mainly for the nouveau-riche and aristocracy, 'special' waters purporting to contain magical minerals for the treatment of a multitude of ailments. The Spas also provided various entertainments such as dancing and gambling, as well as a multitude of grand hotels or apartments where many of the unmarried elite mingled and brushed shoulders in the hope of finding a suitable 'match'. Although the practice of sea bathing dates back to Roman times, it became more popular following the establishment of these inland spas at a time when the benefits of salt water, the sun and warmth were also being recognised. The commonly held belief was that naked bathing in cold natural sea water, and the drinking of it, would cure a whole host of ailments. There is plenty of evidence to be found in books written in the early eighteenth century to suggest that bathing in sea water was beneficial to one's health:

One of these unhappy wretches swollen with the dropsy came to me for my advice. I pitying his penniless condition, gave him a note to Mr Baynes of the Cold Bath, to let him bathe gratis; but having the convenience of a Barge or Hoy, he went to the salt water and by often bathing in the sea, he was recovered: and I am since informed by one of his friends that he did not only bath in the sea, but that he drank the salt water also; and telling of this case to Mr Alexander English chirurgeon to a regiment of horse, he told me that he had known several cured by drinking of salt water, even without bathing.

("Psychrolousia." Or the history of cold bathing, both ancient and modern. Sir John Floyer, Edward Baynard, 1715, pp. 373-374)

Plunging over the head, (says Dr Wainwright) in cold, especially sea water, will do a great deal more in the cure of melancholy madness; and particularly that from a mad dog than any other medicine: It is often (says he) successful in a palsy; and they who use it much, are very little affected with the weather. For the truth of this therefore we choose not to refer to instances, where so good a rationale is grounded. By this remedy all the parts of the body will be sensibly affected, constringed and set in motion and very often, from the first resilitive elasticity, the blood is driven with force to the extremest part of the body the general mass quickened and warmed, rendered less viscid and tenacious, the glands scoured, a greater quantity of spirits generated, and moved with greater celerity through the nerves.

("A new treatise on liquors:" wherein the use and abuse of wine, malt-drinks & water etc, James Sedgwick, 1725, pp. 331-332)

Before he quits this subject, Dr Short takes occasion to advise repairing to Scarborough for the convenience of bathing in the sea, and recommends Dr Wainwright's 'Non-naturals,' with Sir John Floyer's and Dr Baynard's 'Treatises on cold bathing,' to the perusal of all who value their health. The effects of the pressure of water on the body, added to that of the air, are, to straighten the vessels and dissolve the humours: to remove any viscid matter adhering to the sides of the vessels: to scour the glands, and render the motion of the fluids more free and easy, increase the quantity of blood in the brain and viscera, &c. From some experiments made on sea-water, it is concluded to be highly alkaline, that it contains a volatile nitre, the particles of which enter the pores of the skin, mix with the subcuticular juices, and are of eminent service in thinning and dissolving thick or fizzy juices, and of no small benefit in provoking urine.

("The Present state of the republick of letters," Printed for W Innys and R Manby, Volume 13, 1734, pp. 32-33)

By the eighteenth century, due to the decline of its age old economy, a need for change was acknowledged. Local families were finding it increasingly difficult to acquire enough employment to meet their basic needs. Margate's transition was almost certainly due to the motivation and inventiveness of a few local entrepreneurs, who capitalised on the growing interest in the benefits of the sea, as will be explained below. These early pioneers were obviously fully aware of the supposed curative or therapeutic values assigned to ordinary sea water, a commodity to which Margate offered easy access and unlimited supplies. Margate's location in a bay that was flat and protected by surrounding natural cliffs and the close proximity of its buildings in relation to the sea margin made it ideal for the practice of sea bathing.

It is known from the writings of previous visitors that Margate was but a poor fishing village up to 1723. It is likely that soon after this date the village had begun its transition. The following evidence suggests that various modes of entertainment at Margate started to manifest themselves, in order to cater for the increasing company that resorted there.

In 1724 the wealthy owners of the ancient seat of Quex in Birchington had started to provide public breakfasts for the upper echelons of society. It was to become a public place where paying guests could eat, dance and enjoy various other entertainments. Quex became very popular because it used to be where kings and other members of the aristocracy had previously stayed while on their way to Holland. It is quite likely that many of the visitors to Quex made trips to other local places of interest, and Margate being one of them, would have prompted local entrepreneurs to cash in on this opportunity.

As can be seen from the following accounts, by 1730 various modes of entertainment were already showing signs that they could not keep up with demand:

> "...Valentine Jewell, junior, who married Mr Abraham Hudson's daughter of Deal, having taken the sign of the White Hart Inn in Margate, Mr Constant and his wife being deceased, this is to give notice that all gentlemen and others will find good entertainment and may be furnished with good horses at reasonable rates..."

(Extracts from the "Kentish Post," Dec 1729)

> "...We hear Mr Dymer's company of comedians go from this city [Canterbury] today for Margate in the Isle of Thanet, where they intend to open on Tuesday next with that diverting comedy called Busie Body, and on Wednesday that celebrated play called June Shorer..."

(Extracts from the "Kentish Post," June 1730)

> "...We hear from Margate that Mr Dymer meets with so great encouragement that notwithstanding the play house is very large it will not contain the company that resort there..."

(Extracts from the "Kentish Post," July 1730)

The above statements suggest that the number of visitors to Margate, by 1730, was already increasing. I do not believe it is too bold to suggest that Margate already had a fair amount of visitors taking the waters. This may have been due to the ever increasing publicity through treatises, newspapers, magazines etc. praising the benefits of drinking and bathing in sea water. That, coupled with Margate's location to large towns and its perfect bay for bathing, would be prime reasons for a gradual increase in visitors. The following chapter confirms that Margate had begun the transition from being 'just a small fishing village' to an up and coming watering place. There follow written accounts of people's personal experiences, both good and bad, while visiting Margate. These visits cover a period of approximately 33 years, ranging from 1736 through to 1769.

Visitors' reports (1736-1769)

It appears that Thomas Barber, a local Quaker, was probably the first person to introduce natural sea-water bathing at Margate within the walls of an establishment that also provided other necessary facilities such as lodgings, food and entertainment. Barber's establishment seems to have evolved on the strength of the increased publicity and much vaunted benefits of drinking or bathing in sea water.

Barber had an inn fronting Margate harbour, called the Black Horse, which was in close proximity to the sea. Women especially were not comfortable with the prospect of bathing naked in public. With this in mind, in 1736 Thomas Barber combined two important things that the public was talking about – one was the desire for privacy and the other safety while bathing in the sea.

Those early eighteenth century sufferers, resorting at Margate in search of cures for debilitating illnesses, would not have been disappointed, the natural surroundings of Margate providing all the ingredients necessary for a spell of convalescence, particularly so after Mr Barber had devised and provided a facility that could not be found anywhere else within easy reach of London and other big towns. It was a facility that was to provide, not only safety, but especially important for women, that all-important aspect of privacy. In short it enabled people to avoid the age old problem of having to run naked into the sea (if physically able to do so) while being watched by a multitude of sightseers. Barber had decided to cut a 15 foot channel from the sea to one of his private rooms, in which he had built a bath big enough for a customer to bathe privately and in comfort.

The following advertisements from the Kentish Post are confirmation of this facility and are the earliest records I could find that advertised such facilities:

Thomas Barber

"…Whereas bathing in sea-water has for several years and by a great number of people been found to be of great service in many chronic cases, but for want of a convenient and private

22

bathing place, many of both sexes have not cared to expose themselves to the open air: this is to inform all persons that Thomas Barber, a carpenter at Margate in the Isle of Thanet, hath lately made a very convenient bath, into which the sea water runs through a canal about 15 foot long. You descend into the bath from a private room adjoining to it. N.B. There are in the same house convenient lodgings to be let..."

("The Kentish Post, or Canterbury News Letter," 17th July 1736)

The following year Thomas Barber advertised again and it is evident that sea bathing had quickly become popular:

"...His bath [Thomas Barber], which was advertised last year [and which was] not large enough for the number of people which came there to bathe in the sea water [there has now been built] another bath much larger and more commodious, so contrived, that there is a sufficient quantity of water to bathe in it at any time of the tide... [there are also] lodging rooms, dressing rooms and a handsome large sashed dining room [including] a summer house which affords a pleasant prospect out to sea..."

("The Kentish Post, or Canterbury News Letter," 27th April 1737)

Once again, this time in 1740, Thomas Barber found it necessary to advertise his premises, after it was found that many people may have been deterred from visiting, believing that his sea bath was exposed to the open air:

"...As a great many gentlemen and ladies have been deterred from coming to Mr Barber's sea water bath at Margate, by thinking it was exposed to the open air; I have therefore thought it necessary to inform the public that it is quite enclosed and covered by a handsome dining room and that there is a neat dressing room and dresses adjoining to the bath, and as the house fronts the sea there is a most delightful prospect and the number of people that have received benefit from bathing sufficiently demonstrates its usefulness. N.B there are good lodgings and entertainment at my house which adjoins to the bath and a good coach house and stabling..."

("The Kentish Post, or Canterbury News Letter," 14-17 May 1740)

The above advertising over the years 1736-1740 shows how the popularity of sea bathing in private had grown since Barber's first advert in 1736, offering bathing and just lodgings. In 1737 he advertises larger baths, lodging rooms, dressing rooms, dining room and a summer house and lastly in 1740 he offers all the above plus entertainment, a coach house and stabling. In fact Barber could not keep up with demand, despite expanding his business every year until he died in 1753.

It was not long before an independent writer was to advocate the benefits of bathing in sea water at Margate and no doubt this would have boosted the town's popularity considerably:

Margate in 1742

"...The shore from Whitstable and the East Swale affords nothing remarkable but sea-marks, and small towns on the coast, till we came to Margate, noted for King William's frequently landing here in his returns from Holland, and for shipping a vast quantity of corn for the London market, most, if not all of it, the product of the Isle of Thanet in which it stands. There is lately erected here a salt-water bath, which has performed great cures in nervous and paralytic cases, and in numbness of the limbs; and seems every day to become more and more in request..."

("A tour through the whole island of Great Britain," By Daniel Defoe, with additions by a gentleman, 3rd Ed, Vol. 1, 1742, p. 159)

Thomas Barber's wife continued business after his death and in 1753 advertises the facilities of what could have been Margate's first ever assembly room:

("The Kentish Post," 1753)

The Parade at Margate

The above is a wonderfully detailed picture of Margate's harbour area in the 1770s. On the left is one of the old Hoys, behind which is the old iron bridge that crossed the stream coming down from Bridge Street (King Street today). The Black Horse Inn, later renamed the New Inn and finally the York Hotel, is the large building in the centre of the picture, with the pediment. On the right one can see an early bathing machine, like Benjamin Beale's.

Moving forward to Margate in 1755, nineteen years after Thomas Barber set up business, this account displays clearly that sea bathing had come a long way very quickly with the appearance of bathing machines, apparently invented by Benjamin Beale a few years before:

...The diversions used by the country gentlemen are shooting, setting, and hunting. The country people amuse themselves with cricket. The people in this parish depend much on fishing, sending out many vessels in the season to catch mackerel for the London market and in the herring season both for London and to dry and hang them. They also send other boats with skate, thorn-backs, whiting, soles, plaice, dabs and lobsters to London. Some go to Newfoundland on the cod fishing and get home in time to get in the harvest. They are generally robust and healthy and though some parts of the island are aguish it is seldom fatal. This parish lying high is less subject to that distemper. They are excellent sailors.

Of late years since the physicians of London have in several cases proscribed drinking and bathing in salt water the town of Margate has been much frequented on that account as the shore is flat and sandy, and in order to accommodate the bathers they have built a sort of covered wagon which they drive into the sea till the water is about breast high, at the tail of which is a ladder to let down a screen which lets down close to the water so that those who bathe are screened from being seen though they generally bathe in a flannel shift. The ladies have a guide who goes down first and holds them by the hand while they dip under water. The rate of bathing for 6 weeks is £1. 1s for the season, if by the week 4s, paying the guide for every attendance 1s. The machine has benches to sit down on and will contain 5 or 6 people in which they dress and undress…

("MS, Account of Margate 1755, written in 1757," Margate library, pp. 28-29)

A Benjamin Beale bathing machine

It was not long before an eminent doctor would stand up, despite opposition, and publicly support the benefits of the sea. In 1755, Dr. Richard Russell[7] published "The economy of nature in acute and chronical diseases of the glands" and recommended the use of sea water for healing various diseases. Then William Buchan in his 1769 book "Domestic Medicine" also supported the practice and at first, bathing in sea water during the winter months was considered to be the best time to follow the practice.

The following extract by Richard Russell, which was published in 1755, may have been compiled earlier. Many later writers of the period have said that Benjamin Beale's bathing machine was introduced in 1753. Was Mr Russell describing what was happening at Margate or elsewhere? Russell refers to a 'Bathing Chariot' – could it have been one of Benjamin Beale's machines?

Of Sea Bathing

…Sea bathing is another remedy, which may be traced up to great antiquity. Homer makes Diomede and Ulysses use sea bathing to cleanse off their sweat, and strengthen their nerves, after they had brought the spoils of Dolon on shipboard, to dedicate them to Minerva…

…the early use, which different nations of the world made of this purifying remedy: but as this little essay is intended to show, in what cases it may be useful, or hurtful, I have chose to confine myself to the observations I have made upon sea bathing myself, and what has been mentioned by others…

…I distinguish sea bathing into general, and topical; by the former I mean, when the whole body is immersed; by the latter, when sea water is applied to some particular part of the body only. We will begin with the consideration of the first: and that naturally suggests the situation of the place; which, I think, should be clean and neat, at some distance from the opening of a river; that the water may be as highly loaded with sea salt, and the other riches of the ocean, as possible, and not weakened by the mixing of fresh water with its waves. In the next place, one would choose the shore to be sandy and flat; for

---

[7] Richard Russell (1687-1759) was an eighteenth century British physician who encouraged his patients to use a form of water therapy that involved the submersion or bathing in, and drinking of seawater.

the convenience of going into the sea in a bathing chariot. And lastly, that the sea shore should be bounded by lively cliffs and downs; to add to the cheerfulness of the place, and give the person that has bathed an opportunity of mounting on horseback dry and clean; to pursue such exercises as maybe advised by his physician, after he comes out of the bath.

The situation of the place being premised; as to what regards the patient, and his entering upon sea bathing, if he be an invalid, he should not attempt it without advising with some skilful person; as this remedy, like others, may be misapplied. And as all cold bathing acts upon the body according to the coldness or temperature of the bath, so the physician should direct, not only at what period of his disease it is proper, but how long the patient is to remain in the bath; what is to be done at his coming out; and at what time of the day he should enter it. By which means the physician may direct different temperatures of the bath, according to the constitution of his patient. For as the sea is never equally cold with cold spring bathing, so in proportion as the sun grows higher, it becomes still warmer; and you may have the benefit of the temperate bath, with the addition of the salts of the sea…

("The Economy of Nature in Acute and Chronical Diseases of the Glands," Richard Russell, 1755, pp. 212-213)

The extract below refers to a statement made by Benjamin Beale's widow, mentioning 'a covered cart' which appears to pre-date her husband's invention of the hooded bathing machine in 1753. I have been unable to ascertain if this apparent precursor to Beale's machine was sited at Margate.

The precursor to Beale's Hooded Bathing Machine at Margate?

…Margate was the birthplace of the bathing-machine. There seems to be no reason to dispute the claim of Benjamin Beale, a Margate Quaker, to be the originator of these amphibious houses which have contributed so much of the gaiety of nations. Fame was all he got by his ingenuity, for he ruined himself in his attempt to popularise his invention. His successors reaped the harvest. Old Benjamin Beale's widow used to talk in her last days about the covered cart in which visitors were driven into the sea before the bathing machine arrived with its frontal hood. From Margate the bathing machine quickly spread to other resorts. We hear of it at Scarborough and Brighton. Probably the first mention of it in standard literature is to be found in Smollett's 'Humphrey Clinker[8],' where it will be remembered that Humphrey's master, Matt Bramble, bathed from a machine, and was promptly dragged out of the water by his alarmed and faithful servant...

(T Ps Magazine, "The Seaside, Past and Present", edited by T P O' Connor, Vol. 11., No. 11, August 1911)

The following contains an illustration of an early bathing machine. The hood appears to have been copied from Benjamin Beale's Margate invention in 1753, but as this book was printed 7 years later, in 1760, it may not be exactly the same.

Bathing Machine 1760

This is the season for bathing in the sea, I present you with a drawing and description of a very commodious bathing machine used in diverse parts of England but not known here. It consists of a dressing room, A. about seven feet high, and as much square, the sides G panelled with thin deal and the roof, A. covered with painted canvas. The umbrella B. C. D. forms a private bath ten feet long, and gives liberty to such of the male-sex (as choose) to swim, or walk out from under it.

It is made of canvas stretched with iron rods C. C. C. C. which turn upon swivels, the lowermost forming an oblong square, D is a rope which runs thro' the ends of the rods, whereby the whole may be drawn up or let down by a person in the dressing room at pleasure. E the sides of the bath, also made of canvas, which, by means of weights, fall perpendicular into the water. At the end F is the door into the dressing room, there is another at H, with steps to descend into the bath. The whole machine is drawn in and out of the water by means of a running tackle or rope drawn thro' two pulleys fixed to two posts, one on the shore, and the other in the water.

---

[8] "The expedition of Humphrey Clinker," by Tobias George Smollett, 1771.

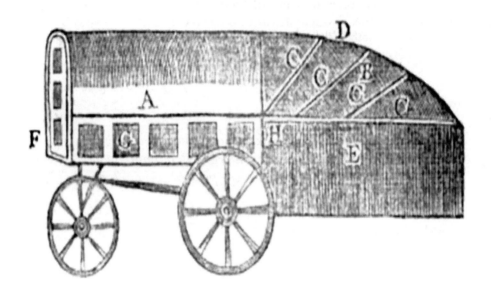

A bathing machine of 1760

The inside of the English machine are furnished with seats, a table and glass. The principal use of the umbrella, or tent, is for the fair sex, many of whom suffer greatly by the wet garments they bathe in, chilling their bodies to a great degree, before they can get dry clothes on. Besides, by these wet clothes adhering close to the skin, all kinds of perspiration is for a time stopped, which has given many persons violent colds and other complaints, as prejudicial to health as those they came to bathe for. To avoid these inconveniences the women in England, by means of this machine, can go into the water without any covering on their bodies; and the moment they ascend out of the sea, the dressing room affords a very commodious place, both for dry-nibbing and putting on their clothes. In short, its use is so very apparent, that it is to be wished several of them may be soon set up at all our bathing places near this city. The room and umbrella may be made for a trifle, the wheels of an old carriage will serve to place it upon and a small gratuity from each lady will soon fully recompense the owner for his charge and trouble.

C S

("The Gentleman's and London magazine," Monthly Chronologer for Ireland, Vol. 29, 1760, p. 345)

The following is just an extract from the first proper guide of Margate to be issued. The guide contains a wealth of other information. There is mention of building works in Margate, suggesting the need for more accommodation to satisfy the growth in visitor numbers.

Margate Guide of 1763

...As the passage from England to Holland is reckoned the shortest from this place, it has often been visited of late years by great personages who have gone over thither; particularly King William [III] often came hither in his way to and from Holland; King George I landed twice here and George II once; the late Queen Caroline with the young Princesses landed and lay here when they first came to England; and the great Duke of Marlborough generally chose this for his place of embarking and landing when he went to and returned from his campaigns.

The lodgings, tho' small are neat and tolerably commodious considering that they are now applied to the reception of strangers, for which purpose they were never originally intended. Some good houses have been built within a few years and others are building. The old ones daily receive all the improvements they are capable of.

Provisions are good but in general dear. Large quantities of fish are taken, the finest of which fetch a good price and the rest are sold cheap enough...

...The principal house of entertainment is the New Inn, kept by Mitchener. The accommodation of it, with respect to neatness and good entertainment, can hardly fail to recommend it. Here is likewise a coffee house as well as other Inns and public houses, in one of which is a fine new billiard table with a very neat apparatus. The bathing rooms are not large but convenient. Here the company often wait for their turn of bathing. The guides attend, sea water is drunk, the ladies dresses are taken notice of and all business of the like kind is managed. There are three of these rooms which employ eleven machines till near the time of high water, which, at the ebb of tide, sometimes run two or three hundred yards into the bay. The sands are so safe and clean and every convenience for bathing is carried to so great perfection that it is no wonder this place should be frequented by such multitudes of people, who go into the sea either for health or pleasure.

As the most useful machine employed for this purpose is the original contrivance of Benjamin Beale, a Quaker, he has undeniably the right of a first claimant to the reward of his ingenuity...

...I do not think myself a proper judge of the efficacy of sea bathing, having never had occasion to consider it but as an amusement. I will, however, venture to say, that in all cases where bathing can be of service, this must be at least equal to any other; and in all disorders of the skin, or where the complaints are external, infinitely superior. Its salutary effects are daily experienced in the rheumatism and in scorbutic and scrophulous habits; nor is it found that patients are more liable to a relapse who have been cured by this method than any other medicines. Nevertheless, it must sometimes happen, from the injudicious use of it, that the sick will go away disappointed of the relief they expected to have received.

Two physicians usually reside here during the summer season.

Here is a boarding school for young ladies, kept in a very decent reputable manner; and another where young gentlemen are taught arithmetic, mathematics, &c. so that gentlemen may now bring down their children for the benefit of the sea without losing time in their education.

As Margate is only a large village you cannot expect that it should be so regularly supplied with shops as a market town; not but that there are several good ones and many very reputable tradesmen. This deficiency is, in a great measure, supplied by the numerous articles to be found in most of them and by their ready and quick communication with London by the Hoys.

Was it not for the assistance of these vessels it would be almost impossible for Margate, and the country round it, to furnish entertainment for the vast numbers of people who resort to it. They are sloops of eighty or a hundred tons burden. There are four of them, two of which sail in alternate weeks...

...Passengers, of whom there are often sixty or seventy, pay 2s. 6d. and the freight of baggage is inconsiderable. They sometimes make the passage in eight hours and at others in two or three days, just as winds and tides happen to be for or against them. The best wind down W.N.W, the best up E.S.E. The Hoy, like the grave, confounds all distinctions, high and low, rich and poor, sick and sound are here indiscriminately blended together. It can be no wonder, if the humours of such a motley crew, of all ages, tempers and dispositions, should, now and then, strike out such scenes, as must beggar every description but the pencil of Hogarth[9]. Upon the whole the passage is

---

[9] William Hogarth (1697-1764), British painter, engraver, pictorial satirist and cartoonist.

32

cheap and in fine weather extremely pleasant and agreeable but I would not recommend it too strongly to ladies of great delicacy...

...The Assembly Room is a part of the New Inn; it stands on the Parade and commands a fine view of the harbour and roads. This prospect is exceedingly pleasant especially when it happens that a large fleet is lying there, waiting for spring tides to carry them up the river. This room, without any pretensions to magnificence is perfectly neat and commodious, being seventy feet in length and twenty in breadth with a gallery for music. Public breakfastings have not been usual, probably, because they would interfere too much with the hours of bathing. Eighteen or twenty couples dance very conveniently. On card assemblies there are generally eight or ten tables and at other times seldom less than four or five. There are two card rooms adjoining but they are seldom used as such, except on the nights of dancing assemblies...

...We have a play house where a company of comedians from Canterbury perform three times in the week. If you expect to see great elegance in the house, scenes, and decorations, or any extraordinary degree of theatrical merit in the actors you may be disappointed...

("Margate Guide, Description of the Isle of Thanet and particularly of the town of Margate," 1763)

Subscriptions and rates for Mitchener's Assembly Room, Margate 1763

	s.	d.
Subscription to the room for the season		
To each gentleman or lady	5	0
Dancing Assembly on Monday night (tea inclusive)		
Each subscriber, gentleman or lady	2	6
Each non-subscriber	5	0
Cards Assembly on Thursday night, whist, &c. each table	6	0
Lottery-table	12	0
Each non-subscriber for admission (tea included)	1	0
Breakfasting		
To subscribers	0	8
To non-subscribers	1	0
Tea in the afternoon		
To subscribers	0	6
To non-subscribers	1	0
Coffee Room		
Subscribers for the coffee room, to each gentleman for newspapers, extra post, pens, and paper	2	6
At The New Inn, the prices of provisions &c. are as follows:		
Each person		
Bread, cheese, or butter	0	1
Welsh rabbit	0	2
Beef steaks, veal cutlets, mutton or pork chops	0	9
Veal or beef collops	1	0
Tripe boiled or fried	0	9
Ditto in fricassee	1	0
Eggs and bacon	0	9
Cold meat	0	8
Servant breakfast, dinner or supper	0	6
Breakfast, tea, coffee, &c.	0	8
Pigeon roasted or boiled	0	8
Ditto boiled with bacon and greens	1	0
Ditto stewed	1	0

Chicken or fowl roasted or boiled	2	0
Ditto boiled with mushroom sauce	2	6
Ditto white or brown fricassee	2	6
Ditto roasted with egg sauce	2	6
Ditto boiled with bacon and greens	3	0
Duck roasted	2	0
Ditto with onion sauce	2	6
Capon roasted or boiled	3	0
Turkey roasted with sauces, &c.	5	0
Ditto boiled with oyster or lemon sauce	5	0
Goose roasted with sauces, &c.	5	0
Wild duck and dressing	2	6
Teal and dressing	1	6
Woodcock and dressing	2	6
Eels and dressing, by the pound	1	6
Trout and dressing, by the pound	2	0
Cray fish by the hundred	6	0
Ditto buttered	8	0
Other fish as it shall be in season at a reasonable price		
Rabbit roasted or fried	1	6
Ditto smothered with onions	2	0
Neck of mutton with onions	3	6
Ditto roasted	2	6
Ditto in chops	2	6
Shoulder of mutton and dressing	3	6
Leg of mutton and dressing	4	0

All other joints of beef, veal, pork, &c. at six pence by the pound dressed.

Made dishes, soups, puddings, tarts, fruits, asparagus, pease, beans, potatoes, greens, cucumbers, pickles, &c. as they come in season at reasonable prices.

Wines &c. as usual.

Explanation of the structure of the machine

Mitchener's bathing room and machines

A. The bathing room to the steps of which machine B is driven with its umbrella drawn up.

C. back view of the machine showing its steps and the folding doors which open into a bath of eight feet by thirteen feet, formed by the fall of the umbrella.

D. The machine, as used in bathing, with its umbrella down.

The entrance into the machine is through a door at the back of the driver, who sits on a movable bench and raises or lets fall the umbrella by means of a line which runs along the top of the machine and is fastened to a pin over the door. This line is guided by a piece of wood of three foot in length, which projects, pointing a little downwards, from the top of the back part of the machine, through which it passes in a sloping direction. To the end of this piece is suspended a cord for the bather to lay hold on if he wants support. The umbrella is formed of light canvas spread on four hoops. The height of each of which is seven feet and each is eight feet wide at its axis. The last hoop falls to a horizontal level with its axis from whence descends the curtain. The piece which supports the hoops is about six feet in length; they are fastened to the bottom of the machine but are extended by a small curve about one foot

36

wider than the body of it on each side. The hoops move in grooves in these pieces. The distance of the axis of the first hoop is more than two feet from the machine; of the rest from each other something more than one foot; but no great exactness is required in these proportions as scarce any two of them are built alike.

Ship spotting!

One of the most popular hobbies at Margate was ship spotting – a widely practiced pastime enjoyed mainly by gentlemen and known to keep the circulation in good order!

An advertisement in 1762

Margate in Kent is esteemed by far the most commodious place for bathing in the sea. John Mitchener from Rochester, for the accommodation of the nobility, gentry and others, has taken and greatly improved the New Inn and Assembly Room at Margate; and in order to make it more convenient and agreeable, both as an Inn and Assembly Room, he has provided the best sorts of liquors, the finest teas, sugars, &c. a good larder and man cook from London. And as he has already completed the improvements of his house &c.

he flatters himself he shall now accommodate the gentlemen and ladies, who shall favour him with their company in such a manner as to merit the honour of their approbation and encouragement, who am their most obedient servant, John Mitchener.

N.B. Not withstanding all ill-natured reports to the contrary, the harbour of Margate is free from all obstructions as usual. The machines and machine houses are fitted up with a decent repair, the Parade much more commodious, and the people in general health.

("The London Chronicle," May 15th 1762, p. 466)

Information concerning this very early period of Margate's sea-bathing history is scarce and most of which I have been fortunate enough to find came in the form of verse. The following mentions the vision one is met with when admiring the "beauties" of the sea in 1760!

"OF THE LADIES BATHING IN THE SEA AT MARGATE"

That from the sea, the bards of old have sung,
Venus, the Queen of love and beauty, sprung;
That on its curling waves the amorous tide,
Safe wafted her to shore, in all its pride;
Soft pleasure revelled thro' the Cyprian grove,
And gladdened nature hailed the Queen of love.
Knowing it false, charmed with the pleasing tale,
We praise the fiction being told so well.

But when on Margate sands, the British fair
Safe in the flood the curling surges dare;
When here so many queens of love are seen,
Bathe in the waves, and wanton in the main;
We justly, Margate, bless thy happier shore,
And bid the fabling poets lye no more;
In madness they their fancied Venus drew;
Of these we feel the power, and know it true.

No more then, poets, in romantic strain,
One Venus call, when here so many reign;
No more invoke her from her Cyprian grove,
But henceforth Margate be the seat of love.

("Notes and Queries" Vol. 8, 3rd S. (191), Aug 26 1865, P. 178)

A cluster of Venuses!

This following verse was written in 1760 by Edward Thurlow, 1st Baron Thurlow, PC (1731-1806). He was a British lawyer and Tory politician who served as Lord Chancellor of Great Britain for fourteen years and under four Prime Ministers. This early mention of Margate and bathing machines is useful especially as it mentions Surflen's room and Surflen's machine. Surflen was, no doubt, a competitor to Benjamin Beale. Miss K. L---- was Kitty Lynch daughter of John Lynch, Dean of Canterbury. Kitty's mother was the daughter of Archbishop Wake

According to an article in Notes and Queries (Vol. 10, 2nd S., 1860), Edward Thurlow was known in his youth to have written amatory verses, and paid attentions to Miss Lynch. The affair ended in the seduction of the young lady, apparently under promise of marriage. Kitty was later taken ill while travelling to London and died after apparently refusing all nourishment. One of her sisters married Sir William Hanham, of Dean's Court, Dorset.

VENUS FOUND

To Miss K. L----
The very first day that to Margate I came,
I saw with delight the fair Cyprian dame;
It was Venus I'm sure, for I well know her face,
I remember the day, and can point out the place.

It was August the 12th, in the morning at eight,
On a Friday – you see I'm exact in the date:
The place, Surflen's room, and in Surflen's machine,
For Venus at Surflen's has always been seen;
The beauties of Margate have ever bathed there,
There is Douglas the mild, there was Ecklin the fair.

Next morning I sought her, but sought her in vain;
The next, too, I came – disappointed again!
The bath-rooms and ball-rooms I daily went round,
Not at bath nor at ball could my Venus be found.

Ah cruel, said I, when a votary comes,
To fly, lovely Queen, from the bath and the rooms!
But heedless alike of my search and concern,
She vanished, and tidings I could never learn,
Till Sunday the last, by good fortune I went
To the capital city of fertile Kent,

Where I found her, I found her: I know your blue eyes,
Dear Goddess, I cried, tho you take this disguise,
And I easily guess why you chose to assume,
Lovely L----'s fair form, meaning face, and sweet bloom.

You're right, said young Cupid, I told her the cause,
Was more notice to gain, and to win more applause,
For I heard her, one day, by dread Styx stoutly swear,
That Kitty excelled her in beauty by far.

("Gentlemans Magazine," Vol. XXXII. P. 495)

'Hazardous Row'

The above is an early illustration of what was locally known as Hazardous Row because of its unsightly buildings with their precarious looking verandas perched on the edge of the old Jetties (shored up cliffs). These were the back doors to the bathing rooms that ran from the bottom end of the High Street by the harbour right up to near the Kings Head pub.

Moving on from sea bathing, Venuses etc, the extract below records a rare occurrence in Margate:

An Earthquake at Margate

Account of the earthquake, felt February 18 [1756], along the coast of England, between Margate and Dover, in a letter from Mr Samuel Warren, supervisor of excise, to John Windham Bowyer, Esq; one of His Majesty's Commissioners of Excise. Communicated by John Pringle.

"I have made inquiry, as therein directed, relating to a shock of an earthquake, which happened on Wednesday the 18th Of

41

February last [1756]; and find, that at Margate it was felt by Mr Valentine Jewell and his family just before eight o'clock in the morning: they being all in their beds, each person observed their respective beds to have a sudden shock, as quick as thought itself. Mr Barber, who lives at the King's Head Inn, and next door to Mr Jewell, at the same time, felt his bed to tremble for the space of half a minute; his wife (who was in child-bed at that time) and her nurse felt the like trembling in another room, and Mr Barber's mother (who keeps the said inn) saw the door of her room to shake, which she thought then to have been caused by the wind; and in like manner it was felt by many other people in Margate. I cannot find that it was felt by any person in Ramsgate. At Deal, Dr St Leger, being in bed on the 18th a little before eight o'clock in the morning, felt the bed to shake under him, which he supposed to be a sudden gust of wind, till he heard other people talk of an earthquake, which they then imagined to be the cause of their beds shaking."

("Philosophical transactions, giving some account of the present," Volume 49, By Royal Society (Gran Bretaña), 1757, p. 579)

Margate harbour in 1805, ten years before the arrival of the steamboats

Within this poem, by an anonymous writer, are some clues as to what Margate was like – no doubt, of course, written by someone from the upper echelons of society!

Occasioned by a lady condemning our choice [editor] of Margate for a place of entertainment.

Happiness Everywhere

Tho' detestable the place;
Mean the lodgings, small and base:
Tho' the crowded Hoy pours forth
Company of little worth:
Coach or chariot, tho' there's none
Rattling thro' the fishing town:
Yet Maria, yet my fair,
Happiness shall find us here.
Happiness our friend shall be;
Ubiquarian Deity!
There's the rapture! In the mind
Dwells the goddess, unconsigned:
Place she scorns; delighted best,
When enthroned within the breast!
Ha – Maria – then I've found
Whence it comes that I am crowned
With such sweet serenity
When accompanied by thee!
Thou thyself art happiness
From thy constant aim to bless,
From thy studious zeal to please,
Cheerful, amiable ease,
Smiling brow and gentle tongue,
I have known, and felt it long;
And I must, I must be blest,
For thou reignest in my breast.
Whether then upon the strand,
Arm in arm we wandering stand,
And the world of waters see,
Dread creator, full of thee;
Whether on the sands we rove,
And talk of Clemantine's love,
Dropping for the pious fair
Now and then a tender tear;
Whether o'er the fertile isle,
Pleasing rides our time beguile;

Whether to rooms we stray,
Bright assemblage of the gay,
Where in social converse joined,
Mirth exhilarates the mind;
Every scene shall sure supply,
An exuberance of joy;
For our constant friend shall be,
Heart enthroned felicity,
There's the rapture – thus, my fair,
Happiness is everywhere.

("The Gentleman's Magazine," Volume 32, By John Nichols, 1762, p.430)

The editor of the magazine which published this poem goes on to say:

This is supposed to have come from the fair objector, but in reality it is far from the truth; since the company is very agreeable, and the carriages and horses so numerous, that there is not room for either.

The above poem from 1762 (or possibly before), has given us an opportunity to picture an early scene at Margate. The writer has started the poem with a negative description of Margate by saying that it is a:

"...detestable place, mean the lodgings, small and base..."

On reflection, if this had been the writer's first visit to the town after having possibly spent many seasons at well established inland Spas, Margate in the early 1760s would have appeared somewhat grim in comparison. The writer then goes on to say:

"...Tho' the crowded Hoy pours forth, company of little worth..."

She appears to be appalled at the influx of lower orders disgorging from the hoys then being allowed to mix with families of her standing. Lastly, she mentions:

"...rattling thro' the fishing town..."

From this description it appears that around the harbour area the herring hangs, boat builder's yards and fisherwomen were carrying on

*with their traditional way of life. The newer society buildings were
being erected around the area which would later be known as Cecil
Square. Further on in the poem the writer says:*

> "…Whether to rooms we stray,
> Bright assemblage of the gay…"

*Depending on the exact date of the poem being written, the writer may
have been referring to the Assembly Rooms at the Black Horse Inn, on
the parade opposite Margate harbour, which was run by old Mrs
Barber in the 1750s, or its successor the New Inn. The Black Horse was
improved and renamed the New Inn in 1761 by John Mitchener of
Rochester, and it retained this name until 1793 when it became the
York Hotel.*

John Mitchener's business card of 1762

*Notice the card above advertises packet boats for Ostend and Dunkirk.
I should imagine that once visitors had experienced the trip to Margate
from London by Hoy the last thing that they would have been
considering would be a trip across the channel to the continent!*

On the clergy's bathing in a Quaker's machine

By a zealous daughter of the church

Tho' the Quakers, poor souls, conscience struck, will not pay,
To the men clad in black, who for foul lucre pray,
And piously suffer for tithes sore vexation,
Yet our good clergy here (men of much moderation)
To win Benjamin over ('tis wife you must own,
And bespeak well the candour befitting the gown)
From Dun and from Surflin church-brethren flee,
That the Quaker may throw them all into the sea,
Which he sure can do cheapest, for he pays them no fee

(The Gentleman's Magazine, Vol. XXX, 1760, p. 432)

No Man's Land, Margate

The picture above shows an island of chalk called No Man's Land. This was what was left in the late eighteenth century of a much larger outcrop of land that in ancient times used to reach out as far as the small boat on the left. It used to protect Margate's harbour

and its small fishing community from the many great storms that battered the coastlines. Its erosion resulted in a good deal of storm damage to Margate's old town and its pier. Today there is no visible evidence of No Man's Land's existence

Margate in 1764

Margate, or St John's, situated on the north side of the island, is a member of the town and port of Dover, to which it is subject in all matters of civil jurisdiction. The principal street is near a mile in length and built on an easy descent, by which means the upper part is clean and dry but the lower end much otherwise. It is difficult to determine at what time Margate pier was first built; but as, since the inning of the level on the south side of this island, the sea has borne harder on the east and north sides, so that the land on each side of the creek was, in process of time, quite washed away by the sea, the inhabitants were obliged to build a pier, to prevent their town from being over flown. This pier was at first but small, and went but a little way from the land; but the cliffs still continuing to wash away, it has been by degrees enlarged to what it now is. This pier is maintained and preserved by certain rates or payments, called Droits, for all goods and commodities shipped or landed.

It is usual to walk for some time after bathing. The places most frequented for this purpose are the Parade, the Fort, and the Rope Walk. When the tide is ebbed, many persons go on the sands, to collect pebbles, shells, sea-weeds, &c. which, although of no great value, are esteemed as matters of curiosity by those to whom such objects have not been familiar. These sands extend for some miles along the shore, quite smooth and dry at low water, and may be passed with safety six hours in the day. Here are those venerable monuments of antiquity, the Banks of Hacken-Down, or Field of Battle-Axes. There are two tumuli or barrows, of earth, the tombs of some of the chief officers killed in a bloody battle fought on this spot between the Saxons, English, and the Danes, in the reign of King Ethelwolf, in the year 853. In the light house, which is a strong octagon building of flint, on an eminence near the cliff on the point of the North Foreland, a fire of coals is kept blazing all night on the top of it for the direction of mariners. As parties resort thither for dining, tea, &c, two booths are built for their reception and attendance is given by the light-keeper.

("The Beauties of England:" or, a comprehensive view of the antiquities of this, Philip Luckombe, 1764, pp. 86-87)

Caves in the chalk cliffs near Margate harbour

The above shows the caves that existed in the early eighteenth century before erosion by sea and high winds caused them to collapse, leaving behind the island called No Man's Land.

Below is a clear description of the devastation caused by a violent storm in 1767 that not only severely damaged much of Margate's seafront and its properties, but it ruined Benjamin Beale as well.

Violent Gale (Isle of Thanet, January 6th 1767)

A violent gale of wind at N W brought on a most furious tide, which bore down everything within its reach. The pier at Margate has suffered damage estimated at £1000. The jetties are almost everywhere much damaged and in many places quite destroyed. The coach road leading to the Parade is almost entirely washed away. The houses on the Parade were thought to be in such immediate danger that the inhabitants removed all their most valuable effects. The low buildings between Hall's Library and the sea are all swept off. Beale's new castle in the air, contiguous to them, shared, in part, the same fate; fortunately it was not so far finished as to be inhabited. The Brooks are again all under water. Great loss and damage has been suffered by many private people. The whole is a scene of the greatest desolation and confusion.

("The Gentleman's Magazine," Sylvanus Urban, Vol. 37, 1767, pp. 23-24)

During the mid-eighteenth century Benjamin Beale had played a major role in the development of Margate as a seaside resort, but two terrible storms in the early 1760s had cost him dearly. A further devastating storm in 1767 finished him off and left him penniless. Sadly, Benjamin Beale died a broken man in 1775 at the age of 58 and he was buried at Draper's Hospital in St Peter's Road, Margate.

Benjamin Beale's Demise – 1767

In the late storm at Margate on the 2nd January 1767 (according to the opinion of some of the inhabitants) the foundation of the building mentioned in the papers by the name of 'Beale's Castle in the Air,' was a great means of preventing a part of the road and several houses being washed away.

Benjamin Beale who, by the invention of the bathing machine &c, has been a principle cause of introducing much company to Margate by this erection, has likewise (under providence) been of great service in the deliverance of a most useful part of the town from destruction. Yet, such has been the consequence of that catastrophe that it may now be said of him, with great propriety, he who was instrumental in helping many, is unable to help himself. Therefore, by the advice and desire of some gentlemen of character and fortune, his case is hereby recommended to the attention of those who may be inclined to assist him in his distress. He has suffered three times by storms, in 1763 his loss was computed at £500, and it was greatly increased by being obliged to sell the principal part of his possessions at a disadvantage. In 1764 he suffered again, but still he laboured to acquire a living by his application and industry, till the late dreadful storm, which has entirely disappointed his hopes of subsistence for himself and wife (though both past the meridian of life) by any other means than by manual labour, unless his case should merit the attention of the humane and benevolent.

His whole loss, on a moderate computation, has been about £1000, a heavy affliction to one who it is very well known was ever studious to serve and give satisfaction to his employers, whose aims in life have been moderate and conducted with the strictest integrity; and his attempts, though unsuccessful to himself, have been beneficial to the public.

Sir John Shaw, Bart, of Harley Street, Cavendish Square; and Dr Hawley, of Great Russell Street (who have long known Mr Beale) have given leave that their names may be made use of on this occasion, they believing the facts as of above stated to be true. Donations for the benefit of Benjamin Beale will be received at Mr Newbury's, bookseller, in St Paul's Church-yard; at Lloyd's Coffee-house, Lombard Street; George's Coffee-house, near Temple-Bar; and at the Salopean Coffee-house, near Charing Cross.

(From a London Paper, April 6th 1767, Margate library collection)

Rise of a Resort (1770-1814)

From the 1730s there was a need to improve the existing buildings in Margate so as to cater for the increasing numbers of wealthy visitors in search of a sea-water cure. By the 1760s it became necessary to start building new modern accommodation at Margate on a scale that had never been seen there before, and it soon became evident that no matter how many properties were being built, when they were finished they soon became crammed with visitors.

It is clearly apparent that from the outset of Margate's rise from being a simple fishing village in about 1723 to a large popular watering place in the 1760s, the town could not keep up with the demand. According to the many writers of the period Margate's proprietors were struggling to cater for the thousands of tourists that flocked down in the Hoys from London every year. By the late 1750s and early 1760s, entrepreneurs like Benjamin Beale, Philpot, Crow, Surflen, and others had established bathing rooms and bathing machines along the bottom stretch of the High Street. At the same time investors from outside Margate with ample funds, like Mitchener, Hall, Silver and Cecil joined in the struggle to meet demand. But once again, even these very wealthy investors in Margate, who financed the building of grand squares with grand houses containing Assembly Rooms, Hotels, Libraries etc., could not, according to the following stories, keep up with demand.

We now reach another epoch in Margate's history as a watering place. By 1770 Margate boasted a fantastic new square, Cecil Square, built in 1769 by a gentleman of that name, in conjunction with Sir John Shaw and Sir Edward Hales. This brought to Margate a taste of London with its grand squares and fine Georgian facades. There was now a magnificent Hotel and Assembly Room, with a wonderful elegant ballroom, which catered for the more elite of Margate's company. It seems that Margate had now become so popular that major investors were queuing up at the door, but all this brought with it other forms of entertainment, the type of entertainment that often undermines the gentility of a place.

Like all new places that evolve when there is money to be spent, Margate appears to have attracted the 'lower orders' of society. With that comes all manner of parasitical elements ready to cheat, steal or cajole the unsuspecting of his hard earned holiday money. This chapter brings together what was being said about Margate after forty years or so of its initial development as a resort. The changes that took place in Margate created a mixture of cockney ribaldry and high society idealism, ultimately a potent cocktail. Some visitors can be likened to the characters in one of Shakespeare's plays 'As You Like It' where 'all the world's a stage.' Margate was a melting pot from which emerged unclassified characters whose temporary anonymity allowed them to mingle and socialise with those outside their usual station in life.

It was not long before the antics at Margate caught the eye of moralists and humorists. Some saw Margate as a den of depravation and degradation, whereas the majority of visitors believed it to be a place where one could throw off the stuffiness and social conformity which was generally a prerequisite in a world of 'knowing one's place' or not being allowed to 'rise above one's station.' Margate became the ideal location where high society and low society, rich and poor, good and bad, famous and nameless could become whoever they wanted to be for a week or so. This will have created a multitude of characters that really did not fit any recognisable mould. Resorts like Margate and the type of character that frequented it were to start cropping up all around England's coast. The famous artist J M W Turner is a prime example of such a character, becoming Mr Booth or Admiral Booth to the locals when at Margate because, some say, Turner was having a clandestine affair with Mrs Sophia Booth, a lodging-house keeper who was twenty-four years his junior.

What follows in this chapter is a collection of writings, some sad, some funny, some angry, and some unlikely. Nonetheless these contemporary writers offer us an insight into the people and events which began to shape Margate into a thriving holiday resort.

An early description of Margate in 1771

Margate is become in great repute of late years, on account of the number of people who resort thither to bathe in the salt water... ...During the summer season this town is full of all sorts of people, whose circumstances will permit them to spend money, and whose health requires bathing for its support. There is a large street above half a mile in length, wherein are some good houses let in lodgings, by which considerable sums are spent in the town; and since the beginning of the present year (1771) several pieces of ground have been let on building leases, and they are now erecting handsome houses to accommodate the company.

Margate High Street in the mid-eighteenth century

This mid-eighteenth century water colour of Margate High Street portrays a kind of village appeal, with its old buildings with small front gardens enclosed by little wooden fences. Notice the masts and sails of the old Hoys anchored in the harbour in the distance.

The water in the harbour is extremely shallow so that ships of great burden cannot get in, although it is constantly crowded with boats carrying different sorts of goods, besides passengers to London. The place has all the appearance of gaiety, during the bathing season, and two or more physicians generally attend in the way of their profession. They have invented carriages for conveying the patients into the sea, and they are constructed in such a manner as to sink down, by which they form themselves into a bath, and rise up again without any danger to the patient. In the year 1763, during the dreadful storm on this coast, the sea overflowed the pier, and threw down the guns mounted for the defence of the harbour, but that loss was soon made good. Margate has neither market, nor fair, and is distant from London 73 miles.

("The Complete English Traveller," or a new survey and description of England, Nathaniel Spencer, 1772, p. 163)

This letter, written in 1771, offers a description of the afflictions suffered by those visiting Margate for the benefits of drinking and bathing in the sea water. It indicates just how busy and popular Margate was by this time.

Margate by an anonymous writer

...I am not quite sure, though, that it may at all times be safe to indulge in these strand walks [along Margate sea front] alone and unarmed; for when the tide is about three fourths in, I have seen the porpoises, which are very common here, often sporting so near the shore, that with half the spring of a salmon leap, they might snap off my head, as I stand on the beach. Whether, indeed, these sea-hogs would eat a man, as the land ones will devour a child, I cannot pronounce, for I have looked into Chamber's Dictionary, and cannot find the word porpoise there, or even any synonym for such an animal.

I go constantly into the sea, here, in my own defence – it is seldom that what is wholesome happens to be pleasant also; but this sultry season renders it both, at present. I am struck with a further sentiment, too, under this regimen – I never come out of the water but I am sensible of a greater love and esteem for myself, than when I went in – whether this be owing to the brisker circulation of the blood, upon such occasion, which, by raising my spirits, may have a natural tendency towards elevating my vanity and affections along with them; or that I may be apt to flatter myself with a better interest in my life and health, upon every immersion, I cannot say.

There is one very extraordinary particular, which superiorly distinguishes this place from any other of the bathing resorts I have ever seen. Everywhere else the female guides, or dippers, as they are called, are a pack of coarse, vulgar, dirty, ragged, oyster wenches, disgusting to sight, touch, and smell.

A Margate beauty

Here they are perfect nereids[10], the very hand maids of Venus, the Anadyomene[11], rendering this Isle of Thanet the fabled Cyprian one. On my word, most of the mermaids of this coast are the handsomest young women I have yet seen here. The habits too they officiate in, are remarkably neat and clean – simplex munditiis[12], verily – and when they retire from their occupations, about noon, they dress themselves out in so genteel

---

[10] In Greek mythology, the Nereids are sea nymphs, the fifty daughters of Nereus and Doris. They often accompany Poseidon and are always friendly and helpful towards sailors fighting perilous storms.

[11] Venus Anadyomene ("Venus Rising From the Sea") was one of the iconic representations of Aphrodite, made famous in a much-admired painting by Apelles.

[12] Simple, in neat attire, not gaudy.

a manner, that they appear on the walks, no other wise to be distinguished from ladies of the best fashion here, than by being taller, better made, handsomer, and of fairer and more florid complexions.

This last circumstance, I own, surprised me, at first, as a sea faring life is apt rather to give a coarser grain, and browner tint to the skin – but the awnings of these bathing machines being let down into the water, screen them from the homely effects of sun and wind; and the element itself seems otherwise of advantage to them, as their hands and arms appear to preserve a plumpness and softness in them, seldom met with in women of so mean and laborious a class of life.

Maidens frolicking at Margate

I observed a singular object in the water t' other morning: – A man issued from a neighbouring machine with a large cabbage leaf in his left hand – accoutred as he was he plunged in, while I stood still, to see what sort of application was to be made of his skimmer – had it been in a lady's hand, I should have supposed it to be a fig-leaf – but I found he only used it as a parasol, to shade his face from being sun-burnt, while he was taking the exercise of swimming; making his stroke with one hand, and guarding his complexion with the other like, and unlike, Caesar saving his commentaries but rather more resembling Pompey's effeminate troops at Pharfalia, which on hearing the word Ferifaciem[13] given, turned their backs to save their faces. This same macaroni[14] swimmer is a fat old gentleman, who has lived a bachelor till his grand climacteric, and with as fair a complexion as any lady in the land, which has hitherto been preserved, I presume, by such like unmanly attentions as this – his limbs, however, are so affected with the gout, that taking him all together, another simile here occurs, of comparing him to Lord Ogleby (a character in The Clandestine Marriage, a comedy by Garrick and Colman), or Lord Chalkstone (In Lethe, a farce by Garrick), which you know is the same thing. This place is grown extremely full, lodgings are risen cent per cent within a week. One would fancy the whole world was here, if one did not hear of other worlds at Southampton, Tunbridge, and a hundred other places...

...But though I cannot supply you with positive character, I can give you an account of negative ones; by mentioning a thing which has given me great disgust here. As soon as the music strikes up for country dances, all the young fellows sit down to loo, with their aunts and grandmothers, or to whist, among themselves; and the young women are left standing on the floor, staring at one another; while a parcel of school boys and boarding school girls hop a cotillion[15] together – and so ends the ball. The natural species of mankind seems to be quite extinct

---

[13] Ferifaciem: During the battle with Caesar, Pompey's inexperienced men could not parry or endure the blows on their faces, but turned their backs and fled with great dishonour.

[14] An eighteenth century British dandy who imitated continental fashions.

[15] The cotillion is a type of patterned social dance that originated in France in the 18th century.

among us, at present – the men and women are metamorphosed into gentlemen and ladies, and the boys and girls transmogrified – I chose the word – into masters and misses…

…I shall soon quit this charming scene, having already received every kind of benefit from it that I came to look for. To drink the water, and to bathe in it, is not enough, alone. The sea itself requires exercise, to preserve its health; and so, indeed, do all the elements – the air, the earth, the fire, need stirring, as well as the water – rest is the death of nature.

("A Physical, Poetical and Classical Account of the Isle of Thanet," Samuel Silver, Margate, 1781, Extracts from letters written by an anonymous author in 1773)

A Margate Macaroni of 1772

In this article the writer appears to be accusing those of a high station of using illness as an excuse for coming to Margate. Once at Margate, these so called 'unfortunates' appear to have engaged in alternative pursuits, doing everything but taking the waters for health reasons. It was not long before more affluent commoners began making the journey, again citing health reasons, thus lowering the status that Margate had enjoyed as a place for genteel people.

Margate in 1773

Being a harlequin of fashion, I left London for this place. Ah! (Said I, leaning over Mrs Fiddes's bow window, in view of the promenade), that it would come to this. What pity (continued I still very moral) that mankind, instead of endeavouring to lessen the number of their real evils, would industriously be increasing the catalogue of them by adding fictitious ones. This Margate is said to be a place of health and they are sick people who are said to visit it, yet of all the crowd who now range before my eye, how few know for what purpose they are come. How few are come for any purpose at all.

One would think (continued I, growing still graver), that the human heart sometimes felt that the human mind sometimes thought; that human kind were not at all times asses. Yet it is the case, one would think, that the experience of yesterday might admonish them today; that the lessons of to-day might be a sharp comment upon the morrow. Yet it is not the case. The experience of yesterday, and of to-day, and of every day, serves only to this purpose; it becomes a load upon our backs, and, to drop or forget the burden, we plunge into new pursuits.

At the least, this same scheme of exoneration is but a sorry one. If, in walking upon yon narrow and clogged path between the two hedges, in my way to yonder style, a thorn pricks me in the foot, my skin is lacerated by brambles, or a serpent winds himself round my ankle; if all or any of these misfortunes, befall me there, the devil's in it if I walk there again tomorrow, or in any villainous place like it. Shall I not, think you, make all the speed I can to yon smooth and level way, which gradually ascends the hill without tiring me; where no thorn will prick me, no bramble lacerate, and no serpent wind round my ankle? – 'Tis a case in point. If, in steering my pathless way over this dreadful ocean which extends itself before my window, I unwittingly wander along the rocks and sands off the North Foreland, endanger my life, and escape only with a very hard struggle, if this misfortune befalls me, shall I not in my next voyage bear far off it as from a hostile shore? Or shall I, to avoid the sands on my right hand, plunge into those on the left, after the example of those good folks who are now walking in my view? If I do, I deserve to be drowned indeed. This also is a case in point.

Fashion! (I still went on) you motley devil, this is all your fault. It is owing to you that these poor people have sweated themselves down hither from the metropolis; it is owing to you that many of them know not for what purpose they are come, and many have come for no purpose at all. Indeed I am not surprised King Cloten[16] was unhappily subject to various diseases. He was once seized with the yellow jaundice. The rapidity with which this disease became fashionable was astonishing. In a trice, not a person was seen at court without the yellow jaundice.

The Assembly Rooms at Silver's Grand Circulating Library, in the eighteenth century.

King Cloten was next seized with the palsy. The palsy was equally destructive among his courtiers. You could not turn a corner without seeing a paralytic, shaking, nodding, and enfeebled. The court was like the court of disease, and the poor king stood in the midst of his courtiers like the king of death.

There was no end to this sickly fashion. As usual, with the other fashions it descended from the court to the commonality; and the king had the

---

[16] Cloten (who reigned in the 7th century) was the king of Dyfed and Brycheiniog in Southern Wales.

melancholy reflection to make, that he had infected his whole kingdom with diseases. It is impossible to tell where this would have ended, had not the king published a declaration, commanding all his subjects to be well again, on pain of his using them ill; and he at the same time threatened, that the first of his subjects who should report himself to be ailing with any of the fashionable diseases, should be sent for to court, and be bled, blistered, and purged into good health again in his own presence.

These were the doings of fashion yet what were these to her other doings? Does no one remember the story of the virgin Queen Rodeluna? She mounted the throne chaste as Dian, and continued so almost three whole months. She was the wonder and admiration of her subjects, who called her the star of modesty, the sun of chastity, &c. &c. It was a very little time after this, alas, when the sun of chastity became pregnant. It was now that fashion displayed her power and the subjects of Rodeluna their good manners; for in a very little time all the young ladies about the court became pregnant too. It was the era of pleasure and joy. It was difficult to walk among so many big bellies; and in a very little time it so fell out, that there was not a virgin in the whole land.

What folly! (Continued I, still moralizing), what madness that we should be the slaves of this same whimsical goddess fashion! That we should wear her ever-changing livery, and suffer her to make what things of us she pleases, that we should have reason, yet use it not; that we should have taste, yet gratify it not; that we should be assiduous to please others rather than ourselves.

Having thus displayed the power of fashion, what wonder is it that she shakes her sceptre over the good company who visit Margate, led by their whimsical and thriftless imaginations! But let us hear them speak for themselves. I left my window, and taking my wooden sword in my hand walked down among the crowd. It was a young lady whom I first touched with my all-powerful and enchanting weapon. "Fair lady" (said I gently), "why comest thou hither?" She replied that it was in consequence of reading a receipt in the family medicine-book which assured her that salt-water was good for – whitening the teeth. Having such bad success with the young, I tried the old reverend lady (said I, touching Mrs Fidders, who has remained at her fortieth year since 1751), "I wish to know the purpose of your journey to Margate." "You do" (replied she, tossing her grey head in my face), "why, what do you think it should be but to dance cotillions?" – I left her.

Who the deuce is yon little gentleman, who sails, up the walk, so placid and so smirking? – Bless me, can it be – It is, by all that's witty and prim it is Colman himself. "Ah! My sincere and excellent friend, *comment vous va?*

61

Surprised – *you* at Margate? – The last person in the world – Why, I left you but Sunday evening in Richmond Gardens! In the name of the muses, what are you doing here so unexpectedly?" – "I am come to get a character" – "A character! – I marvel not at it Mr Colman, for you have long wanted one" – "Not very long 'tis but a month." – "I greatly mistake, or it is much longer since you lost the one you had." – "Pshaw!" (Replied the bard) "you do not know what I mean. The character I want is for my new comedy – an original character – and the company having evacuated the metropolis, I have followed them hither to pick one up among the crowd." – "Oh – now I understand you; and methinks, since you are on the spot, it would not be amiss to carry home some salt also for the seasoning of it, as it is said your comedies have been wonderfully insipid and tasteless since you left Garrick."

I thought it was time to finish my experiments. Three persons were examined: the first visited Margate to get white teeth, the second to dance cotillions, and the third to pick up an original character!

("The London Magazine," or, Gentleman's Monthly Intelligencer, Volume 42, Isaac Kimber, Edward Kimber, 1773, pp 368-369)

The following poem, from 1775, gives us an early insight into what it was like to use the bathing machines at Margate. The young girl, called Flora, had experienced first hand what it was like to bathe in the sea, with an unexpected 'dipper' in waiting! In the sixth verse of this poem the writer mentions Cadogan (1771-1797), an 18th Century physician and writer on childcare and nursing.

Cadogan advocated simplicity in child rearing, including encouraging children to run in the open air with bare feet, light and simple clothing, breastfeeding for at least a year and conversing with them in an adult manner. This regime was said to improve children's health and mind and encourage their intellect. Cadogan claimed that aristocratic children were suffocated with regimented demands, excess clothing and too much food while poor children grew stronger under harsher conditions. In 1764 he published a contentious book on gout, in which he blamed the condition on intemperate living. Many visitors to Margate had gout and, ironically, Cadogan himself suffered from it.

An Invitation to Margate (1775)

The day now opens with a morning fair,
And Speller's boarder's to the sea repair;
With heavy hearts and sleepy heads they go,
Seeming to care not, if they bathed or no.
But now inevitable they see their fate
On that unerring record, Surflen's slate.
"Now" cries the Doctor, learned in bathing laws,
"Ye willing bathers come and take your clothes."
"Dear boasting Doctor! Though you seem so stout
No willing bather comes more willing out."

See – slow and thoughtful, they approach the block
And summon all their courage for the shock;
Among the rest, the tender Flora goes
Watching the sea, as up the steps it flows,
"Indeed I cannot, cannot bathe," she cries;
Then from the steps in timid haste she flies:
And now returning with reluctant pace
Pale horror pictured in her beauteous face,
Sees not the smiling guide in ambush lay;
Ah! Now she seizes on her trembling prey.
Vain are her weak attempts herself to save,
Deep she emerges in the briny wave.

But now she rises, sees her danger o'er,
Affects to laugh at what she feared before:
Wishes to bathe again – pretends to spurn,
At woman's fears, – tomorrow shall she learn
That with their cause the same effects return,
So the rough sailor when he's safe on shore,
Forgets the dangers he escaped before;
But when again at sea, the thoughtless elf
Dreads the impending storm and wonders at himself.
Thus are our passions with exactness weighed,
As hope arises, all our fears are laid:
As either passion weakens in the scale,
In just proportion the other shall prevail.

The clock strikes nine, now Speller's boarders meeting,
With smirking faces bow – each other greeting:
And now the Doctor having drunk salt water,
The girls affect to wonder what he's after.
Nor roll nor tea he values of a farthing,
But quits them both for Speller's pleasant garden.
Breakfast now over – how they pass their time,
How some write prose, and others wretched rhyme!
How various minds to various parts resort,
How some the rooms prefer and some the fort.

"...Then from the steps in timid haste she flies..."

All this, and more than this, in verse I'd bring,
If writing verses was an easy thing:
If as of old the muses would indite,
And poets need learn nothing – but to write.
Was this the case, old volumes I'd rehearse,
Philosophy I'd teach – and all in verse.
But now, alas! Should poets never write;
But when capricious muses will indite:
In helpless expectation wait their leisure
To dictate sentiment and rhyme and measure;
Longing for lines those fickle jades have made,
Starved must our poets be, and lost their trade.

Hark! How Cadogan speaks – he tells ye truth:
Hear him ye sensualist – old age – youth.
Ye Margate bathers, and ye drinkers too,
Would ye my plan of health in truth pursue,
Would ye a trial to the waters give,
Mark me ye eaters! – be temperate and live.
Ye pampered wretches who from London came,
Ye murderers of yourselves, ye sick and lame;
Ye traitors to your king, and this lost nation,
Curst with that load of life – a complication!

In tavern luxuries no longer stay,
This reason calls you, reason points the way;
Eastward direct thy steps – but do it with care
To explore the clearest way to Diggs's Square:
A boarding house there is, well known of yore,
Speller's 'tis now, was Diggs's heretofore.
From me she learns her culinary art,
Cooks by my book – has every page by heart.
Your health her study, temperance all her aim,
No flaming gravies e'er from Speller came,
Nor turtle feasts, nor soups, nor hot chyan,
Shall e'er beguile you from my temperate plan.

Variety! – Of health the greatest bane,
No Margate boarders must of this complain.
Old England's staple here is often seen,

65

Two legs of mutton boiled – a neck between.
Feeding too much on these I heard her say
She thought it best to take one leg away:
And since, I'm told – to give a further check,
In spite of hungry looks – she's moved the neck.
No longer stay,
Ye invalids that can, I allure you,
She shall cure you,
And finish what I began.

("Gentleman's Monthly Intelligencer," Volume 44, Isaac Kimber, Edward Kimber, 1775, pp. 206-207)

Letters of Momus[17]

From its early days as a resort offering the opportunity of bathing in sea water in specially built baths, i.e. from around 1735, Margate had been catering for a genteel company who sincerely wanted a cure for their various ailments. Some 20-25 years later Margate had changed from a prestigious location providing unrivalled benefits as a 'health resort' to a watering place that offered much more! Over that same period people from various walks of life visited Margate with expectations exceeding the usual offerings generally provided by a developing tourist attraction. Extra lodgings were being built every day, entertainment establishments were increasing, and a vast amount of local produce was needed to sustain such a growth. Like many other places where money is in abundance, many discrete establishments appeared to provide for the more sordid indulgences of the visitors!

The following letters by Momus were sent in 1777 to the St James Chronicle for publication, in order to reveal the scandal, degradation and depravation among the various classes of people who often clandestinely visited Margate for its lurid offerings. No one has identified the writer of these letters but the general consensus appears to be that he was a wealthy moralist who, it seems, was from the highest ranks of writers and poets, in Margate for his health. In some of his letters he blatantly, but cruelly, describes the unsightly looks of the women that stay and live in Margate, often describing them with a venomous tongue that could only have humiliated them in public. Notables are also publicly condemned after Momus revealed the real reasons for their visits. In one statement he says of Margate and the 'gentlemen' who visit:

"The whim it has now taken is to prefer raw-boned, scraggy, but very young girls. There is a sickness in the glutted and

---

[17] Momus, or Momos, was in Greek mythology the god of satire, mockery, censure, writers and poets. He was a spirit of evil-spirited blame and unfair criticism.

debauched stomachs of our gentlemen, which will take in nothing but chickens from the eggshell, ducklings, and green geese."

Besides disclosing the debauchery that apparently went on behind closed doors at Margate, Momus also suggested that the libraries were used not for reading but to smuggle contraband goods.

One outraged reader of the St James Chronicle said in a letter to the paper:

"…Public characters indeed are public prey, and vice and folly may be instantly chastised by the satirist; but even then, great delicacy is required, and a Pope or a Horace is a literary phenomenon. But, instead of a probe, or a lancet, this writer, like a butcher, employs a pole-axe, or a cleaver, with which he knocks down indiscriminately all he meets, no private characters escape him and the innocent and virtuous are ridiculed alike…"

From Margate

The editor of these papers has collected them [the letters] from the St James Chronicle; into which the author seems to have negligently thrown them. The spirit and designs with which they seem to have been written appear to be commendable; and the letters highly deserving the little trouble and expense of snatching them from oblivion. They hold up very salutary lessons on the motley groups which crowd our bathing places; and it were well, if men of genius and talents would employ their leisure hours like our author, in restraining the vices and follies of such places; in chastising opulent insolence; and awing the licentious into apparent decency.

Every enquiry for the author at the printer's, &c. has hitherto been in vain. He must therefore excuse the editor for paying him the compliment of asking leave, as well as for some little liberties which have been taken in correcting errors evidently occasioned by haste.

In 1777 Momus wrote the following letters:

Letter I

Sir,

It is become the fashion of your correspondents among other people of fashion and fortune, to resort in the summer to the bathing places. I have been at this place a few days; and I mean to amuse myself, and perhaps your readers, with anything material which may occur to me. Places, like persons, necessarily assume a character, and individuals in a place are like qualities in an individual; they have the same effect, and they combine in the same manner to form the general character. The company at Brighthelmstone [Brighton] consists of persons who are analogous to the qualities of a man of fashion; pride of birth and rank, united with ignorance and knavery; expense without taste; dissipation without pleasure; freedom without politeness, and gallantry without love, are the qualities which give a character of fashion to Brighthelmstone. Margate is furnished with dispositions of a humbler cast; such as might enter into the composition of a country squire, or rather a city alderman. Pride of riches united with sufficient ignorance, expense and dissipation without taste or pleasure; reserve and distance without importance and dignity; and a very little debauchery, gallantry or love.

I have fixed on this as the place where to spend the remainder of my summer. I go to the rooms, where an insipid, and almost a fashionable, dullness prevails, in order to indulge my humour for contemplation. This is seldom interrupted, unless it be by some peculiar manoeuvre of the Master of the Ceremonies who has a strange predilection for haberdashers, mantilla-makers, and milliners, and takes every opportunity of setting them above the wife or daughter of a merchant who hath left off trade; or a quack doctor; or a dentist; or a Lincoln's-Inn lawyer; or a doctor in divinity, or a member of parliament. This sets the whole room, like Cox's museum, in motion, and I have an opportunity of seeing the mechanism and structure of all its particular parts.

I may send you an account of the principal figures, when I have taken them accurately.

A ray of hope dawned on us last week and promised those of us, who knew not what to do with themselves, or what to think about, something to wonder and talk of for some time. In the anxious and corroding silence of the card room an invalid coughed in a note like that of a pig; the astonishment it occasioned made the man ashamed to own his infirmity. Some referred it to evil spirits, and the clergy were desired to go home for their prayer books or to speak Latin, which they declined; and being reduced to difficulties, they started the supposition that the noise was made by a ventriloquist. When this word was explained, the curiosity of the ladies was infinite, to know how the sound was emitted; the place was alive with expectations of wonders from this performer – but neither the sound, nor the author of it, was ever heard of more.

The playhouse is much on the plan of your theatres in London, and in another letter I may give you an account of our Margate Roscius[18] As Roscius's are now springing up like mushrooms, you may let Mr Garrick know from me (and I am sure he will take my word) that his reputation and fame is full as much in danger of being eclipsed by the Margate Roscius as by any other Roscius whatsoever. You will think so when I describe him. As an instance of the manager's judgement, which I desire you will communicate to Mr Colman, even before your paper goes to the press, I must tell you that the playhouse is built over a stable, in order to give a peculiar effect to that striking part in Richard the Third, where he calls out 'A horse, a horse – a kingdom for a horse.' I cannot describe to you the amazing effect produced by the peculiar manner of the actor, and the combustion among the grooms and horses. I mean to write a tragedy on the story of Darius's horse to pay a principal attention to this circumstance, as you do in London to closets, trap doors, and screens and to bring it on at Margate.

---

[18] Quintus Roscius Gallus (ca. 126-62 BC) was a Roman actor.

Letter II

Church Field at Margate, September 6th

Sir,

I have given, in my first letter, only a general description of this place. English benevolence will not be satisfied with general descriptions. It is become so prevailing and powerful a principal in all ranks and conditions, as almost to border on vice, and to become love of scandal. No man now liveth for himself; and almost all his anxiety and concern is for his neighbours. Hence that disposition, not only to pry into the secrets of families, and the wily intrigues of love, while the busy world is in town, but that insatiable curiosity to know how they are employed in the country, and the manner in which they recruit their constitutions, and exercise, and whet up their passions and appetites for future business. While this principal is kept within the bounds of innocence and decency, the St James's Chronicle will be its instrument; when it becomes ribaldry and scandal, there may be other dirty vehicles better suited for its conveyance.

I mean, therefore, in describing Margate, to tell as much truth as I can come at; and where I am left to imagination, contrary to the common rule of writers, to suppose only good. The law, before it decides on paltry property, or on a miserable life, requires positive proofs. Scandal, to decide on reputation, which is dearer than any property, or any life, always gives its most important and fatal decisions from appearances and suppositions. There may be intrigues, and sentimental friendships, and even attachments forming here, but I have yet no evidence of them; and I had rather let two guilty persons escape, than be the means of bringing one innocent and amiable person to infamy and wretchedness.

You must know then Sir, that this place as a place of amusement, consists of a large hotel, containing an assembly

71

room &c. &c. and boarding houses, lodgings, circulating libraries, and male and female coffee houses.

No man of fortune is ever taught to live; and what is called the art of living is truly a method of killing time. I accept anyone who may have risen to the capacity of gambling. If gaming be not a virtue, or an amusement, it requires talents and attention: we have therefore not many who game. Bathing, sauntering, raffling, reading the play bills in the newspapers; giving the appearance of intrigue and love to a tête-à-tête on dogs and cats, and caps and feathers, and getting ready to stare at one another, and to create a general and inarticulate clatter at the rooms in the evening, is our general employment.

Before I come to persons, let me describe to you the places we occupy. The building, which contains the rooms, &c. is upon a large, simple and elegant plan; but so slight that it looks like a temporary one, and wants the necessary appearance of solidity and weight. The business of it, in its various branches, is well conducted, not excepting that of Master of Ceremonies, whose only fault may be charged upon nature. Every man has not Nash's[19] intuitive faculty of discerning the various gradations in the tinges of patrician and plebian blood. Nash was a Welshman, and a Welshman is generally ignorant of every thing but blood. I could furnish Mr Walker[20] with a principle in this manner: 'men and women as they approach to quality (and we have not many people of high fashion here), move further and further from that point of true decency and politeness which are to be found only in middle life. The two extremes of very rich and very poor are equally indecent and vulgar, and are only differently dressed.'

---

[19] Beau Nash (1674-1762), born Richard Nash, was a celebrated dandy and leader of fashion in 18th-century Britain. He is best remembered as the Master of Ceremonies at the spa town of Bath.

[20] Mr Walker was Margate's Master of Ceremonies.

The lodgings here are on the footing of lodgings in other places; but the boarding houses are mostly kept by maidens, verily and truly such, I believe in my conscience. The reason of this I take to be – that as a family mingled by chance, like Epicurus's jumble, is apt to generate unions, nothing can so effectually guard against improper ones, as the daily and nightly watchings of a maiden, verging towards the vale of hopelessness. Excepting this circumstance, many of those houses are on a good footing: that which I now inhabit is in what they call the Church Field: the house itself, and its situation, are charming, and the lady who presides in it, is of an attentive and accommodating disposition.

These boarding houses, besides many other conveniences, produce a peculiar species of gallantry which is truly innocent, and is amusing to those who have cool and dispassionate hearts. There is general ambition of being noticed and admired, and a comical contention among the ladies to obtain sentimental attendants in their walks; danglers at their pleasure; apparent or real admirers and partners at the rooms. This furnishes a good deal of bustle and business, and keeps the houses alive. I have tried to enter into these matters as far as my infirmities would permit; and I have one day gallanted a simpering girl, narrowly watched by her mother; and the next exchanged her for a widow, who has stood the business of many seasons; whom I might take anywhere without danger; and kiss to eternity without stirring a particle of her blood.

The only circumstance, besides a scarcity of books, that distinguishes the circulating libraries is, that the shops are made use of to raffle and smuggle and not to read.

The female coffee houses do not furnish, as they might, their share to our amusement. We want some fair disciples of Mrs Millar, who would lead the way in giving tea, attracting the gentlemen by articulate and intelligible conversation, and daring to sit in company with pretty eyes, sometimes fixed on a book or a paper.

Letter III

Margate, September 13th

Sir,

The company here is divided, as usual, into people of fashion; people of fortune and of genteel professions; and a rabble, consisting, as it may happen, of rich and poor.

Those few who have birth and rank to value themselves upon, being in general destitute of other claims to respect, shut themselves up, on the principles of eastern princes, that familiarity may breed contempt; and that to be often seen is to be despised. Instead therefore of resorting to a good set of rooms, and assisting to give spirits and elegance to our public amusements, they crowd together in select parties in small apartments, and wholly separate themselves from the company. The consequence of this is that our gentry, legitimate and illegitimate, take their place, and affect the airs of fashion. Demi-reps [21] recently made honest women; equivocal appearances, who may be wives or may be mistresses, run into the first stations, and are on a level with the lady of a country gentleman, or of that peculiar species of beings in London who are made gentlemen by a legacy or a lottery ticket. These persons giving themselves the airs of fashion, and keeping aloof in the rooms; the dances, &c. are thrown into the hands of a rabble; and, in spite of the genius, taste, and authority of the Master of the Ceremonies, are the strangest scenes of confusion and even blackguardism, you have ever beheld.

The ladies, as usual, contend for that delusive and fatal object – public admiration; and put in their claims to it by beauty and dress. But the taste for those accomplishments is capricious; and they are often cruelly obliged to accommodate themselves to its variations. The whim it has now taken is to prefer raw-boned, scraggy, but very young girls. There is a sickness in the glutted

---

[21] Demi-rep, a woman of bad repute, especially a prostitute.

and debauched stomachs of our gentlemen, which will take in nothing but chickens from the eggshell, ducklings, and green geese. In this article we are in the fashion at Margate. The present toast of our wretched beaus is a Mrs R---- formed on the model of Scotch beauty, with large ill-set limbs, a long waist, high cheek bones and the vermilion of her countenance and her lips tinged with yellow: but she is very young, very fair, wears her hair very oddly, and is admired; while the real beauties of the place, with faces formed on the truly female model, animated with intelligence, modesty, and love, are neglected and overlooked.

There are others who would be attended to, but cannot obtain attention. Among these is a very remarkable character; Mrs Coniac, widow of a brandy merchant, whose usual place of residence and scandal is Kensington. This comely, staring, assured woman had liked to have had the reputation of an affair with me. She often darted her fierce looks at me with what she deemed familiarity; brushed me in passing; whispered in my hearing, that her husband had been a low bred, provoking, disgusting fumbler; and would have bullied me into some notice of her, if on my first approach I had not been deterred by her breath; which a poet would say, is like a zephyr loaded with the fumes of a distillery, and by a cadaverous exhalation from her skin, which very offensively put me in mind of mortality, consulted my friend Churchill on the cause of this phenomenon; and Churchill for once philosophised. I found that the same cause which gave a fierce fieriness to her features, and a peculiar malignity to her tattle and scandal, was the habit of tasting her late husband's commodities; which had fixed on her a disorder similar to the property of a horse-leech; for all the blood she sucks from the hearts of her fortunate or unfortunate acquaintance, passes by means of that disorder either through her pores or in the manner of that voracious and detestable animal. She is accompanied by a young lady, whom her father on quitting England has been imprudent enough to leave among Mrs Coniac's acquaintance. With a person which would be genteel, if not made too much like a kitchen tongs; with a face which would be passable but for the enormity of its nose; with a middling understanding bloated with pride, and with original sensibility depraved into lasciviousness, this lady aspires to the rank of beauty, and to the honours of a toast. But early signs and symptoms giving her apprehensions of disappointment, she is the echo of the malicious widow; and they are very diligent in their endeavours to depreciate the beauty and tarnish the reputation of others. Repeated mortifications will sour them into saints, and make them proper disciples of that mirror of holiness Sir H Trelawney.

It would be profaneness to contrast trifling objects of this kind, with one who honours this town with her residence; whose beauty is ennobled by her virtues; of whom even scandal is silent, and in whose praise the wise and good are unanimous and warm; or with another, of whose person and the mind which animates it, I can give you no idea. Raphael's finest drawings are harsh to the lines of real beauty which define her neck, her bosom, her waist, her limbs. Her face you will not suppose for the admiration of a modern beau, when I tell you, the features, and especially the eyes, have been formed, disposed, and harmonised by good sense, and an infinite succession of the most natural, tender, and lively affection. If these affections had not been sometimes misplaced, disappointed, and given an impression of regret, timidity, suspicion, and mysterious reserve to her heart, and to her countenance, she would have rivalled the Venus de Medicis; and Wedgwood and Bentley would have sent their copyists in crowds to contemplate that truly Greek and truly natural beauty from a living model, which they so happily imitate from busts, and gems, and vases. But I must not trust myself on this subject, which I find to be caviar to the multitude of high and low people at Margate. And I will not point out to stare of ignorance, or the appetite of lust, which should hardly be contemplated; what certainly should be possessed only by a man of a cultivated mind and of the warmest and most affectionate heart.

After this I can only tell you, that the ladies in general have various degrees of beauty down to deformity; and are dressed in a variety of tastes down to tawdriness and absurdity, of which I could give you no particular account in a letter.

The gentlemen I must pass before you in classes; the first of which being nobility and gentry, and consisting only of a few tattling, gossiping card players, I shall not produce.

The next consists of divines; almost all characters; from the holy sprig of jessamy, which the officiating clergyman stuck up here, when he set out to study the customs and manners of France, to the contemplative and profound curate of St Anne, who having vanquished Dr Hind in a contention for the rights of the most useful division of the clergy, and held him up as a warning to priests, and as an object of pity or contempt to the people, has retired with his intelligent and faithful Pompey, to his favourite amusement; and it is to be hoped, is recruiting his health, spirits and resolution, for the future terror of oppressors, and for the benefit of injured industry and merit.

In this class, or rather in the remove from it, I am under the necessity of placing that divine who is no divine, that religionist who is of no known and acknowledged religion, that priest of nature, and minister of deism whom your correspondent Sappho seems to pursue with the rancour of disappointed love. But as his health appears to be declining, as he seems not to wish to be considered of the company, and is a brother writer, I may as well be silent of him. I only thought he would very properly terminate the view of a small group of divines, as deism and irreligion are the usual limits and boundaries of all the religion in the world.

Lawyers next succeed – with whom this place swarms. Whether washing in the sea be a religious rite, or a physical prescription for the vices and maladies incident to that profession, I cannot take upon me to determine. A counsel is distinguished from an attorney by a peculiar strut, by an apparent attention to an imaginary tail, even when he has not his gown on, and by a harsh and emphatic pronunciation suited only to Westminster Hall. But for these little circumstances Mansfield [22] would be an

---

[22] William Murray, 1st Earl of Mansfield, SL, PC (1705-1793) was a British barrister, politician and judge noted for his reform of English law. Born to Scottish nobility.

entertaining and agreeable man; as would Bearcroft[23], if he had a little more understanding, and a much less opinion of it. There is a sneaking suspiciousness in almost all the attorneys, and they have a habit of contracting their muscles for concealment and chicane, which perhaps electricity would be more effectual for than salt-water, and might spread out and smooth their surfaces into an honest and manly appearance.

But physic is the favourite profession here. We have doctors and surgeons and apothecaries employed here in every way, and it would fill up your paper to give you a history of physic at Margate; my indisposition has furnished me with numerous anecdotes; one of which I will give you as a specimen.

My disorder had demurred to the proceedings of the faculty here, and the lady abbess of our convent entreats me to have Mr Churchill; who, she said, was the pleasantest doctor in the world, and was treated here as such, though he might be only a manager of clyster-pipes [enema tubes] and pestles and mortars in London. I love pleasant things, and sent for Churchill, as much on account of his brother, as on the recommendation of my virgin governess. But judge of my surprise when I learned that I could not see him that day, on account of one of his offices, as deputy manager of an ass race. It seems the highest diversion of the turf here is furnished by asses for fame; wenches for shifts, pigs for peaches, under the direction of Mr Churchill who has a deputation for this purpose from the well-known Mr Godfrey, because he laughs at certain periods with more hilarity, and is supposed to inherit from his family more jokes and merry sayings than other people.

When the fat, burlesque, unthinking figure presented itself before me; it is true, as my governess had told me, I felt pleasantly; and was inclined to laugh from sympathy, because I saw it was what he meant to do, after cracking his jest. I humoured him on account of his brother whom I much loved; slid over my case, as I intended to make no use of him, and

---

[23] Edward Bearcroft, KC (1737-1796) was an English barrister, judge, and politician.

launched into his jests. I found him in wit, exactly what I am in fortune; the second son of a wealthy house, whose brother had run away with the estate. I am cruelly expected to appear as a gentleman, because my brother has a fortune, and has left me only the gleanings of our personal property; and Churchill is as cruelly obliged to affect to be a wit, because his brother was one, and to furnish miserable jokes, from the family shreds and tatters. A similarity of fate has created a sort of friendship between us, and we seldom play our evening rubbers asunder.

These are the principal professional characters at Margate. There are several straggling ones, which are curious enough; and some of which I may possibly send you, if I should not get better subjects to write about, when I am able to make my excursions.

Letter IV

Sir,

I doubt my gambols will be soon over at Margate. My correspondence with you has excited a universal ferment in every breast here, from that of the sublime, easy, and elegant Mr Walker down to the bathing women who all read the St James Chronicle with great eagerness and fury. Various are the conjectures about the author, and droll the menaces on his being discovered. Almost all are afraid and therefore almost all agree that he is an assassin who diverts himself in murdering reputations and in disturbing the quiet of those who are come here to amuse themselves. I have not meddled with real reputations, I play only with shadows; and the devil must be in me to murder them. Churchill affects to laugh while he mutters curses against me; but I have given him his potion, meaning he should taste of what he has often given others and be taught to think before he speaks. It diverts me to see a man accustomed to delight himself in viewing others roasted alive grieved to the heart at being only singed with a paper. The lawyers vow my total destruction if you can be bribed to bring me into Westminster Hall; and what is singular, the most inveterate against me is not any of those whom I have taken notice of but a heavy headed counsellor, whom I had neglected, because nobody could tell me his name. The ladies bounce and speak into a horse laugh at my taste for beauty and bid me seek my Greek forms and expressive countenances where I please, they will go on distorting themselves with high cushions, false curls, false nails, high shoulders, and painted cheeks.

But my most formidable enemies are aged cuckolds and the convenient gallants who are like appendixes and supplements in their families. In a group of these I had like to have been demolished lately. A deadly blow was aimed at me by a wretch who in the black hole at Calcutta assumed the form of a buffalo, gored the heart of a confidential friend and escaped to be exhibited in Westminster Hall: his horns would have reached me but for the officiousness of his assistant, a lottery office keeper, a man of fashion at the watering places and a dealer and chapman in tickets and shares of tickets in the city. This poor wretch fearing I should hang him up to ridicule (for he has got from my servants all the pence and shillings they could procure or pilfer) and eager to show his valour in good company and in the dark, thrust his head between me and the buffalo and received his horns without damage; for his mother having taken the model of his pate from the mop with which she usually washed her house, he may either have horns or receive thrusts from them, without any apparent inconvenience.

These bustles and dangers and the discovery that I was the god of roguery in disguise has obliged me to change my habitation and I am now in a temple of sentimental friendship called a boarding house, under the direction of a widow – and a virgin. Here all is method and order and delicacy. I dare not peep in the morning to call for a bottle of water with slippers on without buttons in my sleeves, or without my garters. The virgin observes and the widow is the disciplinarian. I hope they will never discover I am not a man; for the Mayor of Dover's deputy and the only magistrate here, serves them with small beer; the whole neighbourhood consists of Methodists and they will hasten with inquisitorial alacrity to perch a poor heathen god in a pillory.

I mean, therefore, in my next to write wholly on the fair and pleasant side and to tell you when you become a man of fashion (and it is what all successful printers must come to) on what account you may spend your time very agreeably at Margate.

I am, Sir, &c.

Momus.

Letter V

Margate, Sept. 28

Sir,

I have often been astonished at the extensive capacity and learning of a man in your situation. The printer of a newspaper is addressed and appealed to on all subjects and, no doubt, is a competent judge of all. I need not therefore tell a man of your learning that Momus has ever been as remarkable for his variableness and inconstancy as any woman that ever existed. This is the reason of my quitting the rocky and dangerous road of praise. It is my humour so to do; and I am not intimidated by menaces of being called to an account by a gentleman or way-laid by a laced and embroidered blackguard. All the occasional men of fashion, pawn brokers, lottery-office-keepers and thief-takers, who have left off business are sent out as scouts after me; while I am sat down as peaceably and securely as a poet on the plains of Arcadia, tuning my reed to the music of love and softening my voice to the notes of panegyrick[24] Hail, Flattery! Enchanting goddess of delusion! At thy shrine all beings bend! And in thy religion alone there is no heresy! Thou workest incontestable miracles and reconcilest the most direct contradictions! Thou givest wisdom to the simple, virtue to the

---

[24] A panegyric is a formal public speech, or (in later use) written verse, delivered in high praise of a person or thing, a generally highly studied and discriminating eulogy, not expected to be critical.

Knave and beauty to the ugly! All blessings are bestowed by thee, without even the trouble of deserving them!

You see, Sir, like all great writers, I have invoked a muse, but I plead benefit of divinity and I will not engage to be always constant to my mistress. You cannot easily imagine a sweeter spot than on which this strange place is dropt; only you must dispense with shady groves and purling streams; for there is hardly a tree to be seen, nor a drop of sweet water ever to be tasted. The soil is also chalky, and none but eagles can look at it. Allowing for these exceptions, you may consider Margate is a pleasant place. It is almost central to a great number of little villages which are in nearly the circumference of a circle, which were originally the habitation of farmers and their dependants, but are now the receptacles of contraband goods. Indeed the whole life of Thanet exhibits only a general jumble of lawless confusion; everything is conducted by trick and law and gospel are dispensed by smuggling. 'If I should ever assume the person and station of King of England, I would learn to govern the Isle of Thanet before I thought of conquering America.' These villages, Sir, seem to be built on purpose to terminate our views, and to give variety and interest to our rides and walks, I hate descriptions, or I would tire you. Take this as a specimen: Kingsgate is at a distance of a few miles, where the late Lord Holland spent prodigious sums of money, and those whom he employed showed great taste. The house is in a good style for the situation, on a steep and naked shore; the ruins are for the most part well imagined; but the whole affected me as almost all great objects on earth do. I regretted that virtue had never been so prosperous as to rear edifices and spread lawns, and that the original owner and possessor of so pleasing a spot had not been an honest man. When I have taken these rides, and refreshed myself, as mortals do, at the orderly table of my boarding house, I repair to the circulating libraries, and there find the means either of being introduced into private parties, or of joining company for the rooms. Mr Silver and Mr Hall, presidents of these gambling, gossiping places, men of extraordinary geniuses in their way, and the only persons in Margate who are in the secret of these letters, give me such masterly hints and sketches of all who pass before me, that I cannot only get into any houses, but into any bedchambers and closets of any houses in Margate, and that by managing the foibles of those who have the keys of them.

You will believe me when you know, that without the risqué and infamy of Clodius[25], and without even changing my sex, I am admitted into Millennium Hall, the grave and wise president of which is here attended by some of the chaste sisters of that institution, to purge and check the peccant[26] desires, and to purify their bodies in salt water. This lady is allied to Mrs Montague, famous among the pamphleteers, and monthly subscribers, for assaulting Voltaire, as a gnat would be among its kindred for taking a lion by the nose

Millennium Hall[27] is not yet a perfect institution, for the members of it have not the self denial and generosity to throw their fortunes into a general stock, and quit their several habitations for a common one. It now consists of a circle of neutral beings, with the outward parts of women cast in a masculine mould. They are therefore universally destitute of female beauty, softness, and amiableness and they are as harsh and unpleasant in their minds, as they are ordinary in their forms. You are not to wonder, therefore, that they consist of wives parted from their husbands and old maids who never could get any. Their distinguishing principle is rancour against the men; and their employment reading, writing, praying, and a little charity to the poor. Judge what pleasure I must have in contemplating such expressences in human nature, especially as

---

[25] Publius Clodius Pulcher was a popularist politician in ancient Rome (about 50BC). Clodius positioned himself as a champion of the urban plebs, supporting free grain for the poor and the right of association in guilds. The term Clodius is taken to be a gesture of political solidarity.

[26] having committed a fault or sin.

[27] Millenium Hall was Sarah Scott's most significant novel in 1762. Four editions were published by 1778, and interest in it has revived in the twenty-first century among feminist literary scholars. The book tells how each resident of the female Utopia arrived at Millenium Hall. The adventures are remarkable for their reliance on a nearly superstitious form of divine grace, where God's will manifests itself with the direct punishment of the wicked and the miraculous protection of the innocent.

you must suppose me passing from such society to that of the woman I love, who has retained the female loveliness both of body and mind, unaccompanied by its usual weaknesses and affectations; who has genius without vanity, knowledge without pedantry, and whose natural and exquisite beauty is rendered interesting by a feeling and affectionate heart. Here the pleasure arises from contrast, as it does in another society into which I am admitted, and which is called a female academy for notability and sentiment, under the direction of the late Dr H---kf---th's widow, a little round contented figure, who is too unwieldy to be notable, and whose sentimental apparatus, if she ever had any, has been long since buried in plumpness.

She contrives, however, by tales and novels and histories, united to system of family management, to give her nymphs that singular modern character distinguished by the epithet sentimental, which manages the family by rule; spends and exhausts the natural affections on romantic and imaginary subjects, and which leaves nothing for a husband but an enervated and overstrained mind, insensible to all common and useful attachments.

These are objects of curious speculation to one who contemplates human nature as I do, and Margate always offers such things to observation. When I am not thus engaged, I go to the play, or I partake of the several amusements at the Hotel, the business of which, as far as it depends upon Smith, could not well be better conducted. And if the Master of the Ceremonies were a man of sense, knowledge of the world, and real politeness, this place would soon rival, and perhaps excel the first bathing places in England.

I am yours, Sir,

Your most humble servant,

Momus.

[Editors' notes]

The valour and fury (consisting of male and female clamours) against Momus subsiding; consultations were held on the best means to defend the reputations of those who had none, against the satire and ridicule which he scattered about him. Mr Walker, Master of Ceremonies, and a man as eminent for his wisdom as for his easy politeness, presided at these meetings of alarmed cuckolds, their fawning agents and wanton wives, of superannuated military beaus, of divines, lawyers, and hairdressers. Great was the hubbub of these assemblies; at last a half-pay, half-witted colonel proposed, that all thoughts of force might be dropped, and that he and his nephew, assisted by two or three beaus, might fall on him in the dark. This was thought too dangerous, as the author was appraised of the nature of their courage, and showed himself disposed to sport with it. Colonel Yahoo; the young squire brainless; his eastern greatness the buffalo, and the macaroni rabble of brokers, attorneys and gamblers, were advised to the safer method of calling after him when almost out of hearing, and then to take to their heels. To assist this military measure, it was proposed to look out for some able writer, and repel the insults of this alarming satirist. Colonel Yahoo offered himself; but owned that spelling had been a fatal branch of learning to the family. If it had depended on oratory or bullying, particularly when men advanced in years and hating broils and quarrels were to be insulted, all the governors of the Middlesex Hospital would testify that no man should have been his rival. After many claims, pretensions and debates, it was agreed, that some man, eminent for his learning and talents, should be applied to; and should be complimented for his courage in entering the lists with the title of Defender of the Customs and Practices of Margate. This produced the following letter:

Letter VI

To Momus

Margate, September 30th

Sir,

If it be your delight to destroy that security and repose which are essential to the pleasure of a place like this, or to know that the bare mention of your name excites terror and apprehension, your enjoyment must be exquisite in the effect of your letters from Margate. But I have no idea of a disposition that can be pleased with such malicious gratifications, or that any writer of your abilities can be tempted to prostitute his talents to so base a purpose. I shall rather support vanity to be your motive, than malice; for your descriptions are more witty than just, and your characters like the production of a painter, who is more solicitous to make a fine picture than a good likeness. I very much approve the general plan of your correspondence with Mr Baldwin, am pleased with the liveliness of your colouring, and would cheerfully give my vote to elect you perpetual censor of Margate. For the impertinent airs of gentility, the ridiculous consequence assumed by London tradesmen, and the endless follies which are here common to men of all ranks and professions, are proper subjects for the pen of satire. But the innocent peculiarities of a pretty woman are sacred; and the characters which can defy censure, should be suffered to escape the shafts of ridicule. Margate, like every other public place, is frequented by grotesque women, trifling sops, and designing sharpers, who are fair objects of public ridicule, contempt, or indignation; these if you will scribble, may give full exercise to your wit, and afford sufficient variety for weekly Momus, without touching the reputation of a virtuous woman, disturbing the peace of a worthy family, or giving pain to a well disposed and honest heart. Private scandal is properly understood to be the malicious efforts of envy, or the artful resource of hypocrisy; but wounds inflicted by the hand of genius are mortal, and the blood that flows from them taints everything it touches with infamy. Nothing therefore can excuse a public writer, who exhibits character without that attentive enquiry and authentic information which should always precede the public executions of satire. If you would blame the judge, who from a slight suspicion should condemn a wretched culprit to the gallows; the satirist who wantonly exposes character to infamy or ridicule, upon false and imperfect information, will, with equal justice, be the object of your censure. Yet this must certainly be the case with every man who engages in the undertaking which you have taken for your amusement: for the company which resort to Margate, being collected from every part of the kingdom, are in general strangers to, and consequently unable to communicate the secret history of each other and their stay here is commonly too short, even for the penetration of Momus to discover their real characters. Your descriptions therefore being sketched from imagination, or the fallible rules of physiognomy, should certainly be left to the sagacity of your readers, without the assistance of initials for by avoiding any particular application, you will amuse without offence, and in the true character of Momus, may divert yourself, like a mischievous boy, with throwing squibs and crackers amongst the multitude. You may suspect, perhaps, that my observation upon your letters are occasioned by an intimacy or connection with those you have made the victims of your satire; but they are as little known to me as yourself and I have no motive, but that benevolence and compassion, without which the abilities of Momus are a curse. I hold your mischievous endeavours too deep to apprehend from them any serious consequence, either to myself or my friends; for you have disentitled yourself to a small degree of credit, which the retailers of scandal too easily obtain from the weak and the credulous.

You confess, that an ill state of health hath prevented your mixing with the company, or partaking in the amusement of the place; but you might have spared this confession, for it is very evident, that you are unacquainted both with one and the other, and I think it more than probable, that your descriptions were conceived at your garret in St Giles's than in Church Field, or the Parade at Margate. Whilst a general disposition to civility and politeness, and mutual inclination to please and to be pleased, are the first principles of pleasure in societies of temporary retirement from the fatigues of business; or whilst the most elegant accommodation, recommended by a situation the most delightful, are objects of preferment, the genius of Margate will prevail, and crowded assemblies proclaim her triumph. To as little a purpose is your malice levelled at Mr Walker, for the same assiduity and attention to please, the same readiness to oblige, and the same taste and judgement which have procured him general approbation and applause for years past; will ensure to him the same satisfaction for years to come. The brilliant appearance at his annual ball, the liberality of his subscribers, and the signal marks of respect, which he receives both in public and private, are such arguments in his favour, as neither Momus, his printer, or the devil can gainsay or resist.

Anti-Momus.

Letter VII

To Momus

Sir,

I am rejoiced to hear of your intended retreat from Margate, and I doubt not it will be matter of sincere pleasure to many. For some time I have beheld with astonishment, private reputation tortured by the hands of an unfeeling misanthrope, under the title of a ridiculous figure of antiquity. The satirist who strikes at vice in general is deserving of applause; but the wretch who, without distinction, presents his artillery against private foibles, merits a reception from society of another kind. The good and amiable man, when he perceives a fault in his companion, would admonish in the closet, or pass over the transgression. The haughty temper of the cynic calls forth his venom to the world, regardless of the consequence. A person, sir of your disposition, must either be a very bad or a very odd man, characters universally marked with abhorrence or contempt. This language is too moderate perhaps for a person so distinguished in wit as Momus is; but you should remember that moderation, when heated, is by far more dangerous than the passion of a moment; it has the fire without the flash. These few lines I have written as a preamble; you shall shortly receive a more ample favour.

I am yours, &c.

Philopas.

Letter VIII

Margate, Oct. 5

Sir,

I have been this week so much engaged in contemplating the fruits of my own amorous labours, that I have not given much attention to the events of the place. What is extremely singular in my present case is, that though I am not myself given to making verses, and my mistresses have been mostly what they call guides, who are beings here of an amphibious kind, yet my productions have been all poets. The consequence must be that if I were to write a Momus fit for any of the celestial bathing places, I should not be read, while the company is so engaged with the verses of my children.

Among the most favoured of these is one I have by a handsome smooth-faced creature six feet high. She grew on the hills of Scotland, and in honour to her name and country, I have called the child Macnamolly. I intend to take chambers for him in Lincoln's Inn, to give him the appearance of studying the law; but he is to make his fortune by his face – and a sweet one the ladies say it is! Not a thought shall ever furrow his visage, not a motion in his muscles but what is produced by the smoothest and most unmeaning smiles: he shall walk as if he were going to lie down, and he shall look so languishing, that you would think he were about to sleep. I stuck him up here as a male beauty, and he was making great havoc among those insignificant things called fine ladies, when he almost ruined his own reputation and that of his whole family, by entering into poetic partnership with a female descendant of my loins, called Miss B----. The two simpletons are both pretty, and stared at as such; but they could not be satisfied without first writing anonymous letters to themselves, and then verses to be stuck up in the circulating libraries, in praise of their beauty. Lights are set off by shades, in poetry as in painting. This my children knew; but they were unlucky in the application of the principle; for as a contrast to themselves, they satirized the nephew of a late American governor, who seems to have brought over and transfused into his family, a great deal of the distinguished valour of that country. The young man, a young M----, you would not be able to say which, grinned and chattered at the presidents of the libraries. These gentlemen, not caring to fight with anything, gave up poor Macnamolly, who gave up his poetic sister; at which the young American gave up his blustering, and all three were in a droller situation than any which has been conceived for a comedy these fifty years. The American however went home for his rifle gun, intending to do treacherously what he had no spirit to do otherwise. In the way he was met by the lieutenant of a press gang here, who has the misfortune to be jealous of his wife, and who was then drubbing her for the pleasure he supposed she had received from the coachman. The young American, from the same innate dislike to fighting, interposed with his tongue; but the lieutenant giving him a volley of oaths and contemptuous epithets, made him take his heels, and scramble into his bedchamber; at the window of which he chattered and made grimaces, until his fears and his malice were evaporated. So ended the adventure of my children's verses in praise of themselves.

There are other un-licked cubs of mine to whom I have not yet given a name. They are holding up to ridicule every large bony, plump woman, bearing any resemblance to our family, by attempting to praise her; and they are dishonouring beauty, accomplishments and virtue, by attempting to describe them.

The season here is drawing to a conclusion, and so is my correspondence with you: one letter more will finish it. The first and most active spirits of this season are either gone or going. The buffalo has made an alarming stand against me. He has the courage to postpone his departure for a week, to let the company see that he would not budge at the first smack of my whip; and a whelp in his train, who has repeatedly aimed to snap at my heels, I have been obliged repeatedly to kick out of the town.

My next will be an adieu, and probably very pathetic, as I seldom take leave without weeping.

Yours, &c.

Momus.

Letter IX

Margate, Oct. 12

Sir,

I now mean seriously to take my leave of this place; indeed partly by necessity and partly by choice.

Willing to enter into all the amusements of the neighbourhood, I took to that of shooting, indeed my worthy friend Richard S-m-ns[28], who was here the last season but one, has often told me, that under pretence of one kind of game, he successfully pursued another, and more delicious; and that the little girls of the Isle of Thanet are as easily hit and brought down by a good shot as its pheasants, partridges, and snipes. But this prowling beast of prey was given to boasting. I, tho' a god, found so much of a certain kind of virtue among women, that I was obliged to betake to my gun in good earnest; and should have very agreeably broken in on the formal changes of our table, if the Lord of the Manor had not been a kind of pedlar in civil society, who considers everything on his estate as a commodity, and knows to a farthing what it should bring. This curious cunning man, this fungus, which the caprice of our late season

---

[28] This could have been Richard Simmons (born in 1737 at Bridge, Kent; died in 1802 at Bridge), an English cricketer who played for Kent and All-England in the 1760s and 1770s. He is one of the earliest well-known wicket-keepers. Simmons, who apparently lived his whole life at Bridge, was a useful batsman. He probably began playing in the late 1750s and was active until 1779.

hath forced up among the shoots of a noble and venerable tree, has long owed me a grudge. For one of the means by which he aimed to raise himself was fortune hunting; and he invariably proceeded on the mean principle of quitting a lesser for a greater fortune; even pounds for guineas. He had played on the credulity of several women, when twenty thousand pounds led him to a friend of mine, whom he also quitted in pursuit of a larger sum; but to whom I suggested the following revenge: to invite his lordship to tea and then to affect the utmost remorse and horror at being driven by a desperate passion to poison him and herself. The trick took; my lord went home, and was put to bed. The lady also pretended to take to her bed. The gentlemen of the faculty were brought to him; and he was soundly vomited and purged. The lady instructed her servants to give out that the same practices were used on her: messages were interchanged every day, until the remedies proved ineffectual to kill his lordship, and the joke came out.

I was known to be in favour with the lady; and the name of Momus has been ever since hateful to Lord Cunningham. This is the reason of the prosecution I am now under for killing a hare; and the affront of which I shall settle with his lordship when I come to town, and in my own way. These pretty disasters, like greater evils, seldom come unattended with blessings. All the wits and geniuses in this place are in good understanding and alliance; and those who do great things, and those who say great things, are united by strong and natural ties.

All the poets and players here are ever in my train, ready to transmit my wonderful actions to posterity; to turn my common sayings into blank verse; to rehearse any extempore dialogues I give them; and to eat my dinners. On my general principle of encouraging genius, I bespoke a play; and as all the people of the town and island are occupied in some contraband or illegal practice, I thought the Beggar's Opera would hold up the best lessons to them.

I mustered up my acquaintance, dressed myself finely, was seated in my box and was watching the Margate Roscius in one of the most interesting adventures of Macheath – when I perceived something like a shower of strong scented waters gently dripping over all my clothes. I began to muse on my situation. In Heaven, we know the origin of fragrant flowers, and that they are the tricks of gods and goddesses when they are floating in clouds through the regions of infinite space. I perceived, by what may be called the impregnation of this water, and the wide and scattered manner of its falling, that it came from a female; and if I had been under the canopy of Heaven, should have imagined that Venus or some of her attendants had been hinting to me, in their way, that they were passing. But here, on earth, in a playhouse, covered not only by a roof, but by a gallery, where the women never part with a drop of that precious liquor, but in seldom silence and the deepest retirement – in such a place, to be so distinguished and so blessed, was beyond my comprehension.

It is my custom to make all my accidents known, never to hide anything under a bushel, but hold it as in a candlestick, that it may give either pleasure or pain to all who are about me. I instantly interrupted the performers, and exhibited myself like a Hob just come out of the well. An immediate enquiry was made in the gallery; and the reason was found to be the amazing affect of Roscius's acting, on certain parts of the women's bodies. The most universal and astonishing plaudits were given to the performer – he was ordered to proceed in unlacing and unsphynctering the most retired and exquisite muscles of the sex – while the manager was desired to lay mats, cloths, and any spongy substances on the floor of the gallery, to prevent future accidents to the company below.

This matter has endeared me much to the ladies; for they see I am giving the fullest scope to their sensibility; and that my wit and morality is of the indulgent, not of the severe and restraining kind. If the angelic woman I am devoted to were not tinctured with one earthy failing, which may be called the avarice of love, the universal favour I am in, and the great liberties I might take, would make me defer the appointed time of introducing her to heaven.

On Sunday next at one o'clock, I mean to make myself publicly known to those who do not, or will not know me. I have been promised caning, kicking, stabbing, and shooting from every fool I have exhibited, and every knave I have detected. Those who are not disposed to fulfil these promises, have this notice to take to their horse's heels.

What I have said of Margate, of its inhabitants, and its company, I will maintain, both as a man and a writer – I mean what I have obviously intended as matters of use and matters of fact – what may be couched in allegory, metaphor, irony and transposition, I claim the usual licence of poets for; which will be allowed me by all those of my readers whose opinions I care for.

I hold all private scandal in abhorrence; and I have never hit a villain whom I might not, if I had chosen it, have totally demolished. The place by nature, and by several of its improvements, is airy, healthy, commodious, and pleasant; but its inhabitants, up to its first tradesmen, seem to be kneaded with smuggling dough, and look and act in every little transaction like miserable petty-larceny-men.

The company this season has greatly varied at different times; but in general it has not much pretension to rank, politeness, taste, harmony, or any general circumstance to make such a place happy. It is the resort of those who during the winter are immersed in the frauds of the city, and who would fly here from stinking air and a bad conscience. While I can wield a pen their flight shall not avail them. Villainy is my object; folly only my play; and if the real friends of Margate understood its interest, they would rejoice instead of being angry at the correspondence of Momus.

Letter X

To Momus at Margate

Sir,

I am in the condition of most of your readers here, who have all admired your wit, till they found some inconvenience to themselves from it. That which I and several of my sex complain of is singular, but sometimes distressing; for we are happy enough to be acquainted with men of letters. Every man who is supposed to be an author has been suspected of writing Momus. Whether the real author of your letters has been at Margate this season or not is a question I am far from being clear upon. I am sure, however, that the childish and cowardly marks of resentment which have been shown at random to ingenuous men, and particularly to those ladies who have been with them, are a greater reproach to the place, than anything you have alleged against it.

In consequence of the notice you gave, that you would discover yourself on Sunday, those whom you have most offended, consulted on the best means of insulting you, without danger. No gentleman could therefore undertake the business, and it was consigned to the strangest being that nature, in her freaks, ever exhibited. It was neither a yahoo, a monkey, a baboon, nor a man but a mixture of all of these. I suppose, in the course of many generations. It has the face of a baboon, but seems to have been par-boiled, or rather turned by the scurvy, to the colour of a coddled apple. This is horribly contrasted by silver locks, and legs altogether too small for a lounging ungainly body six feet high. The whole figure, strongly marked with age, is always dressed like a boy, and without a grain of understanding, and with the voice of a castrated monkey, is eternally talking and capering.

This being, always *en militaire*, and always attended with a light-headed relation, whom he has brought here also for the scurvy, was chosen for the champion of all those who have been laughed at by Momus; and he was to call him an assassin, and a villain, the moment he discovered himself, then to show his bare br----ch, and to run away. But all this mighty heroism was defeated; this motley military man will be disappointed in his view of succeeding in the place of the Master of the Ceremonies, and his pretty relation in that of steward of the races.

The talk now assigned these poor wretches is to snarl and groan at every one who may possibly have been Momus. No man of learning and reputed genius can go into the libraries, or pass the streets, but this coddled-faced baboon, and his young cub, provoke him by grinning and chattering; so as to molest without affronting; and then run away in a whole skin. I have felt this inconvenience; and have been often incommoded by these wretches, for they would chatter in a miserable jargon the most injurious things of the supposed Momus, and everybody who associated with him; in such a manner that I might apply them to myself, but could not directly say they meant me, and therefore could not desire my company to kick or cane them away.

This, sir is a serious inconvenience attending your not discovering yourself, marking the time of your departure, or taking some steps which might prevent others, and especially women, from being incommoded on your account. As I hear you are to be at this place next year, and that your letters will be delivered in the same diverting and useful strain, I hope you will attend to these circumstances, and not think you have done enough when you have frightened away beasts of prey, without ridding us of the vermin they leave behind.

I am, sir,

Your humble servant

An insulted woman.

(*"Momus," The most distinguished characters there and the virtues, vices and follies to which they gave occasion in what was called the season of the year 1777*)

Ode to a Margate Hoy

Great is the loss of gentlefolk from Wapping,
Who, fond of travel, unto Margate roam,
To gain that consequence they want at home.

At Margate how like quality they strut!
Nothing is good enough to greet their jaws;
Yet when at home, are often forced, God wot,
To suck like bears a dinner from their paws

Forced on an old joint-stool their tea to take,
With treacle 'stead of sugar for their gums;
Buttering their hungry loaf, or oaten cake,
Like mighty Charles of Sweden, with their thumbs.

But Hoy, inform me, who is she on board,
That seems the lady of a first-rate Lord,
With stomach high pushed forth as if in scorn,
Like craws of ducks and geese o'er charged with corn,

Dressed in a glaring, gorgeous damask gown,
Which roses, like the leaves of cabbage, crown
With also a bright petticoat of pink,
To make the eye from such a lustre shrink?

Yes, who is she the Patagonian[29] Dame,
As bulky as of Heidelberg the tun;
Her face, as if by brandy taught to flame,
In blaze superior to the noon day sun
With fingers just like sausages, fat things;
And loaded much like curtain rods with rings?
Yes, who is she that with a squinting eye
Surveys poor passengers that sickening sigh;

Sad, pale-nosed, gaping, pulling, mournful faces
Deserted by the blooming smiling graces;

---

[29] Patagonia is a region containing the southernmost portion of South America.

That, reaching o'er thy side, so doleful throw,
The stomach's treasure to fish below

'Tis Madam Bacon, proud of worldly goods,
Whose first spouse shaved and bled – drew teeth, made wigs;
Who, having by her tongue destroyed poor Suds,
Married a Wight that educated pigs!

But hark! She speaks! Extremely like a man!
Raising a furious tempest with her fan

Why, captain, what a beastly ship! Good God!
Why, captain, this indeed is very odd!
Why, what a grunting dirty pack of doings!
For heaven's sake, captain, stop the creatures' spewings.

Now hark! The captain answers
Mistress Bacon I own I can't be with such matters taken;
I likes not vomiting no more than you;
But if so be that gentlefolk be sick,
A woman hath the bowels of Old Nick,
Poor souls, to bung their mouths 'twere like a Jew.

Majestic Mistress Bacon speaks agen!
Folks have no business to make others sick:
I don't know, Mister Captain what you mean
About your Jews, and bowels of Old Nick:
If all your cattle will such hubbub keep,
I know that I shall leave your stinking ship.

Some folks have devilish dainty guts, good lord!
What business have such cattle here aboard?
Such gang indeed to foreign places roam!
'Tis more becoming them to spew at home.

But hark! The captain properly replies
Why, what a breeze is here, God damn my eyes!

("Ode to a Margate Hoy," Pindar, 1779)

98

A scene on board a Margate Hoy

George Keate (1729-1797) was a writer and painter. His hilarious rendition of disembarkation from a Margate Hoy in 1790 paints a pretty picture.

The Hoy

...here is the devil and all to do in Margate; half a dozen men tied up in sacks and hopping for a pig. Three jack-asses running for a Cheshire cheese and a smock-race on the sands and all the world there, whilst the prize, decorated with ribbons, is carried in procession on a pole like a popish relic. Every circumstance of life is proportionate; the Golden Pippin on Mount Ida did not more agitate the three Celestial competitors than this little object did our three terrestrial ones here. Happy she who conquers! As the lass with a shift to her back, stands a far better chance for preferment than she who has none. And see the victrix as it slipped over her running dress and marches off triumphant with a drum before her and a mob at her heels!

Disembarkation at Margate

Give that fat lady in the Brunswick[30] your arm my lad; don't you see how lame she is? Poor soul! Scarce a leg to stand on. If the sea can set her up-right, it must work a miracle! I am glad, however, that I have got the start of some of you and am not just setting out on mine.

But this is not half the bustle; for two Hoys are just arrived from London, their decks covered with new comers and all Margate running down to the Pier-head to see them land. I doubt whether I am stout enough to run too but I will be amongst them as fast as I can walk. If I lean over this rail I shall see them all come ashore.

---

[30] A Brunswick gown or Brunswick is a two-piece woman's gown of the mid-eighteenth century.

Mercy on me! I think the whole city of London is aboard of ship! Six! Eight! Ten! Twenty! Thirty! Fifty! Seventy! I can never go on reckoning at this rate. What! Are all the shops shut up? Or have you been all bit Good People? Or are you come here to be bit? The wind has been dreadfully against you the whole way!

Why, as fast as the boats fill, the deck is covered again with new faces that rise out of the hold! There is no end of it! I will positively count no more. Nay ladies, you need not say how sick you have been, your looks will vouch for you. A tedious passage, high sea, all the pumps continually going and no room to stir, even to the ship's side, on necessary calls – it is monstrously inconvenient! But it is a party of pleasure and that is enough.

Ha! What is your Worship come down too? And Madam? And little Miss? Pray take care how you get up the steps. All for the water, I suppose? Bless me, and I see yonder your thrifty neighbour the Common-Council Man on the deck – he has made the voyage, I perceive, in his night cap and is now pulling his wig from his great-coat pocket in order to affect a decent landing.

("Sketches from Nature," A Colourful Journey to Margate, George Keate, 4th Ed. 1790, P. 8)

Margate in 1790

...A great number of nobility and persons of fashion resort to Margate in the summer, both for the enjoyment of its pure and salubrious air and for the benefit of bathing in the sea; for which latter purpose no place in the Universe is so well adapted, the shore being level and covered with the finest sand. Near the sea are several commodious bathing rooms, to which, in the morning the company resort, either to drink the water, or in turns are driven in the machines any depth into the sea, under the conduct of careful and experienced guides; at the back of the machine is a door, through which the bathers descend a few steps into the water, and an umbrella of canvass dropping over, conceals them from the public view. Upwards of thirty of these machines are frequently employed until the time of high water; the public is obliged to Benjamin Beale, one of the people called Quakers, for the invention of them; their structure is at once simple and convenient and the pleasures and advantages of bathing may be enjoyed in so private a manner as to be consistent with the strictest delicacy.

Since so many fashionable families have resorted to Margate, the town has been greatly improved; Cecil Square has within these few years been erected, which consists of many spacious houses and several good shops. On one of its sides is an Assembly Room, finished with great taste and elegance and supposed to be one of the largest in the kingdom. It is situated upon an eminence and commands an extensive prospect of the sea; it is eighty-seven feet long and forty-three broad, of a proportionable height and richly ornamented. Adjoining to this room, are apartments for tea and cards, which are perfectly convenient; the ground floor consists of a good billiard and coffee room which join the hotel and a large piazza extending the whole length of the building. The number of subscribers to these rooms amounts usually to above a thousand. The public amusements are regularly conducted by Mr Le Bas, the Master of the Ceremonies.

The Royal Hotel in Cecil Square, Margate

Besides the Royal Hotel, there is another upon the Parade of equal excellence and several good inns where families may be genteelly accommodated until they have provided themselves with lodgings agreeable to their wishes.

The York Hotel on the Parade, Margate

Hawley Square is nearly completed, one corner of which is occupied by the Theatre Royal, the other by the new Library. This magnificent room, lately built by Mr Hall, consists of a square of forty-two feet, is seventeen feet high and divided near the middle by a screen of columns of the Corinthian order which forms a kind of separation of the Library from the toy shop. In the centre of the latter, a dome of eighteen feet diameter arises to the height of sixteen feet above the ceiling, on the top of which is placed an octagon lantern eight feet high, from which depends a most superb and beautiful chandelier of glass. In the centre of the library (which is furnished with an extensive and valuable collection of books) is another elegant chandelier; the cases for the toys and books are ornamented with the busts of the poets and clusters of glass contribute to the decoration of other parts of the room. A superb mirror is placed over the chimney piece and the space above the mirror is occupied by a figure of Minerva. The chimney piece is beautified with the nine muses (in Mr Thorpe, of Princes Street's patent composition), which, together with the ornaments upon the walls and columns and the decorations on the ceiling, do great credit to the taste and execution of that ingenious artist.

The inside of Hall's library

Without the building, on two sides, is a handsome colonnade, under which the company may walk without being incommoded by the rain or sun. The impressions of magnificence and grandeur which are excited when this superb building is brilliantly illuminated and filled with beauty, taste, and elegance, beggar all description. The nobility and gentry, ever ready to reward merit, have honoured Mr Hall with their most distinguished patronage and have left him no reason to repent of his exertions for their pleasure and amusement. Under this building are very extensive wine vaults, belonging to the same proprietor; who being the importer of his own liquors is enabled to supply the tables of the company with every sort of the first quality and at most reasonable prices. A good engraving of the inside of the library, from a drawing of Miss Keate's of Charlotte Street, Bloomsbury and executed with great taste, by Mr Malton, of Conduit Street, may be had at Mr Hall's. The post office adjoins the library, and is under Mr Hall's direction.

Hall's, later Bettison's, Library on the corner of Hawley Square

An early illustration of the Theatre Royal at Margate

The Theatre Royal, built about three years ago, is a neat and elegant structure after the model of Covent Garden. Its scenery was executed by Mr Hodgins and the patentees Mate and Robson are not wanting in any thing which can render their new undertaking worthy of support. Good actors are retained at large salaries and every attention is paid by the acting manager to the accommodation and entertainment of the public.

Besides the grand library there are two others in the Church Field, kept by Mr Silver and Mr Champion; and a fourth near the water, in a very pleasant situation, kept by Mr Garner, each of which has a good collection of books. There are also several coffee rooms for the reception of ladies and gentlemen where the public papers are read and tea and card parties frequently formed. Indeed nothing is omitted that can in any degree contribute to the convenience or pleasure of the nobility and gentry who resort to this place.

Garner's Library with its precarious veranda

The far left of the picture was known as Horn Corner because of the strong winds that hit as one emerged from the High Street behind Garner's Library.

View from the gallery of Garner's Library

A bank has been for several years opened here by Messrs Cobb and Son, whose fidelity and punctuality in business have rendered their establishment a very great public convenience.

With regard to the efficacy of sea bathing, it is sufficient to observe that in all cases where general bathing can be of service the sea is at least equal to any other bath and in all cutaneous and glandular disorders vastly superior. If warm bathing is necessary, there are at Mitchener's two salt water baths on a very good construction which may be filled in a few minutes and the water brought to any degree of heat with the greatest facility. After bathing in the sea it is usual to walk. The places most frequented are the fort and rope walk although when the tide is out, the company often ramble upon the sands to collect shells and sea weed, many varieties of which are to be found in the neighbourhood of Margate. The sands extend several miles on each side of the town and may be passed with safety four or five hours in a day. The ocean upon the one hand, with a great many ships in view steering different courses and the caverns and grottos worn in the high chalky cliffs on the other, contribute to form a scene at once awfully grand and pleasingly romantic.

Near the fort has been lately erected an exceeding good room where the company often breakfast and drink tea and adjoining is a neat bowling green with alcoves. The prospect from hence is delightful where every vessel sailing to and from London is within a short distance and forms a moving picture beautiful beyond description. Two octagon rooms have been lately built by Mr Booth at opposite corners of the green for the better accommodation of the company and an orchestra for the band of music attends every Monday in the season, at the public breakfasts at Prospect Coffee House. Near this place

Captain Hooper has erected a curious horizontal windmill for the purpose of grinding corn. It is built upon so large a scale and of such wonderful mechanism as to render it well worthy the inspection of all who are fond of the productions of art and ingenuity.

A rare view of Hooper's vertical axis windmill

The above view of sailing ships in Margate's harbour depicts, on the left of the picture, a good representation of Hooper's vertical axis windmill. Built in 1791, it was gone by 1828.

In fine weather, parties frequently divert themselves with fishing or in visiting such ships as are lying at anchor in the road, the company will also be able, with great safety and at an easy expense, to take a view of the most remarkable places in the Netherlands, Holland, and France; as there are packets regularly sailing between Margate and Ostend. The distance is but twenty leagues [about 60 miles], which with a fair wind they run in nine or ten hours. Several pleasant tours may be made within a short time in Flanders, Holland or France and an excursion to the continent for ten or twelve days would afford great entertainment to persons desirous of seeing it. In that time may be visited with great ease, Bruges, Ghent, Brussels, the Hague, Liege, the Spa, Cambray and St Omers; a particular description of which places, with an accurate account of their distances from each other, the best routes, and other articles of useful information is to be found in a small publication entitled the Traveller's Vade Mecum[31] through the Netherlands, Holland, and France, published by Mr Hall.

For the convenience of the company the post comes in from London daily, Monday accepted, and returns thither every day but Saturday and coaches as well as diligences run continually.

There is a good market here exceedingly well supplied with butchers meat, poultry, fish, and vegetables; having an easy communication by water with the metropolis, the shops are well provided with all kinds of articles, in the various branches of trade. The Hoys and yachts sail to and from London every day, and the expense for each passenger is very moderate. They are all well fitted up and in some of them one or two separate cabins may be hired so that families can be as genteelly accommodated as in their own pleasure boats. The passage is frequently made in ten or twelve hours; the most favourable wind to London is East, South East and the best from that place West, North West.

The church of Margate is dedicated to St John the Baptist and was built in the year one thousand and fifty. It was formerly a chapel to Minster but was made parochial in one thousand two hundred and ninety. In it are many monuments of great antiquity and others of a later date to the memory of several families of distinction in the neighbourhood. For the accommodation of the company seats have been erected in the middle chancel; prayers are read every Wednesday and Friday and an additional sermon preached every Sunday during the summer season, for which extra duty the curate is very liberally rewarded by the subscribers to his book at the libraries.

Among the improvements at this place, must be mentioned the schools; there are two for the reception of young ladies and one good boarding school in the town and another in the Church-field for young gentlemen; besides a private seminary lately established by a very respectable and intelligent clergyman so that the health and the education of the children who come for the benefit of sea bathing may be both attended to.

---

[31] A book, such as a guidebook, for ready reference.

There are also several good boarding houses where such gentlemen and ladies, as may not choose the trouble of keeping house, will find themselves very comfortably and genteelly accommodated.

A physician of great ability is resident in the town and several good surgeons and apothecaries.

A charity school has been lately established for the education of forty boys and an equal number of girls; supported by the voluntary subscriptions of the inhabitants and much assisted by the liberal donations of the nobility and gentry who resort to Margate in the summer...

...In the summer of the year one thousand seven hundred and eighty-eight, a female beaked whale came on shore at Margate. It was twenty-seven feet in length and in its girth seventeen. Dale, in his History of Harwich, describes a fish of this kind and Mr Pennant places it among the cetaceous fish without teeth but Mr Hunter, surgeon of this place, in dissecting the head of the fish first mentioned, discovered four teeth just penetrating the gums in the lower jaw, which led him to conjecture that this animal had scarcely attained half its growth and that its common length might, when the whale was full grown, be at least sixty feet.

About three quarters of a mile from Margate is Drapers, an Alms-house, or Hospital, founded by Michael Yoakley of this parish. It was built in the year seventeen hundred and nine and consists of ten very comfortable apartments, one of which is appropriated for an overseer and the other for poor persons belonging to the parishes of St John, St Peter, Birchington and Acol. They are allowed coals and a yearly stipend and have each a strip of ground as a garden. This institution being intended for the relief of indigence, not for the encouragement of idleness; the founder has in his will specified the qualifications of such as are to be admitted; they must be industrious and of a meek, humble and quiet spirit. The company frequently form parties to drink tea at some of the apartments, in all which a great degree of neatness and simplicity is to be found. The humane heart, blessed with sensibility, must enjoy a luxurious repast in observing the effects of that benevolence which has rendered so many worthy objects comfortable in the decline of life after having perhaps weathered many of its calamities and storms. The stipend given at Drapers being found not so fully adequate to the intentions of its charitable founder as formerly, owing to the increase which has taken place in the price of provisions since it was originally allowed; George Keate Esq. has, with his usual benevolence, for several years promoted a subscription among the company by which a considerable addition has been made to the comforts and conveniences of these poor people.

At Nash Court, about a mile from Margate, are the remains of an ancient seat of a good family in the reign of Henry IV. It was in the possession of the Carwintons of Beaksbourne and afterwards, by intermarriages, passed into the families of Haut and Isaack; the memory of which alliances is preserved upon the painted glass in the windows of this mansion, on which the arms of several families are delineated. It has been used lately as a tea garden.

About a mile and a half from Margate is the ruin of a fine old mansion called Dandelion; this was the seat of a family, in ancient times, called Dent de Lion, as appears by divers old deeds, some of which are of such antiquity as to be without a date and some as high as Edward I but about the reign of Henry IV the name appears to have received its present appellation. In this last prince's time the estate belonged to John Dandelion, who is buried in the north chancel of the church at Margate. On the stone over his grave is his effigy in brass and under it an inscription declaring that he died upon the day of the invention of the holy cross, in the year one thousand four hundred and forty-five; the name, from the failure of male issue, upon his death became extinct. This seat was anciently walled round in accordance to the old manner of fortifying against bows and arrows. Part of the wall is still standing with the gatehouse, built with brick and flints in rows, having loop holes and battlements at top. Over the main gate are the arms of Dandelion, namely, sable-three lions rampant, between two bars dancette argent. On the right hand of this gate is a smaller one for common use, at the right corner of which is a blank escutcheon and on the left a demi lion with a label out of its mouth on which is written in the old Saxon characters Daundelion. Under the right side of the gate, as you go from the farm yard, was found, in the year seventeen hundred and three, a room large enough to hold eight or ten men, in which was a great many pieces of lachrymatory urns of earth and glass; under the other side of the gate is a well prison. In the window of the dining room in the mansion house are the arms of Dandelion quartered with those of Petit. The house is now occupied by a tenant who has fitted it up for the reception of parties who walk or ride that way and choose to refresh themselves. A good bowling green has been made planted round with evergreens and flowering shrubs and upon the terrace raised above the green are alcoves for the ladies who frequently drink tea in them while the gentlemen are playing bowls. The walk to this place is extremely pleasant and in many parts of the road, affords a fine view of the sea, of the Isle of Sheppy and of the Reculvers.

There is a public breakfast at Dandelion every Wednesday in the season; a band of music attends and cotillions and country dances beguile the hours on the green until two o'clock. It is but justice to say that Mr Staines, the original projector of this public amusement and the present occupier of the farm, spares neither pains nor expense to render Dandelion one of the most pleasing scenes in the neighbourhood and it is universally acknowledged by those who visit it that they depart with much reluctance from this sweet retreat and derive the greatest satisfaction from the entertainment and attention they meet with there. In order to accommodate a few families who may wish to reside near this delightful spot Mr Staines has, at a great expense, built some very good lodging houses near the grove which must provide a very delightful summer residence.

View of Dandelion pleasure gardens in 1779.

Hengrove, in the parish of Margate, is a manor that formerly belonged to Sir Henry of Sandwich, to whom Robert Abbot, of St Austin's, granted a license in the year one thousand two hundred and thirty to build a chapel or oratory in which he might cause divine service to be celebrated by his own chaplain. The ruins of this little chapel are still to be seen in an open field near the great road leading from Margate to Sandwich, without any house or building near it.

Salmeston or Salmanstone Grange is another manor in the parish of Margate, formerly belonging to the monastery of St Austins. While the monks were possessed of this estate they farmed it themselves and occupied the mansion house as a country residence. Upon the dissolution of the monastery this grange fell to the crown and was given by Queen Elizabeth to the Archbishop, by whom it is leased out on lives. The tenant of this estate is obliged by his lease to pay to the vicars of St John, of St Peter, and St Lawrence every midsummer day two bushels of wheat. And the first week in Lent to twenty-four poor parishioners of Minster, St John, St Peter and St Lawrence, six from each parish, nine loaves and eighteen herrings. And in the middle of Lent the same and also to twelve poor parishioners of the said four parishes three from each two ells of blanket and also to every poor man and woman coming to Salmanstone on Monday and Friday from May the third to June the twenty-fourth, one dish of pease. But this last clause says Lewis, is almost obsolete owing, as it is said, to the tenants taking advantage of the vague meaning of dish, the word used in the lease, and accordingly giving the poor people so few pease that it was not worth their while to go for them. The walls of the chapel and infirmary are still entire but the windows being demolished and the inside ornaments taken away, one of these buildings is now used as a barn the other as a granary.

To the left of Margate, between Northdown and Kingsgate are Hackendown banks where two barrows of earth mark the spot whereon a bloody battle was fought between the Danes and Saxons in the year eight hundred and fifty-three. The concurrent testimony of history, long tradition, and the etymology of the word Field of Battle Axes and more particularly the urns and bone found buried there, leave little room to doubt the truth of this provenance. One of these banks was opened on the twenty-third of May in the year seventeen hundred and forty-three by Mr Thomas Read owner of the lands, in the presence of many hundred people. A little below the surface of the ground were found several graves cut out of the solid chalk and covered with flat stones. They were no more than three feet long and the bodies seemed to have been thrust into them almost double, several urns made of coarse earthen ware capable of holding two or three quarts had been buried with them which crumbled into dust upon being exposed to the air. The bones were large, but not gigantic and for the most part perfectly sound. In June seventeen hundred and sixty-five, the smaller tumulus was opened by order of Henry, Lord Holland, who had purchased the ground; the appearances were similar to the former but no urns were found. The best historians record the battle to have been fought so near the sea that many of the combatants were pushed over the cliff during the action and it seems probable that most of the slain were thrown over afterwards as no other remains of bodies appear to have been found...

("Hall's New Margate and Ramsgate Guide," Joseph Hall, 1790)

Hooper's vertical axis windmill

Hooper's horizontal windmill

The reader may recollect that, a few years since, there stood at Battersea, (on premises once the residence of the great Lord Bolingbroke), a horizontal windmill, so enclosed as to resemble in appearance a gigantic packing case. It was erected by Captain Hooper, who also built a similar mill at Margate. It consisted of a circular wheel, having large hoards or vanes fixed parallel to its axis, and arranged at equal distances from each other. Upon these vanes, the wind could act, so as to blow the wheel round; but had it acted upon the vane at both sides of the wheel at once, it is evident that it could not have had any tendency to turn it round: hence, one side of the wheel was sheltered, while the other was submitted to the full action of the wind. For this purpose it was enclosed within a large cylindrical frame-work, furnished with doors or shutters, on all sides, to open at pleasure and admit the wind, or to shut and stop it. If all the shutters on one side were open, whilst all those on the opposite side were closed, the wind, acting with undiminished force on the vanes at one side, whilst the opposite vanes were under shelter, turned the mill round; but whenever the wind changed, the disposition of the blinds was altered, to admit the wind to strike upon the vanes of the wheel in the direction of a tangent to the circle in which they moved. This mill was long used by a maltster and distiller; but was taken down, in consequence of it having been superseded by the introduction of steam.

("The magazine of science, and school of art," G. Francis F.L.S, 1844, p.107)

Charles Lamb (1775-1834) was an English essayist, best known for his Essays of Elia and for the children's book Tales from Shakespeare, which he produced with his sister, Mary Lamb (1764-1847). The following is Lamb's recollection of a trip to Margate in 1790 where in the first paragraph he makes it clear that he preferred Margate above other watering places (though he would rather be in the countryside).

Charles Lamb

I am fond of passing my vacations (I believe I have said so before) at one or other of the Universities. Next to these my choice would fix me at some woody spot, such as the neighbourhood of Henley affords in abundance, upon the banks of my beloved Thames. But somehow or other my cousin contrives to wheedle me once in three or four seasons to a watering place. Old attachments cling to her in spite of experience. We have been dull at Worthing one summer, duller at Brighton another, dullest at Eastbourne a third, and are at this moment doing dreary penance at Hastings and all because we were happy many years ago for a brief week at Margate. That was our first sea-side experiment, and many circumstances combined to make it the most agreeable holyday of my life. We had neither of us seen the sea, and we had never been from home so long together in company.

The west view of the harbour, Parade and bathing rooms at Margate, 1781

This is a sketch of Margate harbour, drawn by the Rev. John Pridden and would probably have been the Margate that Lamb saw as a boy in the 1790s.

Can I forget thee, thou old Margate Hoy, with thy weather-beaten, sun-burnt captain, and his rough accommodation – ill exchanged for the foppery and fresh-water niceness of the modern steam-packet? To the winds and waves thou committedst thy goodly freightage, and didst ask no aid of magic fumes, and spells, and boiling cauldrons. With the gales of heaven thou wentest swimmingly, or when it was their pleasure stoodest still with sailor-like patience. Thy course was natural, not forced, as in a hot-bed; nor didst thou go poisoning the breath of ocean with sulphureous smoke – a great sea-chimera, chimneying and furnacing the deep; or liker to that fire-god parching up Scamander.

Can I forget thy honest, yet slender crew, with their coy reluctant responses (yet to the suppression of anything like contempt) to the raw questions, which we of the great city would be ever and anon putting to them, as to the uses of this or that strange naval implement? 'Specially can I forget thee, thou happy medium, thou shade of refuge between us and them, conciliating interpreter of their skill to our simplicity, comfortable ambassador between sea and land whose sailor-trousers did not more convincingly assure thee to be an adopted denizen of the former, than thy white cap, and whiter apron over them, with thy neat-fingered practice in thy culinary vocation, bespoke thee to have been of inland nurture heretofore – a master cook of Eastcheap? How busily didst thou ply thy multifarious occupation, cook, mariner, attendant, chamberlain;

here, there, like another Ariel, flaming at once about all parts of the deck, yet with kindlier ministrations – not to assist the tempest, but, as if touched with a kindred sense of our infirmities, to soothe the qualms which that untried motion might haply raise in our crude land-fancies. And when the o'er-washing billows drove us below deck (for it was far gone in October, and we had stiff and blowing weather) how did thy officious ministering, still catering for our comfort, with cards, and cordials, and thy more cordial conversation, alleviate the closeness and the confinement of thy else (truth to say) not very savoury, nor very inviting, little cabin!

Reculver Church

Above, Reculver Church in the 1770s before the building and land to the right of the church disappeared into the sea. Notice the way in which things of interest (written in the top right-hand corner) are depicted by little birds in the sky above them.

With these additaments to boot, we had on board a fellow-passenger, whose discourse in verity might have beguiled a longer voyage than we meditated, and have made mirth and wonder abound as far as the Azores. He was a dark, Spanish complexioned young man, remarkably handsome, with an officer-like assurance, and an insuppressible volubility of assertion. He was, in fact, the greatest liar I had met with then, or since. He was none of your hesitating, half story-tellers (a most painful description of mortals) who go on sounding your belief, and only giving you as much as they see you can swallow at a time – the nibbling pickpockets of your patience – but one who committed downright, day-light depredations upon his neighbour's faith. He did not stand shivering upon the brink, but was a hearty thorough-paced liar, and plunged at once into the depths of your credulity. I partly believe he made pretty sure of his company. Not many rich, not many wise, or learned, composed at that time the common stowage of a Margate packet. We were, I am afraid, a set of as unseasoned Londoners (let our enemies give it a worse name) as Aldermanbury, or Watling-street, as that time of day could have supplied. There might be an exception or two among us, but I scorn to make any invidious distinctions among such a jolly, companionable ship's company, as those were whom I sailed with. Something too must be conceded to the Genius Loci. Had the confident fellow told us half the legends on land, which he favoured us with on the other element, I flatter myself the good sense of most of us would have revolted. But we were in a new world, with everything unfamiliar about us, and the time and place disposed us to the reception of any prodigious marvel whatsoever. Time has obliterated from my memory much of his wild fablings; and the rest would appear but dull, as written, and to be read on shore. He had been Aid-de-camp (among other rare accidents and fortunes) to a Persian prince, and at one blow had stricken off the head of the King of Carimania on horseback. He, of course, married the Prince's daughter. I forget what unlucky turn in the politics of that court, combining with the loss of his consort, was the reason of his quitting Persia; but with the rapidity of a magician he transported himself, along with his hearers, back to England, where we still found him in the confidence of great ladies. There was some story of a Princess – Elizabeth, if I remember – having entrusted to his care an extraordinary casket of jewels, upon some extraordinary occasion – but as I am not certain of the name or circumstance at this distance of time, I must leave it to the Royal daughters of England to settle the honour among themselves in private. I cannot call to mind half his pleasant wonders but I perfectly remember, that in the course of his travels he had seen a phoenix; and he obligingly undeceived us of the vulgar error, that there is but one of that species at a time, assuring us that they were not uncommon in some parts of Upper Egypt. Hitherto he had found the most implicit listeners. His dreaming fancies had transported us beyond the 'ignorant present.' But when (still hardying more and more in his triumphs over our simplicity) he went on to affirm that he had actually sailed through the legs of the Colossus at Rhodes, it really became necessary to make a stand. And here I must do justice to the good sense and intrepidity of one of our party, a youth, that had hitherto been one of his most deferential auditors, who, from his recent reading, made bold to assure the gentleman, that there must be some mistake, as 'the Colossus in question had been destroyed long since;' to whose opinion, delivered with all modesty, our hero was obliging enough to concede thus much, that 'the figure was indeed a little damaged.' This was the only opposition he met with, and it did not at all seem to stagger him, for he proceeded with his fables, which the same youth appeared to swallow with still more complacency than ever, confirmed, as it were, by the extreme candour of that concession. With these prodigies he wheedled us on till we came in sight of the Reculvers, which one of our own company (having been on the voyage before) immediately recognising, and pointing out to us, was considered by us as no ordinary seaman.

The Royal Sea Bathing Infirmary

This early nineteenth century illustration shows the Sea Bathing Infirmary on the right with its fine facade. The Margate Sea Bathing Infirmary, originally known as the General Sea Bathing Infirmary, was founded in 1791 by Dr John Coakley Lettsome[32], and apparently didn't take its first patients in until 1796. So it appears Lamb may have confused his dates. In the distance you can just make out the harbour on the left. Holy Trinity Church is shown above Margate. Built in 1828, Holy Trinity Church was destroyed by German bombs during the Second World War.

---

[32] Dr John Coakley Lettsome (1744-1815) was an English physician and philanthropist born in the British Virgin Islands.

All this time sat upon the edge of the deck quite a different character. It was a lad, apparently very poor, very infirm, and very patient. His eye was ever on the sea, with a smile: and, if he caught now and then some snatches of these wild legends, it was by accident, and they seemed not to concern him. The waves to him whispered more pleasant stories. He was as one, being with us, but not of us. He heard the bell of dinner ring without stirring and when some of us pulled out our private stores – our cold meat and our salads – he produced none, and seemed to want none. Only a solitary biscuit he had laid in; provision for the one or two days and nights, to which these vessels then were oftentimes obliged to prolong their voyage. Upon a nearer acquaintance with him, which he seemed neither to court nor decline, we learned that he was going to Margate, with the hope of being admitted into the Infirmary there for sea-bathing. His disease was a scrofula, which appeared to have eaten all over him. He expressed great hopes of a cure; and when we asked him, whether he had any friends where he was going, he replied, 'he had no friends.'

These pleasant, and some mournful passages, with the first sight of the sea, cooperating with youth, and a sense of holydays, and out-of-door adventure, to me – that had been pent up in populous cities for many months before, have left upon my mind the fragrance as of summer days gone by, bequeathing nothing but their remembrance for cold and wintry hours to chew upon.

Will it be thought a digression (it may spare some unwelcome comparisons), if I endeavour to account for the dissatisfaction which I have heard so many persons confess to have felt (as I did myself feel in part on this occasion), at the sight of the sea for the first time? I think the reason usually given – referring to the incapacity of actual objects for satisfying our preconceptions of them – scarcely goes deep enough into the question. Let the same person see a lion, an elephant, a mountain, for the first time in his life and he shall perhaps feel himself a little mortified. The things do not fill up that space, which the idea of them seemed to take up in his mind. But they have still a correspondence to his first notion, and in time grow up to it, so as to produce a very similar impression: enlarging themselves (if I may say so) upon familiarity. But the sea remains a disappointment. – Is it not, that in the latter we had excited to behold (absurdly, I grant, but, I am afraid, by the law of imagination unavoidably) not a definite object, as those wild beasts, or that mountain compassable by the eye, but all the sea at once, the commensurate antagonist of the earth! I do not say we tell ourselves so much, but the craving of the mind is to be satisfied with nothing less. I will suppose the case of a young person of fifteen (as I then was) knowing nothing of the sea, but from description. He comes to it for the first time – all that he has been reading of it all his life, and that the most enthusiastic part of life, – all he has gathered from narratives of wandering seamen; what he has gained from true voyages, and what he cherishes as credulously from romance and poetry; crowding their images, and exacting strange tributes from expectation. He thinks of the great deep, and of those who go down unto it; of its thousand isles, and of the vast continents it washes; of its receiving the mighty Plata[33], or Orellana[34], into its bosom, without disturbance, or sense of augmentation; of Biscay swells, and the mariner

> For many a day, and many a dreadful night,
> Incessant labouring round the stormy Cape;

of fatal rocks, and the 'still-vexed Bermoothes;[Bermuda]' of great whirlpools, and the water-spout; of sunken ships, and sumless treasures swallowed up in the unrestoring depths: of fishes and quaint monsters, to which all that is terrible on earth

> Be but as bugs to frighten babes withal,
> Compared with the creatures in the sea's entral;

of naked savages, and Juan Fernandez; of pearls and shells; of coral beds, and of enchanted isles of mermaids' grots[35].

I do not assert that in sober earnest he expects to be shown all these wonders at once, but he is under the tyranny of a mighty faculty, which haunts him with confused hints and shadows of all these; and when the actual object opens first upon him, seen (in tame weather too most likely) from our unromantic coast – a speck, a slip of sea-water, as it shows to him – what can it prove but a very unsatisfying and even diminutive entertainment? Or if he has come to it from the mouth of a river, was it much more than the river widening? And, even out of sight of land, what had he but a flat watery horizon about him, nothing comparable to the vast o'er-curtaining sky, his familiar object, seen daily without dread or amazement? – Who, in similar

---

[33] The Río de la Plata Basin, covering parts of Argentina, Brazil, Bolivia, Paraguay and Uruguay.

[34] Orellana is an inland province of Ecuador.

[35] A poetic word for grotto

circumstances, has not been tempted to exclaim with Charuba, [Charoba][36] in the poem of Gebir:

"Is this the mighty ocean? – is this all?"

I love town, or country; but this detestable Cinque Port is neither. I hate these scrubbed shoots, thrusting out their starved foliage from between the horrid fissures of dusty innutritious rocks; which the amateur calls "verdure to the edge of the sea." I require woods, and they show me stunted coppices. I cry out for the water-brooks, and pant for fresh streams, and inland murmurs. I cannot stand all day on the naked beach, watching the capricious hues of the sea, shifting like the colours of a dying mullet. I am tired of looking out at the windows of this island-prison. I would fain retire into the interior of my cage. While I gaze upon the sea, I want to be on it, over it, across it. It binds me in with chains, as of iron. My thoughts are abroad. I should not so feel in Staffordshire. There is no home for me here. There is no sense of home at Hastings. It is a place of fugitive resort, an heterogeneous assemblage of sea-mews and stock-brokers, Amphitrites[37] of the town, and misses that coquet[38] with the Ocean. If it were what it was in its primitive shape, and what it ought to have remained, a fair honest fishing town, and no more, it were something with a few straggling fishermen's huts scattered about, artless as its cliffs, and with their materials filched from them, it were something. I could abide to dwell with Meschek; to consort with fisher-swains, and smugglers. There are, or I dream there are, many of this latter occupation here. Their faces become the place. I like a smuggler. He is the only honest thief. He robs nothing but the revenue, – an abstraction I never greatly cared about. I could go out with them in their mackerel boats, or about their less ostensible business, with some satisfaction. I can even tolerate those poor victims to monotony, who from day to day pace along the beach, in endless progress and recurrence, to watch their illicit countrymen – townsfolk or brethren perchance – whistling to the sheathing and unsheathing of their cutlasses (their only solace), who under the mild name of preventive service, keep up a legitimated civil warfare

---

[36] Charoba was the Young Queen in Walter Savage Landor's (1775-1864) poem, Gebir (1798).

[37] In ancient Greek mythology, Amphitrite was a sea-goddess and wife of Poseidon. To poets – a symbolic representation of the sea.

[38] To behave flirtatiously.

in the deplorable absence of a foreign one, to show their detestation of run hollands, and zeal for old England.

A view from the Parade opposite Margate harbour in 1798

The above is a scene from the Parade opposite the York Hotel in 1798. In about 1806 the Parade was to have a face lift and the wooden fences, which were a part of the old wooden jetty that faced the cliffs below the Parade, were to be replaced with a strong sound stone wall with a solid parapet. Notice the windmills in the distance at Buenos Ayres.

But it is the visitants from town, that come here to say that they have been here, with no more relish of the sea than a pond perch, or a dace might be supposed to have, that are my aversion. I feel like a foolish dace in these regions, and have as little toleration for myself here, as for them. What can they want here? If they had a true relish of the ocean, why have they brought all this land luggage with them? Or why pitch their civilised tents in the desert? What mean these scanty book-rooms – marine libraries as they entitle them – if the sea were, as they would have us believe, a book 'to read strange matter in'? What are their foolish concert-rooms, if they come, as they would fain be thought to do, to listen to the music of the waves? All is false and hollow pretension. They come, because it is the fashion, and to spoil the nature of the place. They are mostly, as I have said, stockbrokers; but I have watched the better sort of them – now and then, an honest citizen (of the old stamp), in the simplicity of his heart, shall bring down his wife and daughters, to taste the sea breezes. I always know the date of their arrival. It is easy to see it in their countenance. A day or two they go wandering on the shingles, picking up cockle-shells, and thinking them great things; but, in a poor week, imagination slackens: they begin to discover that cockles produce no pearls, and then – Oh then! – if I could interpret for the pretty creatures (I know they have not the courage to confess it themselves) how gladly would they exchange their sea-side rambles for a Sunday walk on the green-sward of their accustomed Twickenham meadows!

I would ask of one of these sea-charmed emigrants, who think they truly love the sea, with its wild usages, what would their feelings be, if some of the unsophisticated aborigines of this place, encouraged by their courteous questionings here, should venture, on the faith of such assured sympathy between them, to return the visit, and come up to see – London. I must imagine them with their fishing tackle on their back, as we carry our town necessaries. What a sensation would it cause in Lothbury? What vehement laughter would it not excite among the daughters of Cheapside, and wives of Lombard-Street. I am sure that no town-bred, or inland-born subjects, can feel their true and natural nourishment at these sea-places. Nature, where she does not mean us for mariners and vagabonds, bids us stay at home. The salt foam seems to nourish a spleen. I am not half so good-natured as by the milder waters of my natural river. I would exchange these sea-gulls for swans, and scud a swallow for ever about the banks of Thamesis.

(From "Last Essays of Elia," The Old Margate Hoy, Charles Lamb, 1833)

John Wolcot (1738 – 1819), a satirist who wrote under the pseudonym of Peter Pindar, had a remarkable vein of humour and wit which, while intensely comic to persons not involved, stung its subjects to the quick. This work appears to have been written soon after he visited Margate and its 'attractions' in the early 1790s:

John Wolcot (aka Peter Pindar)

Tales of the Hoy

Twas in that month when nature drear,
With sorrow whimpering, drops a tear,
To find that winter, with a savage sway,
Prepares to leave his hall of storms,
And crush her flower's delightful forms,
And banish summer's poor last lingering ray;

Twas in that season when the men of slop,
The Jew and gentile turn towards their shop,
In alley's dark of London's ample round;
From Margate's handsome spot, and Hooper's Hill
And Dandelion, where, with much good will,
Of buttered rolls they swallow many a pound;

I too, the Bard, from Thanet's pleasant isle,
Where at a lodging-house, I lived in style,
Prepared with gentile and with Jew to wander;
So packed up all my little odds and ends;
Took silent leave of all my Margate friends,
And sought a gallant vessel's great commander;
Who, proud of empire, ruled with conscious joy
His wooden kingdom, called a Margate Hoy!

Lord! How my gaping readers long to know.
Which gallant vessel's valiant lord:
(A natural curiosity I trow!)
Hailed the great poet and his trunk on board!
If Kydd, who nicks the passage to an inch,
Or he, his high and mighty rival, Finch!

No matter! Be it known to my readers, that, on the day of my departure, on the green jap of mother earth, on Hooper's Hill, looking towards dear Dandelion of dancing memory, I thus broke forth into the praise of Margate.

The swing at Dandelion Pleasure Gardens in 1779

The praise of Margate

The tailor here the port of Mars assumes,
Who cross legged, sat in silence on his board;
Forgets his goose and rag-besprinkled rooms,
And thread and thimble, and now struts a Lord!

Here Crispin, too, forgets his end and awl
Here mistress Cleaver, with important looks,
Forgets the beef and mutton on her stall,
And lights and livers dangling from the hooks.

Here mistress Tap, from pewter pots withdrawn,
Walks forth in all the pride of paunch and gear,
Mounts her swollen heels on Dandelion's lawn,
And at the ball-room heaves her heavy rear.

Changed by their travels – mounted high in soul,
Here suds forgets what o'er remembrance shocks;

126

And mistress Suds forgetteth too the pole,
Wigs, bob and pigtail, basins, razors, blocks!

Here, too, the most important Dicky Dab,
With puppy pertness, pretty pleasant Prig,
Forgets the narrow fishy house of Crab,
And drives, in Jew-style, his whirling gig!

And here, 'midst all such consequence am I,
The poet! semper idem – just the same
Bidding old satire's hawks at folly fly,
To fill the shops of booksellers with game.

Dear Margate, with a tear I quit this isle,
Where all seem happy, sweethearts, husbands, spouses:
On every cheek, where pleasure plants a smile,
And plenty furnishes the people's houses.

What's Brighton, when to thee compared! – poor thing;
Whose barren hills in mist for ever weep;
Or what is Weymouth, tho' a queen and king
Wash, walk, and prattle there, and wake, and sleep?

Go bid the whiting the boiled whiting's eye,
In brightness with the gem of Ind compare;
Or bid the skipping Jack-o'-lantern vie
With heaven's keen flash that lights the realms of air:

Go bid the humble thorn the cedars ape,
That to the star their tops sublimely spread;
Go bid a curate in his tattered crape,
Like Doctor Porteus lift the lofty head.

("The Works of Peter Pindar, Esq," by Peter Pindar, 1794, p. 229)

In answer to Peter Pindar, in praise of Margate

Pray, why, friend Peter, didst thou, snarling, hie
To Margate's cheerful strand, in Margate hoy?

Like snake behind a brake, was it to lie,
To spit thy venom – comfort to destroy?

Why, quitting Kings, and Courts, and titled Peers,
Dost shoot thy barbed wit at butcher's wives?
Why at a tailor throw your jibes, your jeers,
When honest industry at wealth arrives?

Tis as when Cockneys, sometimes void of skill,
O'er meads, and even fields, after covies roam,
Spring them and fire, but not a partridge kill,
Shoot a poor sparrow as they journey home!

And, pray, what odds, pert Peter, after all,
'Twixt Cleaver's wife and thou, great Poetaster!
She quits the "beef and mutton on her stall," –
You, lotion, potion, clyster-pipe, and plaster!

("The Sporting Magazine," Vol. 13, Brighton, Oct 20th 1798, p. 60)

George Saville Carey was the son of the celebrated Harry Carey, a successful comic writer in the earlier part of the eighteenth century. Harry Carey is believed to be the composer and writer of our National Anthem "God save the King/Queen." George's description of Margate in the late eighteenth century, is a mixture of praise and disappointment but it has to be said that his last paragraph concerning the immorality of the captain and his crew on board a Margate Hoy is quite telling.

The Balnea[39]

…You no sooner reach Shooter's Hill then the eye is arrested with natural and numerous landscapes of hill and dale, wood and water, until you arrive at Sarre, in the Isle of Thanet. The purpose of your journey is known by every

---

[39] Balnea were facilities for bathing. Whereas Thermae usually refers to the large Imperial bath complexes, *balneae* were smaller-scale facilities, public or private, that existed in great numbers throughout Rome.

inn-keeper, hostler, coachman, postboy, and waiter, on the road; and, like a sheep that has been under the necessity of making his way through a wild of thickets, in order to get at and assemble with the social flock, you are sure to lose a great deal of wool before you get to your journey's end; and when you arrive at the place in question, you are considered as a summer fly, certain of meeting with gaping swallows enough that are always ready to receive you.

Yet I do not know a watering place that is more calculated to gratify a party on a summer's excursion than Margate and its environs; nor is there one where the ladies have been so considered, or so accommodated. The bathing-rooms are not only well situated as to their easy access to the machines, but as a pleasant retreat, at a small subscription, where you are furnished with the news of the day and have a pleasant look-out in the morning over the green ocean, – now a calm, now a breeze; and sometimes presenting itself with all its grandeur in a terrific storm.

The backs of the bathing rooms at the bottom of the High Street

In the evening, parties assemble in the different rooms and what is seldom found in other places of the kind, accord in amity and find an innocent and laudable entertainment for themselves. Each room is generally provided with a piano-forte and is seldom at a loss for a willing and ingenious hand to display its dexterity and give it harmony, nor are the vocal powers restrained in those that are possessed of that enviable ability.

The harbour is sheltered and defended by the pier has a fine sand and a level bottom; so that the bather, unless the wind and the tide be uncommonly high, is seldom annoyed by the turbulence of the waves. The assembly-room is spacious and a good object standing in the centre of the town. The theatre is a royal one, well concerted in respect to size and proportioned to the place. It is remarkably neat and seems to be well conducted; the performers are better, in point of competition in the gross, than most watering-places but are not always so well attended as they sometimes deserve to be. This may proceed from the multiplicity of dice-boxes which are generally rattling at theatrical hours; for at the raffle board everyone is an actor; and, as the spirit of gambling infuses itself into the hearts and minds of men, with a much stronger and more interested propensity than the lines of Shakespeare or the notes of Handel, it is not to be wondered at; when you see the theatre so often empty, or a deserving actor, with all his ability and best exertions, neglected.

There is a tolerable market but it is not so well supplied as might be wished; and, if you are desirous to furnish your table with the necessary comforts of the day, you must get up by six o' clock in the morning and scramble for them, otherwise you may chance to go without your dinner. The pier is a lounging place for many people every evening, but of a Sunday it is a general promenade where you will see a greater diversity of object and a more heterogeneous group than any place in England; which often enables the ingenious artist, when he is disposed to make use of his pencil, to treat the world with a whimsical caricature or two. The libraries are uncommonly elegant, particularly the upper one, which was built by Mr Hall.

Dandelion, about a mile and a half away from Margate, is as pleasant and rural a retreat as can be found anywhere; possessing a grove, an extensive and well-levelled bowling-green, encircled with a voluptuous and variegated shrubbery of the rarest plants and flowers, intersected with seats of accommodation, like to those at Bagnigge[40]-Wells of White[41]-Conduit House.

---

[40] It is documented that Bagnigge was a summer residence for Charles II's mistress Nell Gwynne. The spa was opened to the public around the 1760s, and it became a fashionable meeting place; there was a bowling green and skittle alley, and tea and ale was served.

[41] There has been bathing at Wells of White since 1703.

The dwellings from whence the place takes its name is ancient, formerly belonged to a family of that name, who resided there, and by the stately gateway which is now standing, they must have been people of great respect, being adorned with battlements, as if it had been a place of some defence. The house is now licensed as a tavern, so that the visitor has an opportunity of refreshing himself, if he pleases, while dancing on the green, which is a general practice during the season at a public breakfast, every Wednesday, about twelve o'clock.

There is no proper inlet to the town of Margate from any direction whatsoever; and what they call the High Street is a close contracted thoroughfare, many parts of it is filthy with scarcely a decent habitation and only serves in the present instance to show us what their now-flourishing town was in its original state. The street is too narrow for one carriage to pass another in the day but in the night it is dangerous indeed. Being of considerable length, commencing from the London road down to the old Parade, which is nearly the extent of the town.

What the old Parade might have been is no matter to tell but in its present state and in this improving age, it has little to boast of in respect to elegance, or even cleanliness and in rainy weather it is a mere swamp. The greatest part of it lies between a noisy stable yard, well furnished with manure, and the common sewer of the contiguous market place, as well as all the lower part of the old town, which frequently yield up the most ungrateful exhalations and unsavoury smells to those who choose to regale themselves in this delicious neighbourhood.

Cecil Square is well built; so are the houses in Church Field; but they both turn their backs to the sea, the sight of which one would suppose to be one of the principal attractions which bring summer visitors to this place. The narrow passage, leading from High Street to Cecil Square and the Assembly Rooms, is dangerous both to foot passengers and to those in carriages and serious accidents have often happened there. It is not wondered at, that those who have the management of these things (the principal part of the natives, who are always resident) do not contrive that the new improved parts of the town should have better access to them, or that the visitors, who support the improvement, should not be better accommodated? It should seem as if they acted upon the following idea, – serve but my turn today, and turn out tomorrow.

The lower order of the natives are cunning, avaricious, disrespectful and sometimes malevolent; and, their bread of life is for ever sweetened by the industrious honey-bees from London who yearly distribute the essence of their winter labour among them, yet, from the depravity of their natures, as if they possessed an inward hatred in their minds towards their best benefactors, they seldom discover the least spark of gratitude or even common civility.

Margate High Street during the early nineteenth century

This view of Margate High Street, with the harbour in the background, shows the front entrances to the bathing rooms (which are the low buildings on the left). The backs of these premises were locally named "Hazardous Row" because of the way in which precarious verandas and steps had been built to accommodate customers while waiting their turn in the bathing machines.

Church Field and Cecil Square form the principal part of the new town and there would have been a tolerable opening from thence toward the London and Ramsgate roads, but the intervening ground, in different patches, having been unfortunately purchased by several of the low shopkeepers of Margate, who have conjunctively built upon it a few paltry huts, forming an insignificant row, which they call Cranbourn Alley[42], by which means a very

---

[42] Sometime in the 1960s Cranbourn Alley was totally demolished and replaced with a modern block of flats and various other buildings.

elegant and respectable neighbourhood is deprived of the only eligible egress that was left of making their way into the high road with safety or convenience. The most desirable spot in Margate and where a handsome row of houses might have been judiciously ranged, with all the capability of forming a pleasant, airy, and useful walk in the front, is on the west side of the town at the back of the High Street. It is not only eminently situated but has one of the best aspects of the harbour where there is an everlasting entertainment for the eye from the number of vessels perpetually coming in or going out, with an extensive view of sea and land. But this idea is done away, from the ground being purloined by the proprietors of a rope walk who carry on their business upon the very spot in question and which would be an intolerable nuisance were such an improvement to take place.

The nearest way from Margate to Ramsgate is four miles; but if you should go through Kingsgate and Broadstairs it is more than five. Should you be disposed to go by water to Margate, you will often be under the necessity of arming yourself with a great deal of patience and a good store of victuals; you must shut your eyes from seeing indecent scenes, your ears from indecent conversation and your nose from indelicate smells. The Hoys are a kind of small, much crowded and moving jails; the captain, as he is called, and his men generally assimilate much in their manners and their language to the keepers of Newgate, and other places of confinement about London; and the passengers often, from the time they set sail from Billingsgate till they arrive at Margate, feel themselves under the same state of injunction as those unfortunate creatures who are kept under lock and key in the afore mentioned places of confinement and generally meet with as little degree of respect.

("The Balnea," Or an Impartial Description of all the Popular Watering Places in England, George Saville Carey, London, printed by F W Myers, 1799, Excerpt of Margate, pp 4-16)

This next article fully explains the consequences of travelling in a Hoy when the wind is a bit draughty. Despite the dangers and discomfort people found it well worth visiting Margate, even if it could cost them an extra £20 as the following story points out! (This was almost an annual wage for a farm labourer at the time.)

An Aquatic Excursion to Margate (On August 22nd 1800)

We left Billingsgate on board the British Queen, wind NE by E, about half after one o'clock on Monday last. Our party amounted to one hundred and sixty, the principal of whom were ladies. Expectations of much pleasure during their excursion and other causes produced the most perfect harmony for several hours and many excellent songs were sung with much spirit. We had not been on board above an hour before dinner commenced in the cabin, when all the female part of the company appeared to enjoy their provisions with a good appetite. They next expatiated on the inconveniences attendant on the voyage, as if they were only ideal. The seamen on board encouraged their hopes: 'We shall be down in seven hours and a half; perhaps it may be nine' – at any rate in twelve was the general opinion. This, however, was not the opinion of the Captain and the result was as he expected. The wind at five o'clock was due east and we were then only at North-fleet at seven, we got off Gravesend having made tacks for above an hour and lost ground every tack. We then cast anchor until the next tide, having the mortification of remaining five hours on that station till high-water commenced at twelve o'clock. The steward providing the ladies with hot water and the gentlemen being very attentive in waiting, tea was drank on deck by every judicious person on board; for those who preferred the cabin, soon experienced the ill effects of it and then 'the joys of a sailor's life' appeared no more. We soon understood the situation of those below by the effect on the deck. After we weighed anchor a strong gale sprung up; it was then that sickness was the order of the day.

A common sight to be found on board a Margate Hoy in rough seas

The berths in the cabin were full in a moment and every place occupied under hatch. From them being crowded convulsions succeeded sickness and the scene of horror was heightened by the whistling of the wind and the washing of the decks; all above board were inundated and all below lying over each other huddled together by the rolling of the ship. Every passenger on board was sick – even the ship's steward. The morning appeared with a watery sun; a sure indication of wet weather. At six o'clock we were off Yantlet at the Nore, the atmosphere pouring down a torrent of rain.

A council was held among the ladies (the gale continuing), when it was resolved to petition the captain to put back to Gravesend and on their knees they requested the gentlemen to back their entreaties. A scene of more general misery never appeared on a pleasureable excursion. A twenty-pound note was tendered by one lady to the captain, who, being a good-natured fellow said, 'If the majority of the company wished to return he would comply.' This being the case we tacked about; at seven o'clock the wind being still N.N.E. At eleven, we got back to Gravesend where thirty-five ladies went ashore and several gentlemen. Here we left them to procure post-coaches to Rochester, from whence they proposed taking any casual conveyance to Margate. At one o'clock we set sail to traverse the same course we had left; the wind having veered round to the west we scudded along rapidly and in half an hour Gravesend was out of sight. The favourable gale continuing, we continued on one tack till ten o'clock at night when a dead calm succeeded; being then off the Sisters, about nine miles from Margate. The lights on the Pier and at the Duke's Head Inn were clearly perceptible. A light shower, attended by lightning which was extremely vivid, was succeeded by a gale of wind and at a quarter after twelve we reached Margate Pier and then every one endeavoured to secure a bed after being thirty-six hours on our passage. The town, however, being full, no beds at that hour could be procured; we were, therefore, necessitated to remain on board for another night. We passed it in the manner of the preceding one, lying on the deck as close to each other, for the sake of warmth, as possible; however great our inclination might be for sleep, the cold prevented its taking place. When day-light appeared, we walked round the cliffs and on the pier until the innkeepers arose at six o'clock, when we breakfasted and concurred in one general opinion on the pleasures of a Margate Hoy.

The parties who left us at Gravesend got into Margate at twelve o'clock fatigued almost to death with the journey and put to the expense of five guineas for a chaise (the distance from Gravesend to Margate being fifty miles.)

Margate was never known to be so full; beds are three shillings a night, garrets are cheap at half a guinea per week. The ordinary is two shillings and sixpence a head; last year it was two shillings, and beds one and sixpence. The extravagant charges will do no good to the place.

This morning we left in the new Rose in June (the old one has been broken up). The passengers amounted to 120, returning to London. August 22, 1800.

("Sporting Magazine," or, Monthly Calendar, Vol. 17, 1801, pp. 56-57)

The following is a very sad example of why people were reluctant to travel to Margate by Hoy.

The disaster attending the Margate Hoy near the village of Reculver February 7, 1802

Preliminaries: unfavourable weather – anchor a little distance from Margate, till the return of the tide – the strap of the sounding lead broke – The vessel strikes upon Reculver sand – they let go their anchor; the weather jib-sheet broke, and the lee jib sheet unhooked – the tiller broke, the rudder unshipped, and the vessel unmanageable – fruitless endeavours – the hoy sinks – melancholy result – narrow escape of the ship-carpenter and others – names and number of those who were saved.

The Hoy, named Margate, of Margate (John Goodborn, master, and J. Sacket, owner), was deeply laden with corn for the London market, and had on board twenty-eight passengers, besides the crew consisting of four men. They sailed about three o'clock in the afternoon of Saturday the 6th, though not with very flattering appearances as to weather; yet all of them apparently in the greatest cheerfulness, except Goodborn the captain whose dull countenance seemed to indicate a presentiment of the succeeding calamity and who, during the whole scene, gradually sunk under its horrors.

As the tide was on the ebb and the wind unfavourable when they sailed, they were obliged to come to an anchor at a little distance from Margate where they remained till eight o'clock waiting the return of the tide. However, the master, apprehending blowing weather, judged it most advisable to get under way before the flood-tide made; fearing they should not be able to purchase their anchor as the wind was increasing and by its blowing on the shore rendered their situation dangerous. When the tide made, the wind continuing to blow fresh from the N. N. W. and the night being dark it was resolved that

136

they should turn up under the hook of Margate sand; hoping to have anchored there, but this resolution, prudent as it might be, was entirely frustrated.

After conflicting with the wind and waves until about eleven o'clock, upon making their last tack inward, and sounding, the strap of the sounding-lead broke; an accident which very rarely happens and what is more remarkable, this strap had not been in use more than two voyages. This disaster, apparently trifling, proved to be the foremost in a train of others as unforeseen as inevitable. They now attempted to get the vessel about and to provide themselves with another lead, but before they could accomplish either she struck upon one of the banks below the Reculver sand. Alarmed by the shock and stimulated by a desire to use every possible exertion to preserve the vessel, they let go their anchor as the only remedy in this afflictive situation and the tide flowing she soon rode afloat. However they got their anchor again; but in hauling in the weather-jib sheet, owing to the fury of the wind, it broke; and the lee-jib sheet being greatly agitated became unhooked.

The master having stopped the tiller to leeward sprang forward in order to assist in getting the jib in. At this time it was that the vessel struck again and again they let go their anchor; but now as the height of their distress was advancing the disastrous incidents which contributed to it succeeded each other more rapidly for the tiller broke and whilst they attempted to repair it (the vessel still beating vehemently on the sand) the rudder was unshipped and she became totally unmanageable. In this perilous condition they tried the fore pump, which being choked was rendered useless. They then sounded and found between two and three feet of water in the hold which very soon rose above the floor of the forecastle. As they apprehended the vessel was now sinking they slipped the cable, hoisted the foresail and dropped the gaff in order to let her drive in shore; but as she could not be governed she presently came with her broadside to the beach and there sunk; and the tide still making, the ponderous waves rolled over her in a most tremendous manner. No language can describe the dreadful scene which now presented itself.

The mariners, when they perceived they could do no more to save the vessel and that they must resign her to the winds and waves, directed all their cares towards the passengers. The water had been for some time pouring into the cabin from the scuttle, the companion and the chimney; and all attempts to stop these avenues were totally defeated by the constant dashing of the seas over them. They therefore endeavoured to seize the tarpawling which covered a stack of corn upon the deck, hoping to place it over the cabin to prevent its being inundated; but as several of the affrighted passengers had taken refuge on this stack they could not speedily remove the tarpawling and no time was to be lost, for the water in the cabin was increasing very rapidly and many unhappy creatures were there fainting with fear and almost dying with the sea-sickness. Some of these, with the assistance of the seamen and others, were immediately drawn out of this watery dungeon.

The demise of the 'Margate' Hoy

It was now that Mr Thornton was heard in great distress uttering the most pathetic cries for his dear wife who was in the cabin. He succeeded in extricating her from thence – but to add to his painful anxiety his son, who was a passenger with them, was left to perish there. The unhappy husband did not long retain the clear object of his affection for he was found soon after upon the stack lamenting for the loss of her, and saying: "Alas! She is gone, we shall all soon follow her." which observation proved too true in his case, having been by the impetuosity of the waves suddenly swept away.

When the cabin was pretty deep in water, John Wood, one of the mariners, drew up a female but the seas being very heavy he could not keep his hold with one hand in order to assist with the other; he therefore grasped with both, and let down his foot among the struggling victims which was presently seized by one of them, whose hand he caught hold of, hoping to rescue the almost dying creature from the jaws of death; but the waters swelling higher with every rolling sea, he lost his hold and was obliged to relinquish his generous efforts and abandon the rest of the drowning sufferers to their dismal fate in order to provide for his own safety.

Mr Field, the ship-carpenter, was assisting to repair the tiller, but the rudder being carried away during the attempt and the vessel becoming unmanageable, he immediately anticipated what would happen and turned his thoughts to his own safety and that of his beloved wife for whom he became all anxiety: he ran to a part of the vessel where he found some rattling stuff, out of which he provided two lashings for himself and her. Expecting to find her in the cabin he hastened thither but was disappointed, for she had taken refuge on the stack. When in the cabin he found himself nearly up to the breast in water with the poor creatures struggling around him. His own situation here became critical; for two or three of the despairing creatures clung so fast to him that he could not extricate himself. They were therefore drawn up together by (as he supposes) the exertions of the seamen; but owing to the darkness of the night, dashing of the waters and his own perturbation he could not distinguish who were their deliverers; it is thought that those who were drawn up with him were soon washed off the deck.

Having found his wife on the stack he lashed her to the boom with one of the cords he had provided but in his trepidation, not being able to find the other, he bound his arm to her with the end of that with which she was fastened and in this position they remained whilst two or three heavy seas came over the vessel which by degrees removed the stack from under them and at length carried them both together into the sea. However, Mr Field, either by laying hold of the side of the vessel or some ropes, got back again and lodged himself in the shrouds from whence, in the anguish of his spirit, he could not forbear calling after his dear companion who was now perishing and who just before had embraced him saying, "O, my dear, what will become of our dear children," expecting that they would be left orphans.

According to Mr Field's report, there were with him and his wife on the stack only Mr Thornton and Mr George Bone; the former was first washed away and then his companion, who was a local preacher among the Methodists and who endeavoured to calm the fears of the wretched crew by pious exhortations.

As for the unfortunate captain, he was seen hanging by the reef-tackle; but he soon lost his hold, fell upon the deck and was immediately washed overboard.

John Beazley, a working gardener near Paddington, was seen leaning on the winch to which the fore-halliards had been brought and the fore-sail hove up. The sea falling heavily upon him, in this situation the halliards came off the winch and occasioned the fore-sail to run down upon which he was carried overboard.

This unhappy man was afterwards found under the vessel from whence he was with great difficulty drawn out. The others were strewed along the shore, except Mrs Owen and her servant Mrs Tatnell, Mrs Jacobs, Mrs Edmund's son and John Taylor, a youth, whose bodies were found in the cabin.

From the general account given, by both mariners and passengers who were saved, it is probable that many were washed away at an early period of the distress as they came up out of the cabin debilitated (especially the females) by their exertions to save themselves, their fears and the sea-sickness; and the waves which went over them soon became so heavy that a strong man in full possession of his vigour, could not retain his hold, unless he were so situated as to be beaten against some parts of the tackling of the vessel, or so high in the shrouds as to be above the heavy pressure of the water.

The singular preservation of Mr Jesse Carroway deserves particular notice for being almost exhausted with hanging a considerable time by the boom, he was conveyed on the surface of a violent sea alive to the shore, whilst the same sea, as we have reason to think, hurried some to a watery death.

The preservation of those who had taken refuge in the shrouds was equally surprising when we recollect the state of weakness to which they were reduced by long watching and fatigue; which would have proved fatal to them also, had they continued in their critical situation only a few hours longer. One of these, John Busbridge, a passenger, and a youth used to the sea, being so worn out as to be unable to use his arms any longer, was actually suspended for a short time by his feet from which position he was removed in a state of insensibility by the assistance of his fellow-sufferers. John Wood too was so debilitated that having a little stream to pass in his way to Reculver, whither most of them went when they got ashore, took the precaution of going sideways through it, fearing he should be thrown down by this feeble obstruction and apprehending if he fell he should rise no more.

Names and number of those who were lost:

From Margate:

>Mr John Goodborn, captain.
>Mr George Bone, carpenter, left a widow and four children.
>Mr Henry Thornton, carpenter, and Sarah Thornton, his wife, who left five orphans. Henry, their son, aged 13 years.
>Mrs Crow, a widow.

Thomas Edmunds aged 9 years, son of Mr Thomas Edmunds of the White-Hart Inn.

Miss A Smith Nesbit, Holley-street, Clare-Market, London.

Mrs Owen of Rathbone Place and Elizabeth Wood of Little Chelsea her servant.

Mary Hoof of Rotherhithe.

Sarah Watson of Folkestone; servant at the White-Hart, Margate.

From Ramsgate:

Mr Tatnell of Ramsgate – who left a widow and four children.

Sarah Jones of Vere-street, Clare-Market, London & Robert Offspring of Mount Street, Grosvenor-square, both servants to Miss Millar.

Robert Melville of London, hostler.

Thomas Farndon of Guilford, from Mr Pierce's, shoemaker.

John Smith, Pentonville, from Mr Spurgeon's, butcher.

An American sailor, who said he had been cast away before.

From Broadstairs

Mrs Jacobs, who left a widower with eight children.

Mrs Field, who also left a widower with four children.

John Taylor, son of J. Taylor, shipwright, of Wapping.

John Beazley, of Lisbon-street, near Paddington, working gardener who left a pregnant widow and three children.

Total 23

Names of the Persons saved:

Mr J. Carroway, Margate.

Mr Nuckell, librarian, Broadstairs

Ed. Sayer, mate, Broadstairs.

John Smith.

Mr Taylor, Margate.

John Wood.

Mr Field, Broadstairs.

Wm. Singleton.

J. Busbridge, St Peter's.

Mr John Dear, Ramsgate.

Total 10

The vessel, not having suffered a great deal of damage, was brought into Margate pier within two or three days after her stranding; from whence she was taken to London to undergo a thorough repair.

("Chronicles of the sea," issue number 5, 1838)

This anonymous writer asserts that one of the reasons why some heads of large families come to Margate is to secure a match for their daughters:

Different Sensations, 1812

The homeward bound Packet sailed this day for London at the same time that the outward bound reached the pier after a short and pleasant voyage. The appearance of the passengers by the two was an amusing contrast. Those destined to quit Margate:

> "Down where yon anchoring spreads the sail,
> That, idly waiting, flaps with every gale,
> Downward they move, a melancholy band,
> Pass from the shore, and darken all the strand."

Every countenance wore the same gloom of sorrow, but although the effect was similar, the cause different. The father of a large family, having been over persuaded by his coaxing spouse and importunate daughters, 'cursed with fair faces' and little prudence, to visit Margate, grumbling hurries his wife and family on board the packet with heavy heart and light pocket. The youth, having escaped from his apprenticeship behind a linen-draper's counter, 'remote, unfriended, melancholy, slow,' paces towards the Hoy, anticipating the dreadful effects of his master's kindled ire and picturing, to his disordered fancy, all the tenors of the Court of Aldermen and all the horrors of Little Ease[43]. The tender maiden, 'lovelier in her tears,' with white handkerchief mopping her flowing eyes, takes her last leave of her darling Jemmy, who, though equally unhappy, sustains his loss with all the silent manliness of grief. The ruined spendthrift, now no longer proud, who had dashed down to Margate in his tandem, fallen, fallen, fallen, from his high estate, ashamed of his degradation, rushes impatiently to the pier, cursing horses, dogs, and

---

[43] The place of confinement in Guildhall for disobedient apprentices, so ingeniously contrived that the culprit can neither sit, stand, nor lie down.

Margate. All these, and more, await the Hoy that is to convey them to their cheerless homes and soon as the parting signal is given, they hurry on hoard.

Far different are the appearance of those who had arrived from London. With bounding heart and heels they leap on shore, with a fixed determination to be, what they call, happy. Fathers, mothers, and children, alike thoughtless, hasten along the pier, to plunge themselves instantly into the very centre of the hustle and dissipation of a Watering Place. Alas! They never heed the dismal faces of those whom they meet on their way to London; if they did, it might afford them a useful but unwelcome lesson:

> "Thought would destroy their Paradise,
> No more! Where ignorance is bliss
> is folly to be wise"

After having reached their lodgings, the first thing they do is to dress themselves as gaily as possible; the next, to run to all the libraries, where they shake the dice-box till both their hearts and their elbows ache; and thus, in one half-hour, they are in full possession of all the enjoyments that Margate, delightful Margate, can afford them.

It cannot be denied, that Margate is the most convenient of all the watering places in the kingdom for single men to visit, for whether they be or be not known, they can readily make acquaintances, such as they are; and a young gentleman of enterprise, by a very small share of adroitness, a few soft speeches to the young, and a few compliments to the old ladies, may soon mix with a very large circle, and coquette with single or married, mothers and daughters, on the most intimate footing. The fact is that many of the heads of large families come to this place on speculation, and bring with them their marriageable daughters as marketable commodities which they are willing to dispose of to the best advantage. On this account they are never averse to making new acquaintances, in the hope that by means of a smart dress and a winning glance they may be able to strike a bargain and get rid of those goods here, which have been long old shopkeepers and unsaleable in London. This is the true secret of the free and easy manners to be found in Margate; and this is the reason that mothers and daughters, *una voce*[44], declare that it is the most pleasantest place they ever set their blessed eyes upon. We have long thought that the name was miscalled and that, instead of being written Margate, our

---

[44] una voce: with one voice

topographers should have spelt it Market, and doubtless the latter is the original and proper mode, the former being only a corruption.

("Sporting magazine," Volume 40, 1812, pp. 270-272)

A 'Hoy' was a vessel with one mast, sometimes with a boom to the mainsail and rigged very much like a cutter. Hoys are said to have taken their name from being hailed "Ahoy" to stop to take on passengers. London travellers of the eighteenth century did not relish the prospect of travelling long distances in a Hoy, or at least wished to venture no further seawards than Gravesend. Ramsgate and Margate were classified as long voyages, as in rough weather it may have taken two days or more to make the passage.

On board a Margate Hoy

'The British Queen,' a Margate Hoy detained full of passengers for having accidentally had communication with a vessel performing quarantine, has been since released by orders from the Admiralty. The distresses of the passengers partook of the serio-comic; at first provisions were very scanty, and they had no prospect but seven weeks of durance.

("Drakard's Paper," for October 3, 1813, The Annual Register, Vol. 53, January 1811, Chronicle section, p. 2)

The Margate Hoy in Quarantine

Vone Mister Vill Vilkins, vone wery fine day,
Called up Mrs Vilkins, and to her did say,
Vhat think you, vife, Molly, if ve start avay,
On board of the hoy, to Margate.

There's board and lodging in the ship,
There's wictuals to eat, and vine to sip,
Then, Molly, vill you take a trip,
On board of the hoy, to Margate?

Like a dutiful vife, she complied vith his vishes,
And packed up his linen, coat, vaistcoat and smallclothes,

And avay they sailed ower salt vater and fishes,
On board of the hoy to Margate.

The sailors vere swearing and smoking pig-tail,
Weering the wessel and vetting the sail,
Vhilst 'gainst vind and veather the captain did rail.
On board of the hoy to Margate.

Now, vhen Mr Vilkins lost sight of St Paul's,
He trembled, for fear of the sea-faring squalls,
Vhich are dangerous for those who are not born vith cauls,
Going by vater to Margate,

The vinds blew high, and the vaves did roll,
'Gainst a wessel in quarantine they ran foul,
The vatchmen saw it, and stopped every soul
Going their voyage to Margate.

Six veeks in limbo the wessel must stick,
Sure never vas packet e'er served such a trick!
It made Mister Vilkins confoundedly sick
Of going by vater to Margate.

Such camphorating, fuming and smoking,
Passengers sickening, and sailors joking;
Oh, I vish, said Vilkins, I'd never been poking
On board of the hoy, to Margate.

The whole forty days Vilkins grumbled and swore.
Oh, a plague take the plague-ship! I'm sick and I'm sore!
Vhen the quarantine's finished I vill go on shore
And not go on a voyage to Margate.

The camphor and winegar vhirl in my brain,
Retching and heaving my bowels do strain,
Oh, blow me! you vont catch me going again,
On board of the hoy, to Margate.

("Universal Songster," 1825, p. 112)

145

To those going to the seaside for a week this would have been a serious affair. I wonder whether the vessel they had contact with was the large Dutch vessel mentioned below?

This morning a large Dutch vessel, performing quarantine off Margate, drove from her anchors, and after making several attempts to gain the harbour, came on shore in Westgate Bay, when, it not being possible to afford them any assistance, all the crew perished. In the course of Friday night another vessel was also wrecked on the Margate sand. The bodies of the unfortunate men above mentioned have since been picked up on the shore.

("The Edinburgh Annual Register," Part 2, Sir Walter Scott, 1813, p. 8)

Steamers arrive (1815-1853)

This chapter begins at a very important time in maritime history as well as a very exciting time for the ordinary hard-working lower classes of London. Previously, when travelling by Hoy down to Margate, the passengers, and the crew, really had little idea of how long a voyage was going to take. This would have raised two questions to a working-class passenger: Firstly, would there be enough time left to spend at Margate when he got there? Secondly, would he be back in time for work? If he did not turn up for work he could lose his job. It had been known to take more than a week just to reach Margate due to the unpredictable weather, let alone get back again.

When steam boats became the order of the day it was almost guaranteed that a boat would reach Margate within twelve hours. This of course opened the doors to those classes of people who were concerned about the length of time spent travelling, let alone spending what may have been their only annual holiday being sick on a Hoy struggling to reach its destination. Steam did have its draw-backs though: it was always a worry that the boiler might blow up, as it sometimes did; also, steam had unsavoury side effects: depending on the class of ticket purchased, on deck one risked being plastered with bits of black soot or, if one's ticket was third-class, one would be sent to the far back of the boat where, in a short time of setting off, the passenger (often the servants) would not only end up looking like a chimney-sweep but may have had to fight for breath, choked by the sulphurous emissions. First class passengers, of course, would have the option of spending the journey on the lower decks being entertained, dining, etc or sleeping in their cabins

By 1815 Margate was trying to put behind it the ill effects of the war with Napoleon and France. The consequences of war, and the dire prospects for soldiers returning to a land of high unemployment and high food prices, had affected Margate's new-found holiday industry as much as it had affected many other industries in the country at the time. However, it was not long before the working classes were finding enough time and money to fill the new steam boats for a rowdy time down at Margate. As the nineteenth century advanced, a larger proportion of the working classes were now able to spend their holiday time at Margate without the fear of losing their jobs. This influx had the effect of almost squeezing the upper echelons of society out of Margate and on to local towns such as Broadstairs or further afield to Brighton to utilise the sea water. Their absence led to the town developing a London 'East-End' ambience, the entertainment needs of the new holiday makers being somewhat less refined.

The writings from this period include some from the famous early 'Punch' magazines: a magazine that captured the very essence of why people came to Margate!

This book will cease to travel beyond the bounds of 1853 because the railways brought with them a new era for Margate, including the day trippers. The railways also had the effect of subdividing Thanet into little hamlets which were to continue catering for the more affluent visitor, such as Westgate.

One of the first recorded eye-witness accounts of a steam vessel entering Margate harbour was from Sir Rowland Hill, who was staying in Margate on the 3ʳᵈ of July 1815:

The Early Steam Boats at Margate

We went to see the steamboat come in from London. It is worked by means of two wheels, resembling water wheels, one of which is placed on each side of the vessel and about half-sunk in the water. It comes from London and returns three times in each week. It generally performs the voyage in about twelve hours. In the best cabin there is a handsome library, draught-board, etc. It is surprising to see how most people are prejudiced against this packet. Some say that it cannot sail against the wind if it is high; but when it entered the harbour the wind and tide were both against it and the former rather rough, yet I saw it stem both. There was a great crowd, and much enthusiasm, though carpers predicted failure and sneered at 'smoke-jacks'.

("The New Margate, Ramsgate, and Broadstairs Guide", 6ᵗʰ Ed., Margate, 1816, p 59-60, extract from The Times, 8ᵗʰ July 1815)

The Thames steam yacht in 1815

This is an illustration of the Thames steam yacht, the first to ply between London and Margate in 1815. By the 1820s the old sailing Hoys, such as the one pictured ahead of the steam yacht, were being replaced by the steam boats.

I have been unable to establish if Peter Splitfig really existed and this anonymous account seems somewhat exaggerated. Still, this story, sent to a Margate paper by a poor chap who spent some time at Margate with his family and fell victim to a multitude of calamities makes good reading.

Peter Splitfig's trip to Margate

To the editor of the Thanet Magazine

Gentlemen

I have to request that you will communicate my sad story to the community at large; and let the public judge whether my case is not truly deserving of commiseration.

I am an eminent grocer and keep a respectable shop within Temple-Bar. Having married a poor girl early in life, I was compelled to labour hard at my business to gain a livelihood for her and the young ones. Consequently, I have had but little time to waste in frivolous pleasurable pursuits; and until this unlucky year 1817, I have scarcely ever quitted London for a moment. Would to God gentlemen, that I had still been contented to serve out butter and cheese behind my snug little counter, without venturing to visit a town where I have been broiled, beaten, bubbled, kicked, half-picked and made the laughing stock of thousands. My wife having unfortunately scraped an acquaintance with Mrs Waddleboom, a Fellmonger's wife at Shoreditch, was easily persuaded to coax me for a trip to Margate during the season. As the jade had never troubled me much to go on excursions of this kind, I even consented to waste a few pounds for her amusement. Alas! Little did I imagine what a set of devils inhabited the shores of Thanet, and, that they treated all strangers even worse than the cannibals which one reads about in Robinson Crusoe.

Everything being at length prepared for a start, we left our house early in the morning and went towards Billingsgate where we hoped to get on board one of the Margate Hoys. We had not proceeded far, before a little dapper fellow accosted us with great civility and enquired whether we were going down to Margate? We replied in the affirmative, "Oh then" said he "of course you will prefer going with the Regent, give me leave to conduct you on board." "Why Sir" said I, "as we are out upon pleasure, we may as well see all the fine sights, therefore as you are extremely polite in undertaking to escort us we shall all be very glad to go down in company with so illustrious a personage." The little man bowed very obsequiously and having handed us into a boat, took his leave; observing that he should soon have the felicity of meeting us again. My wife declared that she had never beheld a more finished gentleman "and who knows" continued she "but that this pink of good breeding is one of the courtiers appointed to attend his Royal Highness on his excursion to Margate. Mary my dear, pull that curl a little more over your left eye and draw your shoulders back child, for consider the vast consequence of appearing to advantage in the presence of so great a man."

Arrived on board, we were very politely received and handed into a cabin, fitted up in a style fully adequate to all that we had conceived of the Prince Regent's magnificence. At length I ventured to enquire of the company assembled below, when they expected his Royal Highness would embark? Some laughed, some startled, some whispered, some tittered and all appeared highly diverted at my question; although no one attempted to answer it. "Lord husband" cried my wife "here comes his lordship who procured us a passage and who offered to convey us to Margate with the Regent; maybe he would be polite enough to explain matters to our satisfaction." The little man now came forward almost bursting with laughter and informed us that we were on board the 'Regent' steam packet, of which he was merely the steward or cabin servant. Words cannot describe our confusion and disappointment. The whole of the passengers displaying their wit in some sarcastic observation, on Mr Splitfig's intimacy with the Prince, Mrs Splitfig's influence with the Queen, &c. &c. &c.; and my daughter Mary could scarce hold up her head, she was so much mortified at having 'cocked her cap' at the humble steward of a steam packet.

We proceeded for a considerable time very pleasantly and had actually obtained sight of Margate pier when every person on board was alarmed by a cry of fire. In an instant all was bustle and terror; the women shrieked, the children squalled, the sailors cursed and the gentlemen raved – A thought struck me that I might suggest the means of allaying this tumult. Accordingly I walked cooly up to the Captain and requested him to dispatch a messenger for the Sun Fireman! To my great astonishment he called me 'a damned ignorant Cockney fool,' and ran forward to hasten the passengers into a boat that lay alongside – Seeing no other prospect of deliverance, I also hurried Mrs Splitfig and my daughter Polly into the boat and landed at Whitstable with no other damage than a slight scorching.

On the following day we reached Margate and went into pleasant lodgings upon the Fort where I was soon visited by a gentleman who requested me to bear witness, that the Steam

Packets were by far the most pleasant and safe mode of conveyance between London and Margate. "Sir" said I, "it will be impossible for me to deny that they are excellently adapted for a winter passage but certainly for summer, you make them rather too hot to hold us." With that I showed him my left arm which was considerably inflamed, and my visitor immediately walked off grumbling to himself.

A few days after our arrival at Margate, it being the Sabbath, which my family had always been taught to reverence, we sallied forth to visit some place of public worship. Chance happened to direct our steps towards a chapel of Swedenburghian Dissenters, and it having always been my opinion that the horizons of a true Christian are as likely to find their way upwards from one place as another, we walked into the chapel, and were immediately accommodated with comfortable seats. The Preacher, who I understand is also a Tailor, was exceedingly earnest in his exhortations, and have no doubt, but the good man argued from the very bottom of his heart; but the language of his sermon appeared to me extremely lax and unceremonious, "beware" said he, "of persons affecting sanctity, they are all d-----d hypocrites, yes, mark what I tell ye, they have a sting in their tails." Upon thus hearing the Preacher absolutely swear in his pulpit, my hair bristled up, and I began to meditate a precipitate retreat, but unwilling to disturb the congregation, I loitered in my seat, when suddenly the Preacher clapping his fingers to his nose, exclaimed with great vehemence, "Good God! What an abominable stink! For heavens sake gentlemen open the door, or we shall all be suffocated." I could contain myself no longer, but catching Mrs Splitfig and my daughter by the hand, we rushed out of the place, and returned home to offer up our devotions in private.

Having partaken of a frugal dinner, towards evening we again left home with the intention of going to one of the Dissenting Chapels, with which the town of Margate is said to abound. As we passed through Cecil Square, a door under the Piazzas stood open, apparently for the reception of genteel devotees. We walked up the staircase, but were stopped by a polite powdered gentleman, who demanded eighteen-pence admission money for each person. I accordingly threw down four shillings and sixpence, but requested to be informed to what peculiar sect the place was appropriated, "Lord Sir," said the smiling door-keeper, "this is the *O Rare Tory O*" "Good, good," cried I with exultation, "my grandfather was a staunch Tory, and I reverence his memory too much, to depart from his principles." With these words we entered the inner door, and were surprised to find ourselves in a magnificent chamber, hung with several beautiful chandeliers, and filled by an assemblage of elegant company. Several persons of both sexes whom I took for Priests and Priestesses, stood on an elevated platform, by the side of a handsome organ; and an old grey-headed Druidical personage, sat playing a solemn air upon the Harp – Wrapt in profound meditation, I became insensible to all around; and when the divine chords of the Minstrel ceased to vibrate, I dropped upon my knee, and in an audible voice began to repeat the Lord's Prayer. A universal burst of laughter interrupted my adoration, and perceiving that I had committed some blunder, I hastily resumed my seat. Not long after one of the Priestesses rose and sung an anthem; but conceive gentlemen my consternation when I heard the congregation applaud her holy labour, by clapping their hands like the audience of a London Theatre. Determining not to acquiesce quietly in this public breach of religious decorum, I mounted on one of the forms, and loudly remonstrated against such palpable indecency. The company became once more convulsed with laughter and my daughter Polly kept pulling me down by the sleeve; but in spite of all opposition I still maintained my post, and continued to harangue the tittering crowd.

At length two or three young bloods of fashion came up and addressed me as follows, "Sir, the ladies and gentlemen are extremely obliged to you for this advice; but would have no objection to its termination; they have therefore deputed us to insist on your immediate departure, or in the event of a refusal, we shall be under the truly disagreeable necessity of tossing you in a blanket! The females in the Orchestra are not Priestesses, as you suppose, but merely actresses hired by the master of this Hotel to amuse the visitors by the performance of sacred music." "Hotel," shrieked out my wife, "and have the pious family of the Splitfigs, been lured into an Hotel, to spend their money and their Sabbath?" "Come, come, my dear," said I, "it is now too late to complain, this is all you have gained by your intimacy with that vile Mrs Waddleboom, for she it was who recommended this uncomfortable town for a summer's excursion." Saying this, I speedily sallied forth from the accursed place, and returned once more to our lodgings, where we passed away the remainder of the evening in deploring the blasphemous conduct of the *O Rare Tory O.*

The following day I was walking down the High Street, a very civil little man enquired in the most humble manner if I chose to take a cold bath? I consented to go in one of the machines, but having been very fond of swimming in my youth I crept out from under the umbrella, and took a long turn round the bay. On my return it puzzled me much to conjecture which was my own bathing machine; at length however, feeling tolerably certain that I had found the right, I lifted up the canvass, and to my utter astonishment found myself in the midst of five beautiful nymphs, who were sporting in all the playful wantonness of naked simplicity. Four of them it is true had a sort of flannel garment round their waists, but the fifth wanted even this inefficient covering to conceal her pre-eminent loveliness. The streaming hair hung floating at their backs, and their exquisitely formed bosoms crested the briny waves with snowy lustre.

The moment my head appeared, the naked sylph ran up the steps into the machine, and immediately banged the door; the other ladies attacked me with all the violence of language and action; nay, one gypsy even carried the joke so far as to dash a trundling mop in my face. It was in vain that I apologised, protested and entreated, as it was utterly impossible to convince them that my intrusion was wholly unintentional. At length they all four began to labour my bald pate with wet hand towels, which compelled me to make precipitate retreat; but, as the devil would have it, I had no sooner escaped from the merciless fangs of these harpies, than the rascally driver saluted me with several severe cuts a posteriori. It is most probable that I was indebted for the latter salutation to the information conveyed by the little witch who ran into the machine on my first appearance.

Oops! Wrong bathing machine

Smarting under the effects of this disagreeable encounter, I fortunately happened to find my own machine, the driver of which had become exceedingly impatient at my long delay in the water. Having dressed myself and drove up to the block, I was accosted on leaving the vehicle by a fierce looking naval officer, who demanded my name and address, adding, that he expected to have the pleasure of exchanging shots with me before twenty-four hours had elapsed; as he was determined to wash out the insult which his sister had just received, in the blood of her brutal assaulter!!! Need I describe to you gentlemen the horror of my mind, on hearing this sanguinary ruffian thus coolly arrange my passage to the other world? Falling humbly on my knees, I begged of him if he had any compassion, to pardon my inadvertent mistake, for said I "you can hardly suppose that a poor miserable old grocer, with a wife and family of his own, would entertain any improper ideas of your sister." The blushing son of Neptune looked scornfully on my prostrate figure, and tweaked my nose with some violence, walked contemptuously away, exclaiming "Curse the old Honey and Treacle, he is unworthy of a gentleman's resentment." Never did I feel more endeared to my sweet profession, than at the moment when it rescued me from this terrible thunderbolt.

Walking slowly homewards I could not resist the following monologue, "Oh Splitfig, Splitfig are these the elegant pleasures for which thy fellow citizens crowd by thousands to the shores of Thanet?" "If you are for pleasure Sir," said a stout athletic man, putting a card into my hand, "I hope soon to see you in my Tea Gardens at Minster." "Aye" replied I, "any place would suit me better than this vile town." The man solicited me to visit him the next day, to which having assented, we parted, apparently well pleased with each other.

Not to detain you too long gentlemen, suppose us mounted upon the best of Bennett's stud; and, after many wonderful escapes, arrived at Minster. The Tea was good, the gardens delightful, and the music excellent. My daughter Polly having met with an old sweetheart, footed it away upon the platform among the merriest of the dancers; and my blood was so warmed at the sight, that I was unluckily induced to get into a swing, erected for the amusement of the London visitants. Alas! It was predestined that I should experience nothing but vexations and misfortunes; the rope happening to break whilst I was in full motion, it precipitated me headlong through the glass sash of a cucumber bed, and had nearly dislocated the joint of my neck! I had no sooner recovered the shock, than the master of the gardens demanded payment for the broken panes of his cucumber frame, which, after some altercation, I was silly enough to pay; although this foolish compliance ultimately produced a severe curtain lecture from Mrs Splitfig.

Returning homewards from this unfortunate expedition, my daughter had the misfortune to fall from her donkey; and as the roads were very muddy, she entirely spoilt her new velvet pelisse, which of course, papa could not refuse to replace. So that altogether our ramble to Minster cost me

	£	s	d
For three donkeys one day	0	15	0
Donkey boys	0	3	0
Tea, wine, waiter, &c	0	13	0
To breaking cucumber frame	1	0	0
Paid man for swinging	0	1	0
New Velvet Pelisse for Polly	10	0	0
	12	12	0

Twelve guineas!!! Merciful powers, it would have purchased rushlights enough to have illuminated half London!

The shock that I received in my fall from the swing, gave me a violent pain in the side, for which I was recommended to try a warm bath. Accordingly I did venture into one of those marble coffins, and it was with the utmost difficulty I could again crawl out of it alive. The heat of the bath threw me into such a profuse perspiration, that I attempted to moderate its temperature, by turning in more cold water; but chancing to mistake the cock, I let out such a flood of boiling lava, as flayed all the skin off my back and legs. Jumping madly out of this diabolical contrivance, I roared, stamped, swore, and raved, until the whole house was in uproar. Men, women, and children flocked into the room; when observing that I was in reality par-boiled, each person humanely attempted to alleviate my torments, by applying their own remedy. Oil, vinegar, brandy, melted butter, and water, were instantly poured in copious streams over my suffering body; and to save myself from utter suffocation, I was absolutely compelled to catch up my clothes, and run stark naked into the street. A good natured fellow assisted me to huddle on my garments, and to regain my lodgings, where I was immediately conveyed to bed, and carefully anointed by the fair hands of my daughter Polly.

I passed a restless night, and wishing in the morning to procure a soporific medicine, Mrs Splitfig purchased a powder for me of a druggist who, as I observe by an advertisement on the wrappers of one of your numbers, professes to be the only vender of genuine drugs in Margate. Would it be credited gentlemen that either owing to some mistake of my wife, or of the honest dealer in 'Galenicals [45]' my poor bowels were absolutely drenched by a vile draught, intended to cure horses of the staggers! This gave the finishing stroke to my perambulatory miseries, as immediately after its dreadful operation had ceased, I packed up my 'bag and baggage' and returned to Temple Bar, with a full determination never again to venture within fifty miles of a fashionable watering place.

I am, Gentlemen,

Your afflicted servant, Peter Splitfig.

("The Thanet Magazine," 1817, by a society of gentlemen, published and sold by I Denne, Albion Printing Office, Queen Street, Margate)

The Sea Bathing Infirmary or Royal Sea Bathing Hospital had been a great institution for over twenty years by 1818 but after one of its founder members, Dr Lettsome, had died, grievances arose among the subscribers, creating a rift that lasted for many years. The grievances concerned the plight of many local poor people who were facing sickness and hardship but who were denied access to the benefits of the Sea Bathing Infirmary. Money for the Infirmary was raised both locally and from London patrons, but many local subscribers to the cause were denied the right to nominate a sick local person for a place in the hospital, therefore may have considered withdrawing their subscriptions.

Sea Bathing Infirmary 1818

(Disagreements)

---

[45] A medicinal preparation made up chiefly of herbal or vegetable matter.

...Almost contiguous to Margate, in the small hamlet of Westbrook, stands the Sea-bathing Infirmary, a commodious building erected by the voluntary contributions of a number of benevolent persons, who were desirous of affording an opportunity of sea-bathing to the poor and indigent resident in the inland parts of the country, who, without such a provision for their accommodation, must be precluded a participation of the benefits to be expected in various diseases from the use of salt-water baths, and a saline atmosphere.

The late Dr Lettsome, who was an active promoter of this benevolent plan, and to whom the merit and ingenuity of its original design has been ascribed, laid the first stone of the building on the 21st of June, 1792, in the presence of most of the company assembled at Margate, who, after an impressive oration delivered upon the occasion by the Rev. Weeden Butler, senior of Chelsea, subscribed so largely towards the undertaking, that it was completed, and opened in 1796 for the reception of patients – His Royal Highness the Prince of Wales having graciously condescended to become its Patron.

The success of the managers of this establishment, in obtaining the support necessary for its maintenance, appears to have equalled the expectations of its warmest friends; and it is said, that numerous patients have derived great benefit from it. Whether, under all circumstances, the situation were well chosen, or possesses superior advantages over other parts of the coast, excepting merely in the very cheap conveyance by water, which enables the lower classes of the inhabitants of the metropolis the more easily to avail themselves of the charity, may perhaps be doubted.

The affairs of the institution are conducted by a Committee of Trustees and Governors, principally, if not entirely, resident in London; the chief and original intention of the founders being evidently to afford to persons who live at a distance from the coast benefits which, it was supposed, the indigent could not otherwise obtain; but the circumstance of a collection in aid of the funds having been annually made at the doors of the parish church, unfortunately gave rise of late to a dispute respecting the right, both of management and of admission into the infirmary, which was followed by such heats and animosity between the parties engaged in it, that it may not be altogether improper to introduce a few words upon the subject for the information of those visitors of Margate, who by ex parte statements might be liable to have their opinions of the merits of the institution diminished, in consequence of the events which have recently happened.

It was contended on the one side, that the poor of Margate and its neighbourhood were equally eligible as the poor of any other parish whatsoever, and that subscribers to the Sea-bathing Infirmary, resident in the Isle of Thanet, had a right to participate in the direction and government of that institution, and to enjoy the power of admitting such persons amongst the native inhabitants, whom they deemed fit objects of the charity. It is assumed, on the other hand, that the inhabitants of the Isle of Thanet, however indigent their circumstances, or in other respects proper objects for admission into the infirmary, could never be considered equally in need of such assistance as that which this establishment was designed to afford: because they could, at all times, partake of the benefits of the water and the air, and, perhaps more advantageously, without being confined within the walls of an infirmary. That the principal design in view was not the medical aid to be obtained there (for without disparagement of the skill, or abilities of the medical attendants, it must be confessed that at least equal skill and equal abilities might be found elsewhere, and in hospitals constantly open to the whole public) but the accommodation of appropriate lodgings, sustentation, and attendance, in a situation better adapted for the enjoyment of sea-air and sea-bathing, than in places at a remote distance from the coast.

With regard to the direction of the affairs of the establishment, and the right of every subscriber to partake in the management of it, such right was not denied, although the expediency of it might be justly doubted; but the greater number, both of original benefactors and annual subscribers, being inhabitants of the metropolis (to whom, by-the-by, the town of Margate is chiefly indebted for its opulence and prosperity, and almost for its support) it certainly must appear reasonable that the acting committee of an institution supported principally by their bounty, and designed for the use of their poor neighbours rather than the natives of the coast, should be selected from amongst themselves, who must be, at least, as capable of forming a proper judgment of the fitness or unfitness of those who were desirous of obtaining admission into the infirmary, as the local inhabitants, however respectable, or however impartial, of Margate, or the Isle of Thanet. Such appears to have been the nature of the dispute by which, for a season, Margate was rendered a scene of continual inquietude and animosity. The original question was soon forgotten in the tumultuous jargon of vehement and noisy altercation. This circumstance is noticed in these pages, not with the remotest design of arousing those passions which ought never to have been manifested by either party in the dispute, or to inflame prejudices which every friend of harmony and good order must unfeignedly lament to have at any time existed, but for the purpose of allaying the ferment which has been raised by partial and erroneous statements, and unfair views of the subject. It is introduced also, that the benefit of mutual good-will may be inculcated, between those whose character must essentially suffer, and whose ingenuous feelings must have been outraged by the rash and inconsiderate, the hasty and mischievous efforts of many of their respective partisans, who eagerly rushed into the dispute, from no commendable motives, and certainly without forming any just estimate of the merits of the question at issue.

Reasons and persuasions can not compel any one to recede from the assertion of his rights, whether real or supposed; but upon liberal minds, they can scarcely fail to make an impression if properly urged and timely introduced. It is hoped that these remarks will not be deemed impertinent, or misapplied; and that a due consideration of the evils which arise out of vehement disputes – from jealousy and rivalry – from intermingling too much of secular concerns with ecclesiastical affairs – of mixing the magisterial with the clerical office – of refusing to others that right of private judgment, respecting matters of general concern, which we ourselves desire to exercise, and would not relinquish without a painful struggle – and of the necessity and importance of meekness, forbearance and charity, amongst 'all who profess and call themselves Christians,' will operate a becoming change in the minds of both parties, so that all those bickerings and animosities which have converted kind friends into bitter enemies, and introduced confusion and turbulence into the tranquil recesses of peace and concord, will henceforth, and for ever cease…

("A Journey Round the Coast of Kent," L Fussell, 1818, pp. 89-91)

William Cobbett (1763-1835), was the son of a farmer and innkeeper. He was in the army between 1784 and 1791, but blowing the whistle on military corruption forced him to flee to America. There he began his career as a journalist, publishing 12 volumes of attacks on American democracy and becoming known as Peter Porcupine. He returned to England in 1800 and began publishing a weekly newsletter, the 'Political Register' in 1802. He saw himself as a champion of traditional rural society against the changes brought about by the Industrial Revolution. He was active in grassroots radicalism and supported labourers' riots in 1830, leading to him being tried and acquitted for sedition. He was elected to Parliament in 1832 but died in 1835. The following extract from Cobbett's 'Rural Rides' can only be described as a very scathing account of Margate and its surroundings:

Sept. 3rd to 6th, 1823: From Dover to the Wen. [London]

…Deal is a most villainous place. It is full of filthy-looking people. Great desolation of abomination has been going on here; tremendous barracks, partly pulled down and partly tumbling down, and partly occupied by soldiers.

Everything seems upon the perish. I was glad to hurry along through it, and to leave its inns and public-houses to be occupied by the tarred, and trowsered, and blue-and-buff crew whose very vicinage I always detest. From Deal you come along to Upper Deal, which, it seems, was the original village; thence upon a beautiful road to Sandwich, which is a rotten borough. Rottenness, putridity is excellent for land, but bad for boroughs. This place, which is as villainous a hole as one would wish to see, is surrounded by some of the finest land in the world. Along on one side of it lies a marsh. On the other sides of it is land which they tell me bears seven quarters of wheat to an acre. It is certainly very fine; for I saw large patches of radish-seed on the roadside; this seed is grown for the seedsmen in London; and it will grow on none but rich land. All the corn is carried here except some beans and some barley.

Thursday Afternoon, Sept 4

In quitting Sandwich, you immediately cross a river up which vessels bring coals from the sea. This marsh is about a couple of miles wide. It begins at the sea-beach, opposite the Downs, to my right hand, coming from Sandwich, and it wheels round to my left and ends at the sea-beach, opposite Margate roads. This marsh was formerly covered with the sea, very likely; and hence the land within this sort of semicircle, the name of which is Thanet, was called an Isle. It is, in fact, an island now, for the same reason that Portsea is an island, and that New York is an island; for there certainly is the water in this river that goes round and connects one part of the sea with the other. I had to cross this river, and to cross the marsh, before I got into the famous Isle of Thanet, which it was my intention to cross.

On the marsh I found the same sort of sheep as on Romney Marsh; but the cattle here are chiefly Welsh; black and called runts. They are nice hardy cattle; and, I am told, that this is the description of cattle that they fat all the way up on this north side of Kent. When I got upon the corn land in the Isle of Thanet, I got into a garden indeed. There is hardly any fallow; comparatively few turnips. It is a country of corn. Most of the harvest is in; but there are some fields of wheat and of barley not yet housed. [There are] a great many pieces of lucerne[46] and all of them very fine. I left Ramsgate to my right about three miles, and went right across the island to Margate; but that place is so thickly settled with stock-jobbing cuckolds, at this time of the year, that, having no fancy to get their horns stuck into me, I turned away to my left when I got within about half a mile of the town. I got to a little hamlet, where

---

[46] Lucerne, another name for alfalfa

I breakfasted; but could get no corn for my horse, and no bacon for myself! All was corn around me. Barns, I should think, two hundred feet long; ricks of enormous size and most numerous; crops of wheat, five quarters to an acre, on the average; and a public-house without either bacon or corn! The labourers' houses all along through this island are beggarly in the extreme. The people dirty, poor-looking; ragged, but particularly dirty. The men and boys with dirty faces, and dirty smock-frocks, and dirty shirts; and, good God! What a difference between the wife of a labouring man here, and the wife of a labouring man in the forests and woodlands of Hampshire and Sussex! Invariably have I observed that the richer the soil, and the more destitute of woods; that is to say, the more purely a corn country, the more miserable the labourers. The cause is this, the great, the big bull frog, grasps all. In this beautiful island every inch of land is appropriated by the rich. No hedges, no ditches, no commons and no grassy lanes: a country divided into great farms; a few trees surround the great farm-house. All the rest is bare of trees; and the wretched labourer has not a stick of wood, and has no place for a pig or cow to graze, or even to lie down upon. The rabbit countries are the countries for labouring men. There the ground is not so valuable. There it is not so easily appropriated by the few. Here, in this island, the work is almost all done by the horses. The horses plough the ground; they sow the ground; they hoe the ground; they carry the corn home; they thresh it out; and they carry it to market: nay, in this island, they rake the ground; they rake up the straggling straws and ears; so that they do the whole, except the reaping and the mowing. It is impossible to have an idea of anything more miserable than the state of the labourers in this part of the country.

After coming by Margate, I passed a village called Monckton, and another called Sarr. At Sarr there is a bridge, over which you come out of the island, as you go into it over the bridge at Sandwich. At Monckton they had seventeen men working on the roads, though the harvest was not quite in, and though, of course, it had all to be threshed out; but, at Monckton, they had four threshing machines; and they have three threshing machines at Sarr, though there, also, they have several men upon the roads! This is a shocking state of things; and in spite of everything that the Jenkinsons and the Scots can do, this state of things must be changed. At Sarr, or a little way further back, I saw a man who had just begun to reap a field of canary seed. The plants were too far advanced to be cut in order to be bleached for the making of plat; but I got the reaper to select me a few green stalks that grew near a bush that stood on the outside of the piece. These I have brought on with me, in order to give them a trial. At Sarr I began to cross the marsh, and had, after this, to come through the village of Upstreet, and another village called Steady [Sturry], before I got to Canterbury. At Upstreet I was struck with the words written upon a board which was fastened upon a pole, which pole was standing in a garden near a neat little box of a house. The words were these: 'PARADISE PLACE. Spring guns and steel traps are set here.' A pretty idea it must give us of Paradise to know that spring guns and steel traps are set in it! This is doubtless some stock-jobber's place; for, in the first place, the name is likely to have been selected by one of that crew; and, in the next place, whenever any of them go to the country, they look upon it that they are to begin a sort of warfare against everything around them. They invariably look upon every labourer as a thief...

(Extract from 'Rural Rides,' William Cobbett, 1830, pp. 207-8)

The following diary of a cockney who had spent a week at Margate mentions a Mrs Stains, wife of Sir Thomas Stains Captain in the Royal Navy, who lived at Dent-de-Lion or Dandelion at Garlinge near Margate. Apparently a duel took place in 1817 between Sir Thomas Stains, and Major Halford, brother to Mr Halford, Banker, of Canterbury, the outcome of which was that Sir Thomas Stains was seriously wounded in the right arm. What was particularly unfortunate is that he had already lost his left arm, in defence of his country, in 1808.

One intriguing revelation in this account is that a roller coaster, known as the Russian Mountains, was actually set up on the Fort above Margate harbour. The first proper timber roller coaster was built in Belleville, France, in 1812 and was named Les Montagues Russes ('Russian Mountains') This was apparently the first ride to have cars fixed to the track. In 1817, in France, the first two roller coasters to operate on a continuous circuit were built. This suggests that the one on the Fort above Margate harbour in 1823, as mentioned below, may have been the very first roller coaster to be exhibited in England. Would this not make the proposed development of Margate's Heritage Amusement park at Dreamland with its old roller coaster, the Scenic Railway, even more interesting?

A week's journal at Margate

By a cockney in 1823

'The evenings are getting lengthy now,' quoth I to myself, a brief time back, and I do not think that I can amuse myself more harmlessly than by going to

164

pay my long-promised visit to my good friend Mr Tobias Simpkin. The affair was no sooner arranged in my own mind, than in an active train for being put in execution. Off I bundled, straight up the Strand, and through Temple-Bar, till I fairly found my way to the domicile of my respected elderly friend in _____ Row, not many miles from 'Bow Church Steeple.'

I was received with the customary warm welcome; no professions – no flummery – none of the active, endless talkativeness of being so glad to see me, and all that sort of thing; but almost as soon as I had entered, the little party, consisting of my friend, his wife, two daughters, and self, assembled round a roaring fire, and there was not a single expression in any of their visages which did not loudly assure me, that I was considered as one of the family.

Mr Tobias Simpkin had been lately visiting solus, that place of great fame and renown ycleped[47] Margate. He had hinted to me that it was his intention to make a few dotchings – an idea which I warmly patronized; and accordingly, after a few words of gossip upon indifferent subjects had been exchanged, he hauled out his MS, and, enjoining silence, commenced, with a face of much importance, the following journal, which is characteristic of the worthy citizen, and shows the man to the life; while it gives at the same time no bad general idea of the place which he visited:-

Tuesday morning. – Started in the Albion steam-boat from the Tower, at a quarter past eight o'clock precisely, glad to escape from the counter, and leave my wife and all my cares behind me – deuced good things these steam-boats, beat the old hoys all to nothing – never shall forget being forty-eight hours a few years ago, with Mrs S. and girls, in the Greyhound – sure to get down in glorious time – found the deck crowded – all merry faces – few invalids – plenty of loose cash floating about – sure sign of the badness of the times – found myself excessively voluble – joked, laughed, and chuckled with everybody and at everybody – couldn't find out any originals to twig – blessed fat gentleman, who seemed to know every one on board – very jocose with the ladies thought to cut me out, forsooth – gave him his own, and was looked upon as somebody – old girl and six daughters very loquacious – evidently angling for matches – saw the wenches in the act of making some desperate attempts to inveigle the greenhorns – recognized 'Mamma' as our fishmonger's wife – adjourned to the neighbourhood of the bowsprit to explode at the discovery – good humour the order of the day – music – rising

---

[47] By the name of; called.

generation knocked up a dance – enjoyed the fun, tho' an old prig – elegant fine day – blue sky above and breeze freshening around us – vast exhilaration of animal spirits at every bound of the vessel – send all the sons of Esculapius[48] to Jericho, and wish all his gracious Majesty's hard working subjects were just inhaling the same fine air – edified two middle aged gentlemen and a venerable matron with my profound knowledge of the coast – enlarged upon Tilbury Fort – Gravesend – the Nore – and when a shout from many voices proclaimed the Reculvers in sight, began an erudite account thereof, and finished the same very much to my own satisfaction – appetite marvellous – increased to a ruinous degree – eating all day – arrived in the Bay – vile landing-place – thanked stars I had no womankind with me – chucked myself, portmanteau in hand, into a boat, and soon put foot once more upon mother earth – stalked up the High-street with great dignity, boy behind with portmanteau – saw the vagabond's head half off with laughing – anchored at the King's Head, being always a loyal subject – said inn not to be squinted at – fair accommodations – no disparagement to the Duke's Head, which has a most enticing sea view, besides other excellencies – Adonised[49] – took a cup of bohea, and sallied out for a walk on the Pier – beauteous dames, and gentlemen with reputable calves to their legs, not a few – query, more legs than understandings – met some knowing frequenters of Change – cut them – sundry waddlers too – bless us! – sauntered home, and took a warm bath – flesh-brush very much at my service and the public's – fancied how daintily it might have been scouring the clay of my fat friend the fishmonger's wife, previously to its rejoicing mine eye-lids – bah! – set my stomach in fine order with a bottom of brandy, and went to roost.

Wednesday – Weather still bobbish – up betimes – scandalous to go to the seaside, and lose the most healthy part of the day, perspiring at every pore in a feather-bed – walk on the Fort – scarce a soul stirring but myself, or body either – sun-rise – became thoughtful – caught myself in something of a devotional frame – not displeased thereat – tried how memory would serve me to con Addison's hymn – couldn't remember any of it, but

> "For ever singing as they shine,
> The hand that made us is divine."

---

[48] Esculapius is the god of medicine and healing in ancient Greek religion.

[49] Adonise, to adorn oneself.

Crawled as far as the preventive service establishment, then sat down, and began to muse on the mighty ocean – small white sails popping about in every direction – detected something within me of the sentimental – got cruelly hungry, and turned my nose towards my good-looking King's Head – 'did all that might become a man' to an excellent breakfast, and spent the morning in scouring the town and its outskirts – no change in my old friends – every stone in the same place as when I last was here – a few houses repaired and beautified on the Marine Parade – some new ones rising on the Fort, but still the same old place – all unchanged in the main, amid the many calamitous and eventful changes jammed together in the nutshell of two or three short years, that rise up in my mind's eye – when I think – but "I'll not weep" – Met an old friend, who proposed a trip to Broadstairs – no objection – mounted a " Tally-ho," and drove off with a pair of donkeys in a style that astonished the natives – friend a very passable whip – self having no pretensions that way – gravelled the outworks of a neat mansion near St Peter's, and were all but spilt – landlady bustled out in a furious heat – red as a turkey-cock – managed to appease her – friend did the handsome, and paid damages – laughed a mortal half hour, by St Peter's clock, at the joke – got muzzy with some singularly fine Burton ale at Broadstairs – friend affirmed poz, that he would go and have a cup of fine flavoured souchong[50] with the wrathful landlady, ere he quitted the Isle of Thanet – was as good as his word, and (as he afterwards informed me) being well received, they laughed the matter over, and:

> "Twice he drove in donkey gig,
> And twice knocked down the rail."

Concluded the day at the Ranelagh Gardens – delightful spot, rhyming with cool grot, charming cot, and such like sweet associations – evening passed away with much hilarity – music, dancing – sweet sights and pleasant sounds – in good sooth, I have often spent pleasant hours there, which may not soon be forgotten – and at Dandelion too, the old place – but that hath departed; the merciless plough has gone over it, and alas, my dear Mrs Stains[51] we shall

---

[50] Souchong is a black tea

[51] Sarah Stains the wife of Sir Thomas Staines, (1776-1830), Captain in the Royal Navy, Knight Commander of the Bath, and of the Sicilian Order of St Ferdinand and Merit, and Knight of the Ottoman Order of the Crescent. It was his service as captain of the Cyane, which cost him his arm that led to his knighthood and the Order of Saint Ferdinand.

never, no never, have the felicity of sipping our afternoon's early cup of tea there again!

Ranelagh Gardens

Thursday – First morning of the races, and such a morning! – delicate Scotch mist, alias an unquestionable English drizzle – nothing could be more annoying – managed to procure a crick in my neck, not to mention a decided head-ache, watching for a scrap of blue among the heavy clouds that were sailing over us.

12 o'clock – A regular fixed day raining frying-pans and gridirons – reconciled to remaining in a dry skin for the next twelve hours at least – hurled the settee near the fire, and sprawled at full length thereon, and seizing 'The Guide to the Watering Places,' commenced reading – I am much filled with compassion, like my Lord Falkland, for unlettered gentlemen, on a wet day – fell fast asleep – roused by waiter hinting that dinner was ready – soon took up a position, and evinced as much alacrity as could rationally be expected in the discharge of the various duties to which I was called – thought with complacency of the Clonakilty[52] lads, facetious remark, that the public was much indebted to the man who first invented eating – had recourse again

---

[52] Clonakilty: Irish: often referred to by locals simply as Clon, is a small town in West County Cork, Ireland.

to my settee, and did not require 'The Guide to the Watering Places' to encourage my afternoon's nap – was amused the rest of the evening with beholding the triumphal entry of those, my worthy friend Mr Simpkin, although a man of but slender education, is possessed of some acquirements, with considerable shrewdness and observation. He thinks himself a literary character who had been at the races. Into Margate – ladies much like unto drowned rats, and gentlemen like fricaseed[53] porcupines – calculated upon colds and catarrhs not a few, and wished much I was in the physic line – must speak about it to my old chum Mr Bolus.

Friday – Morning fine – up with the larks – never have yet forgotten the two lines in my Primer – 'Early to bed, and early to rise, Will make ye both healthy, wealthy, and wise.' Scuttled off betimes to the race-ground – a good stiff walk – must be a mile and a half beyond Dandelion – all the conveyances engaged – couldn't have got even a wheelbarrow for love or money – fagged and hot – stood still and looked around me – wondered where all the people could have come from – received a smart, well-aimed blow between the shoulders – looked up, and rapping out an oath (as an acquaintance passed me with a shout at a hard gallop, on a grey Rosinante[54]), repeated those lines of Cowper's:

"The man that hails you Tom or Jack," &c

With considerable feeling – mounted an old dust-cart, in the twinkling of a gingerbread-nut, and had an enviable view of the race-course – made friends with some of my neighbours, regular old files like myself, and entered into the spirit of the thing with infinite promptitude – if I could have reconciled betting to my conscience, I might have won in two out of three courses – considerably tickled with my skill in horseflesh – never was aware of it before – passed for a knowing one among a few in the vicinity – got into a brown study – wax tired, and descending from my exalted station, 'homewards trudged my weary way.'

Saturday – Lots of exportation – went early to Ramsgate, and paraded the surrounding places, not forgetting Pegwell Bay – glorious pier for a

---

[53] Fricasee: a dish consisting of meat cut into pieces, stewed or fried, and served in a sauce of its own gravy.

[54] Rosinante: the name of Don Quixote's horse, taken as the type of a poor, worn-out, and elderly horse.

promenade – recognised an old acquaintance – never shall forget the appearance, the tout ensemble, as the French have it, of his inexpressibles – must have changed them with a scarecrow – hadn't the grace to ask me to take a chop and a tankard with him – resolved to cut all Margate gossips for the future – no heart about them – came home in the dumps.

Sunday – Steered towards Zion Chapel – Mr T, of Ramsgate, in the pulpit – marvelled that he seemed to have the sacred writings, chapter and verse, upon all occasions, at his fingers' ends, and yet more marvellous, that he made withal a sermon at utter variance with the beauty and sublimity of the book with which he appeared so well acquainted – can't endure the jocose school of preaching – visited the parish church in the afternoon, and heard a sober and plain address, certainly suited to the meanest capacity – fine evening walk on the Fort – Pier crowded with people – music playing – beautiful way of 'remembering the sabbath day to keep it holy' – O! For the Rev. E. Irving[55] to uplift his voice among them! With a slick of brimstone lit at both ends in one hand, and an Irish sprig of shilelah[56] in the other, he might perchance work a reform.

Monday – Fell in, as I was lounging on the Pier before breakfast, with a respectable elderly gentleman, not altogether unknown, or unremembered in the 'days of yore' – told me his womankind was with him, and that he had seen one or two old fools who had been spinning over the Russian Mountains[57] on the Fort, at the manifest risk of neck and limb, to procure an appetite for breakfast. Spent the entire day very pleasantly – obliged to omit visiting Minster, with its fine old church and tempting tea-gardens – went to roost with my chin much increased in longitude, that my time was up, and I must return to my wife and the smoke, din, and business of London.

Tuesday – Rose with a face of alarming length – Cheapside a fool to it – went on board the steam-boat, much out of temper – a touch of the pathetic in blank verse, by way of farewell to Margate, while the music struck up 'Off she

---

[55] Edward Irving (1792-1834) was a Scottish clergyman, generally regarded as the main figure behind the foundation of the Catholic Apostolic Church.

[56] Shilelah or shillelagh: Irish, a cudgel with a strap; is a wooden walking stick and club or cudgel, typically made from a stout knotty stick with a large knob at the top, that is associated with Ireland and Irish folklore.

[57] Russian Mountains were a predecessor to the roller coaster.

goes,' by way of keeping up our spirits – saw more faces in which flatness was legible on board, and some about as long as my own – contrived to keep my chin out of my waistcoat pocket, and knocked up a smile at having some companions in affliction – sad difference between going to Margate and returning from it – money all spent – fought manfully every inch of ground for the odd sixpence – horrid row with the boatmen at the Tower-stairs – managed to throw myself at length in a hack, and arrived at home just in good time to express my veneration for a chine of beef, which was smoking on the table.   EDGAR

("The Mirror of Literature, Amusement and Instruction," Vol. 2, Oct 16 1823, PP. 373-75)

Russian Mountains

The Russian Mountains, or Roller Coaster, was first introduced into England in the 1820s and I have spent some time trying to establish when and where they were first introduced. I have put together all the earliest archive evidence of the Russian Mountains existing in Great Britain that I could find. Possibly the earliest mention of the Russian Mountains in England can be found in an advert for a play at the Sadler's Wells Theatre which appeared in The Times newspaper in 1823:

Sadler's Wells Theatre:

> ...This little theatre opened last night for the summer season...
> ...A new pantomime followed called Harlequin's Trip to Paris, or the Golden Flute, in which were introduced the gardens of Tivoli, with the favourite Russian amusement of descending in sledges on inclined planes, which planes or Russian Mountains as they are termed, were erected from the extremity of the stage to the back of the pit. Two sledges, with two persons in each, descended at the same time, one on each plane with great velocity and when they stopped, they were hauled up empty for two other couples to descend in the same way. They seem to afford considerable amusement. The house was filled, but not crowded...

("The Times," 1ˢᵗ April 1823, p. 3)

> ...The Russian Mountains, introduced for the first time in this country, on their present extensive scale, having produced the novel and unexpected event of many of the audience nightly descending in the cars, they will continue their rapid and safe career from the extremity of the stage to the back of the pit every evening till further notice...

("The Times," April 7ᵗʰ 1823, p. 2)

The above appears to be a small, straight, simulation of the Russian Mountains, small enough to fit on the stage. The real Russian Mountains completed a circuit with undulations. The play appears to have lasted for a couple of months. The next reference I found was from someone suggesting that the first person to display the Russian Mountains in England in its entirety was Mr Thomas Rouse of London. I have been unable to confirm the exact date that Rouse did so but the following data may produce some clues:

…This mount [at Northfleet in Kent] has been preparing all the winter for the amusement of the 'Russian Mountains,' for those persons who have courage to partake of such velocity; and similar to those mountains, which were very prevalent in Paris a few years ago, and also first introduced into England by Mr Thomas Rouse, the spirited proprietor of the Eagle Tavern, City Road…

("Pierce Egan's Book of Sports, and Mirror of Life," Pierce Egan, 1832, p. 260)

…The Shepherd and Shepherdess appears to have been pulled down about 1825, at which time Thomas Rouse built on or near its site the Eagle Tavern…

("The London Pleasure Gardens of the Eighteenth Century," Warwick William Wroth, Arthur Edgar Wroth, 1896)

…But at the time when my friend and I spent our evening here, the original house yet stood. It was an old-fashioned inn, called the 'Shepherd and Shepherdess', with skittle-grounds attached, and a few ill-conditioned arbours where the company smoked their pipes and quaffed their ale. At the back part of the premises, the 'governor' had raised (what he called) 'Russian Mountains,' with steep circuitous pathways, made corkscrew fashion, and running from top to bottom: down which the adventurous public travelled in chairs with considerable velocity. The charge for this amusement was something very trifling – I believe a penny, or twopence; but the numbers made it a profitable speculation. From such small beginnings did 'Governor Rouse' elaborate that famous resort known to the world as the 'Eagle Tavern' in the City-road…

("Sixty Years Gleanings from Life's Harvest:" A genuine autobiography, John Brown, 1858, p. 297)

…At half-past five on Monday afternoon, Mr Green accompanied by one of his brothers, ascended in a balloon from the Eagle Tavern, the site of the still remembered 'Shepherd and Shepherdess,' in the City-road…

("The Every Day Book, or, a Guide to the Year," Volume 1, William Hone, 1826, p. 221)

The above two extracts give us an approximate date as to when the Mountains were first exhibited: The first informs us that the Shepherd and Shepherdess pub was still in existence when the Russian Mountains were exhibited: our narrator informs us that they were erected at the back of the premises. The other tells us that the pub had gone by the time The Every Day Book was published in 1826. It is therefore safe to say that the Russian Mountains were introduced before 1826. Although it is still not known how long before 1826, it is possible they were erected when the new Shepherd and Shepherdess gardens were created in 1825 as mentioned below:

...The site of the Theatre is interesting as the building was not only a reconstruction of the Grecian Saloon, originally built by Thomas Rouse in 1841, but was also attached to a public house called the Eagle Tavern which was named in the, still well known, song 'Pop Goes the Weasel'. The Eagle Tavern was constructed next to the Pleasure Gardens known as the Shepherd and Shepherdess Gardens which had been created in 1825...

("Shoreditch Theatres and Halls," www.arthurlloyd.co.uk/Shoreditch.htm)

It appears then, that Margate may be able to claim the kudos of being the first location to exhibit the Russian Mountains in the UK. The article below indicates they were in use there in 1823.

...Monday – Fell in, as I was lounging on the Pier [at Margate] before breakfast, with a respectable elderly gentleman, [...] he had seen one or two old fools who had been spinning over the Russian Mountains on the Fort, at the manifest risk of neck and limb, to procure an appetite for breakfast.

("The Mirror of Literature, Amusement and Instruction," Vol. 2, Oct 16 1823, PP. 373-75)

The following extract also confirms the presence of the Russian Mountains at Margate, albeit for a short period of time:

...There was at one time an attempt to make the Russian Mountains an entertainment at Margate, and they ran for a short time, the locale being in some fields out beyond Zion Chapel; whether they, however, did not come up to Bob Fudge's description, "I've tried all these mountains, Swiss, French, and Ruggieri's, and think for digestion there's none like the Russian," or whether the doctors of the period, who were mighty autocratic, finding them too provocative of health, ordered them off, this deponent saith not; they went and left no mark…

("Turner's Margate Through Contemporary Eyes" – The Viney Letters, Stephen Channing, 2009, p. 23)

The following is an example of what may have been seen on the Fort at Margate in 1823. If it is the case that this was the first appearance of the Russian Mountains in Great Britain, then not only can Margate boast the oldest working wooden roller coaster in Great Britain but the town may well have had the very first one as well. There follows what appears to be an application for a patent, lodged on behalf of 'certain foreigners residing abroad', for the apparatus, submitted and sealed in April 1823:

Graulhie's Portable Conveying Machine

To Gerard Graulhie, of Castle Street, Holborn, in the City of London, Gentleman, for communications made to him by certain foreigners residing abroad, of a machine or apparatus upon a new and portable construction, capable of being inclined in different degrees, adapted to the conveyance of persons and goods over water or ravines, for military or other objects, and applicable also to purposes of recreation and exercise.

(Sealed 16th April, 1823)

Many of our readers have witnessed a species of amusement practised in Paris, consisting of sliding carriages, passing up and down inclined planes, which are called the Russian Mountains. The present project is something of the same kind now first imported into this country. Without expressing any opinion as to the merits or usefulness of the invention, we cannot but regret that a foreigner, probably unacquainted with the English language, should have been so ill-advised as to enrol such an unintelligible document as the specification of his invention now before us. We have perused this rare production with considerable attention, but are totally unable to point out its features, or to comprehend in what it consists. We are therefore, compelled in this instance, to deviate from our usual practice, and to give the specification literally.

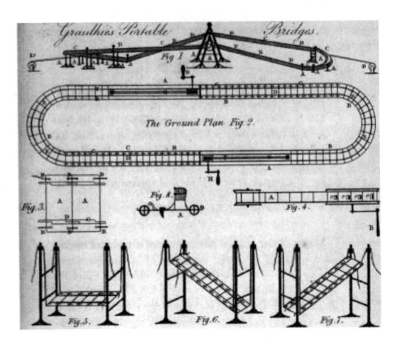

Could this depict the 'Russian Mountains' erected on the Fort at Margate in 1823?

This invention is composed of the following parts, viz. First: Frames and posts more or less elevated and placed at a distance from each other, See drawing fig. 1. A (Plate X.) to support the tables with thin ropes, ways, and balustrades, (hereafter mentioned) and to form with them flying bridges, and other machinery, portable and flexible, and susceptible of different undulations, and degrees of inclination; with the facility of changing at pleasure the inclination or declivity from one direction, to the opposite direction. (fig. 5, 6, and 7.) and to form with the tables an ascending part, which is the shortest (fig. 1, B. and fig. 2, A.) and a descending part, which is the longest, (fig. 1, C. and fig. 2, B.) with the double floor either at the top, or bottom of the inclined planes, consisting of two tables, one sliding over the other, to fill up the space produced by slackening the main ropes or chains.

Second: Wood, metal or any other usables, (fig. 2, D. and fig. 3, A.) made of any convenient length and width, with one edge of each table made convex, and the other edge concave; so that when the tables are drawn close they may work together like a joint attached to each other by ropes, or chains, passing above, or below, through holes made at each side of the said tables, (fig. 2, C. and fig. 3, B.) These tables are supported by main chains, or ropes, tightened at pleasure by windlasses, (fig. 1, D.) giving the facility to change the declivity, and to diminish the motion at the commencement of the circular tables.

Third: Semi-circular tables, (fig. 2, E.) made of the same materials as the straight tables before-mentioned, and supported by a circular frame, (fig A.) with posts high enough to receive the hand rails (hereafter mentioned,) and having (in addition to the general declivity) a particular inclination, or declivity, in the inside of the semi-circles, so as to balance the centrifugal force, by the power of gravity, by proportioning the inside particular inclination of the semi-circular tables, to the general declivity of the whole, and to the velocity required in consequence.

Fourth: A circular projection of iron rod, or wire, or other material affixed to the inside of the posts, surrounding the circular frame, and hanging over the extremity of the axle-trees, outside of the wheels, so as to prevent the possibility of the wheels rising and running over the ways; such circular projections giving facility to form an endless circuit, or ellipsis, where the cars (hereafter mentioned) running with great ease and perfect safety, may be kept in a continued and uninterrupted motion.

Fifth: Ways fixed to the tables on each side, to connect together the boards forming each table, and likewise to direct the wheels of the cars running on the connected tables, (fig. F and fig. 3 C; and to prevent any side motion of the said tables, bare face tenons or rebates, (fig. 3. D.) are formed at the end of each way, so as to join half of the ways of one table, to half of the ways of the next table, without destroying their flexibility, or their backward or forward motion; and also moveable ways at the bottom of the descent to turn the cars off the machine, when it is necessary for them to stop.

Sixth: Balustrades at each side of the connected tables formed of a hand-rail of ropes, running through the tops of the posts; the said hand-rails connected with the tables by means of other smaller ropes, in the form of network, (fig. 1, D.)

Seventh: Cars with two axles moving on the bolts which attach the said axles to the pivot, allowing the wheels to accommodate themselves to the parabola of the circles, so as to prevent their friction on the circular ways. The bodies of the said cars are made to move backwards and forwards on another axletree, which gives to a hooked lever underneath, (fig. 8, A.) the facility to pull down, or bring forward the front of the cars, and place the body of the cars and the rider in a horizontal position on the ascending part, by the action of the rope or chain-ladder (hereafter mentioned) on the lever, in catching the iron steps of the ladder, and by the re-action of the hooked part of the lever,

177

on the front part of the cars; and at the commencement of the descent, the body of the cars and the riders returning backwards by their own gravity are equally in the descending part in a horizontal position.

Eighth: An endless rope or chain-ladder on the ascending part, with iron-rod steps, (fig. 2, G. and fig. 4, A.) turning or revolving by means of persons turning the handles of the large wheels, (fig. 2, H. and fig. 4, B.) on two wheels, one small at the bottom, the other large at the top; the large wheel with cogs or catches, (fig. 4, C.) to prevent the ladder from slipping while drawing up the cars, which is performed by the steps of the ladder catching hold of the hooked lever, before-mentioned, (fig. 8, A.) of iron, fixed underneath the said cars; the lever moving in one direction only, so as to pass over the iron-rod steps of the ladder in going up, and catching them in the tendency of the cars to go back. The cars being thus drawn to the top of the ascending part or commencement of the descending part are then impelled forward by their own gravity.

Finally, it is for the flexibility of the tables; for the circular ends, ways, and tables; for the susceptibility of the cars assuming a horizontal position in ascending the machine, and for the mode of bringing up the cars, that this patent is obtained.

[Enrolled October, 1823]

("The London Journal of Arts and Sciences:" Vol. 7, 1824, p. 180)

The Pier at Margate

OH! Margate is a charming place,
'Tis full of beauty, life and grace,
And I've met many a lovely face
Upon the pier at Margate.

When Cynthia sheds a silver beam,
And London belles on down-beds dream,
'Tis sweet to hear the foaming stream
Beside the pier at Margate.

I love to see the dashing wave
The snow-white cliffs of Britain lave;
I love to hear the night storm rave
Around the pier at Margate.

Though Ramsgate boasts a splendid pier,
More happy we in humbler sphere,
More sociable, more friendly here,
We walk the pier at Margate.

Oh! Margate is a charming place,
'Tis full of beauty, life, and grace,
And I've met many a lovely face
Upon the pier at Margate.

("The Spirit of Public Journals," new series, George Crickshank, Robert Crickshank, 1824, Vol. 2, p. 427)

Margate Health Hunting

"Come to Margate," says Mrs Abrahams," "there you will get a colour and an appetite, bless you." Well, down they all go. First they take a warm bath, then a cold bath – floundering about for an hour in the water – stay out sauntering about in the night air… poke themselves into crowded libraries and dancing-rooms – go to bed at break of day – and then come to town in a fever! Thus it has been lately with several; and we at present visit a case which has had a narrow escape from death – all brought on by *health-hunting at Margate.* – Let people, if they go to watering places for health, go to bed at ten o'clock – rise early, – immerse themselves in the water daily, and instantly leave it – live moderate – and mix with the amusements only at proper hours, and they will return with improved health and spirits; but Margate now a-days, since steam came into fashion, is the place to become an invalid.

("The Atheneum," or Spirit of the English Magazine, Vol. 2, 2ⁿᵈ Series, 1824)

I bet this vapour bath at Margate had a long queue!

The Vapour Bath

As the ceremony of a Vapour Bath may not be generally known, a short account of it may be acceptable. We learn from the encyclopaedia, that

Vapour Baths are used when sick persons are made to receive the vapours arising from some liquid, placed over fire, also, the Vapour Bath is commonly used in Russia and other Northern countries not for any medical purpose, but as a luxury. Ladies or gentlemen go into closed rooms or stoves heated to a very great degree with steam, where they luxuriate for some time, under the hands of the attendants who rub them down. The Vapour Bath at Margate is a flannel tent, the interior of which appears hung round with flannel sleeves. The patient (or luxuriator, as the case may be), is seated in the middle of the tent, and as the process of steaming goes on, hands are introduced through the flannel sleeves, which (like 'the hands' in the entertaining Fairy Tale of the White Cat,) rub with a 'lightness and gentleness' that is extremely delightful.

(From "A Week at Margate", 3rd Ed, 1825)

This sign apparently hung over Bennett's door in Margate's High Street:

Bennett (the Donkey Man)

Cow's milk and asses too, I sell,
And keep a stud for hire,
Of donkeys famed for doing well,
And mules that never tire.

An Angel honoured Balaam's ass,
To meet him on the way;
But Bennett's troop through Thanet pass,
With Angels every day.

(From "A Week at Margate", 3rd Ed, 1825)

This article contains information on costs incurred while staying at Margate in 1825, as well as mention of many local businesses and their proprietors.

"A Week at Margate"

At Howe's, Wright's, the Fountain,
White Hart, or Duke's Head,
Or at Croft's you'll be welcomed, and famously fed;

And I have not a doubt you'll be treated as well
At the Queen's Head in Duke Street, the London Hotel,
Or the Liverpool Arms, which few taverns excel;
Or, if you prefer Social Boarding-House fare,
Try Cecil, or Hawley (no matter which) Square;
And for daily enjoyment, what more would you seek,
Than five meals and a bed at two guineas a week.

The Coffee-rooms, Dancing-rooms, Card-rooms, the Play,
Or the Libraries call you, and tempt you to stay;
At Bettison's, Beauty and Harmony join,
And allure you to stay till three quarters past nine;
Then go other beauties in High Street to view,
Where Bettison's Junior amuses you too,
And does all to attract that politeness can do.

Treat your eyes then at Levy's (if you're inclined)
With the toys on the stands, and sweet faces behind;
At Bettison's, then, you rejoin the gay throng,
And arrive just in time to encore the last song.
If you wish to see Kingsgate, and, all in one day,
Foreland, Broadstairs, and Ramsgate, and then Pegwell Bay,
To Johnson, or Hewitt, or Bennett repair,
You will meet with a choice of conveyances there;
Chairs, Ponies, and Donkeys of spirit and power,
That will trot you five miles at two shillings an hour.

If (mixed with economy) pleasure you seek,
On Wednesday, dear Wednesday, in every week
At Ranelagh Gardens – St Peter's – the fun
Go taste in perfection precisely at one;
Tea, Coffee, and cream, butter, bread white and brown,
With Concert and Dance for a single half crown:
And the sweet smiling faces you constantly meet,
Enjoying the bliss of a national treat,
So enliven the heart, and so light up the features,
That you quit with reluctance the charms of St Peter's.

At Minster, gay rational scenes of delight
Are offered at Buddell's and Well's every night;

And if so far off you're unwilling to rove,
At a sweet pretty place which they call 'Shady Grove,'
You may go and enjoy – but the Bellman will cry,
And say all about it much better than I.

At five in the morning to see the sun rise,
Go down to the beach, and enrapture your eyes;
There gaze with delight as his beams mildly shine,
And illume the bright East with his radiance divine;
Then hail the glad fisherman, meet the strong tide,
Your line and your bait he will amply provide;
A mile off the Foreland your anchor let go,
And fish till the tide is beginning to flow;
Then gaily return and more fish bring away,
Than those who go later and toil the whole day.

And now is the time when delighted you feel,
To accept the politeness of Philpot and Beale,
Hughes, Cleveland, or Hubbard – a frown do not dart
Mrs H. for tho' last, you are first in my heart:
From your name in my childhood such joy have I known,
Your 'Poor Dog' (if I know it) shall ne'er want 'a bone.'

A bathe in the sea will for breakfast prepare
An appetite, some would give hundreds to share;
And appetite, pleasure, contentment, and health
May be purchased by temperance – cannot by wealth.

These luxuries, comforts, and blessings invite,
To the Margate Steam-Packets then haste with delight;
You may stay out a week, taste the pleasures all round,
And carry home change from a Note of Five Pounds.
                    Probatum est

("A Week at Margate," 3rd Ed, 1825, London: Published by Smith, Elder, & Co. Cornhill, 1825)

Philpot's Warm Salt Water Baths

'Hazardous Row' showing the premises of Philpot's warm salt water baths advertised on the side of his bathing room above.

Various bathing machine proprietors

The next article gives an idea of how much it would have cost in travel fares and to stay at Margate for a week in the 1820s, that is, if you wanted to keep your expenses down to no more than five pounds.

Summary of occupations, amusements and expenses, from Saturday morning, on embarking at the tower for a week at Margate, until the return on the following Saturday in time for dinner.

	£	s	d
Saturday:			
Poor Jack at the Tower Stairs	0	0	½
Boat	0	0	6
Luncheon	0	1	0
Music	0	0	6
Ship's Company	0	0	6
Passage Money	0	12	0
Porterage on Landing (two parcels)	0	0	6
Walk on the Pier at night	0	0	1
Sunday:			
Bathing Machine	0	1	0
Go to church, or some place of worship.			
Charity Sermon	0	1	0
Sacred Music at Howe's, at night	0	1	6
Monday:			
Walk to Kingsgate, from thence to the North Foreland, from the summit of which enjoy the Panorama	0	0	6
And home by the obelisk on North Down in time for Luncheon: after which walk down the road to Buenos Ayres, and to the Sea Bathing Infirmary; if the tide serve come home on the sands. At night, Shady Grove	0	1	6
Tuesday:			
Ride to Broadstairs, Ramsgate, and Pegwell Bay.			
Two hours in a Donkey Chaise	0	3	6
Or go per Stage to Ramsgate (1s.), from thence on the sands to Broadstairs; walk home and save half a crown: to which at night add 1s. 6d , and go to the play in the boxes	0	1	6
Wednesday:			
Public breakfast at St Peter's	0	2	6
Conveyance there	0	1	0
Walk home. At night, Bettison's, both libraries	0	2	0

Thursday:

		£	s	d
If on Tuesday you adopted the saving plan, ride to Pegwell Bay per Donkey Chaise		0	2	0
Walk home through St Lawrence.				
At night, Assembly at Howe's		0	4	0
Friday:				
Sail in the morning and fish; go in company; (a party of four for two hours); your share		0	1	0
Drive to Minster in a Caravan at a shilling a head		0	1	0
Tea and amusements there		0	1	8
Walk home in the cool of the evening. At night pay your bill:				
Boarding-House one week		2	2	0
Servants, Cleaning shoes 6d.		0	2	6
A parting gift to the happy Fiddler		0	0	2
Passage home		0	12	0
Luncheon		0	1	0
Ship's Company		0	0	6
Music		0	0	6
Boat		0	0	6
		4	19	11½
Change from your £5 Note to poor Jack at Tower Stairs		0	0	½
		5	0	0

("A Week at Margate," Economy of Time and Money: Showing a traveller to the Isle of Thanet how to dispose of both to the greatest advantage, London, 3rd Ed., 1825, published by Smith, Elder, & Co. Cornhill, 1825)

An invitation to Margate (1825)

Of Margate's attractions I fearlessly boast,
Of Sea-Ports in England possessing the most:
For ease of conveyance, or pleasures when there,
Can Hastings, or Worthing, or Brighton compare?
NO – Margate's improvements shall now be my theme,
Now Margate is held in the highest esteem.

And first, the conveyance – ah! What can exceed
The beauty of prospect, the comfort, the speed?
Full eighty-four miles, the whole distance between us
Takes only seven hours by the Eclipse or the Venus;
While those who would glide in less time o'er the water,
By the Albion, or Dart, go in six and a quarter.

The Captains are men of politeness and science,
On Jones, Large, and Rule, you may place full reliance;
In them you will find (what Captains should be,)
The 'in modo suaviter-fortiter-re. '⁵⁸
And yet, I acknowledge, they do not exceed,
In manners or skill, our new Captain – REED.

(I somewhat misname him in calling him new,
He commanded the FAV'RITE, and comes with this view,
To be one himself, ladies, favoured by you.)

From the Tower, at nine, every day you may start
By the Venus, the Albion, Eclipse, or the Dart;
And (to show how the public convenience they seek)
To accommodate those at the end of the week,
Who think that on Saturday nine is too soon,
One Packet will also set off about noon.

If the weather be fine, upon deck you may stay,
And enjoy lovely prospects the whole of the way;
But if showery weather should force you to go,
Or if you prefer to sit reading below,
Through fear of sea-sickness, for fancy, or pride's sake,
Buy 'Smiles for all seasons' and laugh to your sides ache.

With such strong inducements to Margate to come,
Say, can you decline a week's pastime from home?
From the moment you first put your foot on the pier,
Amusements in multitudes welcome you here.
But ere to the numberless pleasures you run,
I advise you to fortify well 'Number One.'

("A Week at Margate," Third Edition, London, published by Smith, Elder, & Co. Cornhill, 1825)

---

⁵⁸ Suaviter in modo, fortiter in re. is a Latin phrase: Gentle in manner, Firm in deeds

The Dart steamboat

After reading this sad story written by a donkey I have decided never to ride one again...but what a clever donkey!

The Sorrows of a Donkey

I am the most unfortunate of an unfortunate race. The most wretched of the wretched who have no rest for the soles of their feet. Mistake me not – I am no Jew – would I were but the meanest amongst the Hebrews! – But my unhappy, despised generation labours under a sterner, though a similar curse. We are a proverb and a bye-word – a mark for derision and scorn, even to the vilest of those scattered Israelites. We are sold into tenfold bondage and persecution. We are delivered over to slavery and to poverty – we are visited with numberless stripes

No, tender-hearted Man of Bramber[59]! We are not what thy sparkling eyes would seem to anticipate – we are, alas! No negroes – it were a merciful fate to us to be but Blackamoors. They have their snatches of rest and of joy even

---

[59] Bramber is a village and civil parish in the Horsham District of West Sussex, England.

their tabors, and pipes, and cymbals – *we* have neither song nor dance – misery alone is our portion – pain is in all our joints – and on our bosoms, and all about us, sits everlasting shagreen[60]. – Dost thou not, by this time, guess at my tribe? – Dost thou not suspect my ears?

I am, indeed, as thou discernest, an inferior horse – a Jerusalem colt; but why should I blush to 'write myself down an ass?' My ancestors at least were free, and inhabited the desert! – My forefathers were noble – though it must rob our patriarchs of some of their immortal bliss, if they can look down from their lower Indian heaven on their abject posterity!

Fate – I know not whether kindly or unkindly – has cast my lot upon the coast. I have heard there are some of my race who draw in sand-carts, and carry panniers, and are addressed by those Coptic vagabonds, the Gypsies – but I can conceive no oppressions greater than mine. I can dream of no fardels[61] more intolerable than those I bear; but think, rather with envy, of the passiveness of a pair of panniers, compared to the living burdens which gall and fret me by their continual efforts. A sand-bag might be afflictive, from its weight – but it could not kick with it, like a young lady. I should fear no stripes – from a basket of apples. A load of green peas could not tear my tongue by tugging at my eternal bridle. All these are circumstances of my hourly afflictions – when I am toiling along the beach – the most abject, and starved, and wretched of our sea-roamers – with one, or perhaps three, of my master's cruel customers, sitting upon my painful back.

It may chance, for this ride, that I have been ravished from a hasty breakfast – full of hunger and wind – having at six o'clock suckled a pair of young ladies, in declines – my own un-weaned shaggy foal remaining all the time unnourished (think of that, mothers!) in his sorry stable. It is generally for some child or children that I am saddled thus early – for urchins fresh from the brine, full of spirits and mischief – would to providence it might please Mrs D---- the dipper, to suffocate the shrieking imps in their noisy immersion! The sands are allowed to be excellent for a gallop – but for the sake of the clatter, these infant demons prefer the shingles; and on this horrible footing I am raced up and down, till I can barely lift a leg. A brawny Scotch nursery

---

[60] Shagreen is a type of leather or rawhide consisting of rough untanned skin, formerly made from a horse's back or that of an onager (wild ass), and typically dyed green. Shagreen is now commonly made of the skins of sharks and rays.

[61] Fardel: a burden or bundle

wench, therefore, with sinews made all the more vigorous by the shrewd bracing sea air, lays lustily on my haunches with a toy whip – no toy, however, in her pitiless red right hand; and when she is tired of the exercise, I am made over to the next comer. This is probably the Master Buckle – and what hath my young cock, but a pair of artificial spurs – or huge corking-pins stuck at his abominable heels. – No gentle knight comes pricking o'er the plain.

I am now treated, of course, like a cockchafer – and endeavour to rid myself of my tormentor; but the bruteling, to his infernal praise, is an excellent rider. At last the contrivance is espied, and my jockey drawn off by his considerate parent – not as the excellent Mr Thomas Day would advise, with a Christian lecture on his cruelty – but with an admonition on the danger of his neck. His mother, too, kisses him in a frenzy of tenderness at his escape – and I am discharged with a character of spitefulness, and obstinacy, and all that is brutal in nature.

A young literary lady – blinded with tears, that make her stumble over the shingles – here approaches, book in hand, and mounts me – with the charitable design, as I hope, of preserving me from a more unkindly rider. And, indeed, when I halt from fatigue, she only strikes me over the crupper, with a volume of Duke Christian of Lunenberg – (a Christian tale to be used so!), till her concern for the binding of the novel compels her to desist. I am then parted with as incorrigibly lazy, and am mounted in turn by all the stoutest women in Margate, it being their fancy, as they declare, to ride leisurely.

Are these things to be borne?

Conceive me, simply, tottering under the bulk of Miss Wiggins (who, some aver, is 'all soul', but to me she is all body), or Miss Huggins – the Prize Giantesses of England; either of them sitting like a personified lumbago on my loins! – Am I a Hindoo tortoise – an Atlas? Sometimes, Heaven forgive me, I think I am an ass to put up with such miseries – Dreaming under the impossibility of throwing off my fardels – of ridding myself of myself – or in moments of less impatience, wishing myself to have been created at least an elephant, to bear these young women in their 'towers,' as they call them, about the coast.

A Donkey Chaise

Did they never read the fable of 'Ass's Skin,' under which covering a princess was once hidden by the malice of fairy Fate? If they have, it might inspire them with a tender shrinking and misgiving, lest, under our hapless shape, should, per adventure, be oppressing crushing some once dear relative or bosom-friend, some youthful intimate or school-fellow, bound to them, perhaps, by a mutual vow of eternal affection. Some of us, moreover, have titles which might deter a modest mind from degrading us. Who would think of riding, much less of flagellating the beautiful Duchess – or only a namesake of the beautiful Duchess of Devonshire? Who would think of wounding through our sides the tender nature of the Lady Jane Grey? Who would care to goad Lord Wellington, or Nelson, or Duncan? – And yet these illustrious titles are all worn – by my melancholy brethren. There is scarcely a distinguished family in the peerage – but hath an ass of their name.

Let my oppressors think of this and mount modestly, and let them use me – a female – tenderly, for the credit of their own feminine nature. Am I not capable, like them, of pain and fatigue – of hunger and thirst? Have I, forsooth, no rheumatic aches – no colic and windy spasms, or stitches in the side – no vertigoes – no asthma – no feebleness or hysterics – no colds on the

191

lungs? It would be but reasonable to presume I had all these, for my stable is bleak and damp – my water brackish and my food scanty – for my master is a Caledonian, and starves me. – I am almost one of those Scotch asses that 'live upon a brae!'

Will you mention these things, honourable and humane Sir, in your place in Parliament? Friends of humanity! – Eschewers of West Indian sugar! – Patrons of black drudges – pity also the brown and grizzle grey! Suffer no sand – that hath been dragged by the afflicted donkey. Consume not the pannier-potato – that hath helped to over burthen the miserable ass! Do not ride on us, or drive us – or mingle with those who do. Die conscientiously of declines – and spare the consumption of our family milk. Think of our babes, and of our backs. Remember our manifold sufferings, and our meek resignation – our life-long martyrdom, and our mild martyr-like endurance. Think of the 'languid patience' in our physiognomy!

I have heard of a certain French Metropolitan, who declared that the most afflicted and patient of animals was 'de Job-horse' – but surely he ought to have applied to our race the attributes and the name of the man of Uz[62]!

("The Mirror of Literature, Amusement, and Instruction," containing orginal essays, 1825, pp.200-202)

---

[62] The Land of Uz, was Job's homeland, according to The Old Testament Book of Job.

The Mermaid Of Margate
By Thomas Hood, (1799-1845)

The Mermaid of Margate

On Margate beach, where the sick one roams
And the sentimental reads;
Where the maiden flirts, and the widow comes
Like the ocean – to cast her weeds;

Where urchins wander to pick up shells
And the Cit to spy at the ships,
Like the water gala at Sadler's Wells,
And the Chandler for watery dips;

There's a maiden sits by the ocean brim
As lovely and fair as sin!
But woe, deep water and woe to him,
That she snareth like Peter Fin!

Her head is crowned with pretty sea-wares

And her locks are golden loose,
And seek to her feet, like other folks' heirs,
To stand, of course, in her shoes!

And all day long she combeth them well
With a sea-shark's prickly jaw;
And her mouth is just like a rose-lipped shell,
The fairest that man e'er saw!

And the fishmonger, humble as love may be
Hath planted his seat by her side;
'Good even, fair maid! Is thy lover at sea,
To make thee so watch the tide?'

She turned about with her pearly brows,
And clasped him by the hand;
'Come, love, with me; I've a bonny house
On the golden Goodwin sand.'

And then she gave him a siren kiss,
No honeycomb e'er was sweeter;
Poor wretch! How little he dreamt for this
That Peter should be salt-Peter:

And away with her prize to the wave she leapt,
Not walking, as damsels do,
With toe and heel, as she ought to have stept,
But she hopped like a Kangaroo;

One plunge, and then the victim was blind,
Whilst they galloped across the tide;
At last, on the bank he waked in his mind,
And the beauty was by his side

One half on the sand, and half in the sea,
But his hair began to stiffen;
For when he looked where her feet should be,

She had no more feet than Miss Biffen[63]!

But a scaly tail, of a dolphin's growth,
In the dabbling brine did soak:
At last she opened her pearly mouth,
Like an oyster, and thus she spoke:

'You crimpt my father, who was a skate,
And my sister you sold – a maid;
So here remain for a fishery fate,
For lost you are, and betrayed!'

And away she went, with a sea-gull's scream
And a splash of her saucy tail;
In a moment he lost the silvery gleam
That shone on her splendid mail!

The sun went down with a blood-red flame,
And the sky grew cloudy and black,
And the tumbling billows like leap-frog came,
Each over the other's back!

Ah me! It had been a beautiful scene
With the safe terra-firma round;
But the green water-hillocks all seemed to him
Like those in a churchyard ground;

And Christians love in the turf to lie
Not in watery graves to be;
Nay, the very fishes will sooner die
On the land than in the sea.

And whilst he stood, the watery strife
Encroached on every hand,
And the ground decreased, – his moments of life

---

[63] Sarah Biffen (1784-1850) was a Victorian English painter. She was born to a family of farmers in Somerset, 94 cm tall, with no arms and only vestigial legs.

Seemed measured, like time's, by sand;

And still the waters foamed in, like ale
In front, and on either flank,
He knew that Goodwin and Co. must fail,
There was such a run on the bank.

A little more, and a little more
The surges came tumbling in,
He sang the evening hymn twice o'er,
And thought of every sin!

Each flounder and plaice lay cold at his heart
As cold as his marble slab;
And he thought he felt, in every part,
The pincers of scalded crab.

The squealing lobsters that he had boiled
And the little potted shrimps,
All the horny prawns he had ever spoiled,
Gnawed into his soul, like imps!

And the billows were wandering to and fro
And the glorious sun was sunk,
And day, getting black in the face, as though
Of the nightshade she had drunk!

Had there been but a smuggler's cargo adrift
One tub, or keg, to be seen,
It might have given his spirits a lift
Or an anker[64] where Hope might lean!

But there was not a box or a beam afloat
To raft him from that sad place;
Not a skiff, not a yawl, or a mackerel boat,

---

[64] Anker: *(obsolete)* a measure of wine or spirit equal to 10 gallons; a barrel of this capacity.

Nor a smack upon Neptune's face.

At last, his lingering hopes to buoy
He saw a sail and a mast,
And called 'Ahoy!' – But it was not a Hoy
And so the vessel went past.

And with saucy wing that flapped in his face
The wild bird about him flew,
With a shrilly scream, that twitted his case,
'Why, thou art a sea-gull too!'

And lo! The tide was over his feet
Oh! His heart began to freeze
And slowly to pulse: in another beat
The wave was up to his knees!

He was deafened amidst the mountain tops
And the salt spray blinded his eyes,
And washed away the other salt drops
That grief had caused to arise:

But just as his body was all afloat
And the surges above him broke,
He was saved from the hungry deep by a boat
Of Deal (but built of oak).

The skipper gave him a dram, as he lay
And chafed his shivering skin;
And the Angel returned that was flying away
With the spirit of Peter Fin!

("Whims and Oddities:" in Prose and Verse, with forty original designs, Thomas Hood, 1826, pp. 44-49)

Margate Regatta of 1827

On Monday in August 1827, at the above lively watering place [Margate], the announcement of the Regatta attracted a large assemblage both from London and the adjacent country; but, owing to the disappointment of a 'Great Man,' nothing else but a match took place between four six-oared cutters belonging to the town of Margate, for a cup, the sole gift of the late highly-respected and liberal individual, James Taddy, Esq. The cup, an extremely handsome one, though small, representing on one side the passengers and crew of the Hindostan East Indiaman saved by the intrepidity of the Lord Nelson Margate lugger in 1803. The following boats started: – Reculver Queen, Rose, Polly Peachum, and Queen; but the distance of rowing was so badly arranged, that one boat had to row several hundred yards less than another, which gave the Reculver Queen the advantage and she has now had the good fortune of winning two successive years. The Margate men, however, cannot row, it is quite out of their line, and immediately the heat was over, six Deal men challenged any six men in Margate, from £50 to £100, which was not accepted. Expectation had brought together several gentlemen's pleasure vessels, and as nothing was given to be sailed for, a sweepstake of 10 guineas each, for the sole purpose of making sport, was proposed upon the spur of moment, and the following yachts entered:

Names	Owners	Tons
Cameleon	W. Nettlefold, Esq	23
Royal Eagle	T. Stokes, Esq	11
Will-o'-the-Wisp	W. H. Harrison, Esq	16
Pearl	James Heighington, Esq	16

Just as the boats took their stations, the Will-o'-the-Wisp, apparently to take some gentleman on board, stood in to the pier head, and the others started without her; she, however followed, and a most beautifully contested match took place, round the buoy off the Hook, the wind being dead at W, with a two-reefed mainsail breeze. It was with some difficulty won by the Pearl, the Royal Eagle being second, the Cameleon last, very much against the general opinion. With this material addition to the sport, the day which was very fine, passed off merrily, and apparently to the satisfaction of every one. Eleven hundred persons were brought down by steam on the Saturday previous to the Regatta.

("Pierce Egan's Book of Sports, and Mirror of Life," Pierce Egan, 1832, p. 323)

The Margate Regatta

Note the reference to the distinctive 'pea green' colour of the pier – the colour green appears to have been well used in Margate at the time, as the following extracts indicate:

Arrival at Margate

...The buildings of Margate now became evident, and every minute developed some new feature in the landscape; all the party abandoned their sitting to enjoy the view. The curved pier painted pea green and covered with Cockneys, now was disclosed to our eyes, and my old friend from Leicester was again staggered into a profound silence, by being told that a row of houses with a windmill at the end of it was Buenos Ayres. I saw his amazement, but he did not betray his ignorance in speech as the French actress did, who was in London some years since, and when dining on the Adelphi Terrace was shown Waterloo Bridge. After gazing at it, with a degree of pathos, partly national and partly theatrical, she heaved a sigh for the brave fellows who had perished in the neighbourhood, and feelingly inquired whereabouts the farm of Haye Saint was – this is literally a fact and is vouched for – nor is the absence of geographical knowledge in the natives of France, confined to the lady – she is by no means a solitary instance of the most glorious ignorance of localities. – The Turks too, talk of Ireland as a disorderly part of London; and an American, during the last winter, lecturing in Germany, referring to the great improvements which have recently taken place in England, enumerated, amongst other stupendous works of art, the Menai Bridge, which he informed his hearers united Ireland with Wales.

As we approached the harbour we seemed to fly – the jetty and pier became more and more crowded – it was evident we had created 'an interest;' the hurry and bustle on board appeared to increase as we neared the shore, and the sudden tranquillization of the hubbub by the magical words, 'stop her,' of the master evidently excited a mingled feeling of wonder and satisfaction in the breast of our Leicestershire companion, whose countenance had previously indicated a strong suspicion that it was the captain's intention to try the relative strength of our vessel's bow and the nob end of Mr Jarvis's jetty. Of the landing-place, nor his violent indignation when stepping out of the boat in a pair of jockey boots, and selecting, what appeared to his ruralized vision, a verdant spot; his feet slid from under him, and he got a fall unmodified in its disagreeable results by the excitement of the sport so prevalent in his native country.

Jarvis's Jetty, in the early nineteenth century.

"Who built this fine stone affair?" said R----, pointing to the pea-green promenade on our right. "The people of Margate," said someone.

"I thought nobody in England but the king could make a pier," said R----. "Come, come," cried B----, "let us be grave for a minute or two; we look more like a parcel of boys landing than a grave and learned body." "Youth is the time for punning," said R----. "It is no great crime when one is older," said B----. "That I deny," answered our wag; "it may be good in youth, but it is bad in age." The groan which followed this last pun of the voyage re echoed along the shore, and it was not until we reached Howe's hotel, a sort of Bath York House stuck in the middle of Golden Square, London, that the tumult died away...

("The Mirror of Literature, Amusement, and Instruction," Volume 14, No. 387, August 28th 1829)

More pea green

...This place of cockney resort is very pleasant now, breezes fresh, and life and spirit the order of the day. By the way Siddall's library at which I am now scribbling is one of the novelties this season, and from its situation, and the unwearied civility of its conductors, worthy of the patronage of the public. Directly fronting me is the pier, and of course a noble view of the green ocean, one of the most magnificent objects in nature, and of which the eye seldom or never wearies. The bathing rooms, where music, and love, and beating hearts, &c. are in full action from morn till night, are seen with their green painted fronts, and the bay here where the Londoners have their annual dip, with the tide just coming up, and the white chalky tinted element, can really furnish my mind at present (although poetically disposed) with no finer simile than a capacious basin of pease soup. Don't turn away fair ladies at my vulgar and odious comparison. This here Margate is after all a place not to be sneezed at by any means. Here you have fine air, fine walks, noble donkeys, sea breezes, lots of fun, frolic, and vulgarity, and what more would you have? Here Liquor pond-street at least may be forgotten pro tempore – desks, quills, reams of paper, ledgers, may be whisked to 'auld Hornie,'[65] and – all the horrors of a London winter may be lightened by the pleasant recollections of these things, in each and all of which however, it must be said that many are more merry than wise; but I have spent at this same place many a merry day and more thoughtful ones, many in the bustle, but more in the stillness of retired life, and upon the whole, Margate, as I may never see thee again, we part in peace and friendship. St Peter's, Minster, Reculver, Canterbury will return with its merry faces and sunny remembrances to my mind's eye, when Margate and all its scenery are far enough remote from the retina of my visible optics...

("The Mirror of Literature, Amusement, and Instruction," containing original essays, 1825, p. 211)

---

[65] The devil

The following extracts are from the many letters written to the local Keble's Gazette by Stewart Warrender Viney. Viney lived on Bankside, an area that overlooked Margate harbour. He was born in 1820 and as a youngster spent many a day playing under the window of Mrs Booth's lodging house, where the artist J M W Turner stayed when in Margate. Viney's letters are full of detailed descriptions of Margate and the people who lived and worked there. Many of his descriptions are humorous but written in a very intelligent manner:

The letters of Stewart Warrender Viney (1820-1897)

A Margate resident

…as the summer solstice commenced, there was a general smell of green paint, a Margate man seemed to have a craze for green paint and used it incongruously and anaesthetically in everything from shutters to boats…

…Women shook themselves together and rubbed, scrubbed, and furbished up everything capable of being scoured, and by the time the season was just comfortably aired by the north coming sun, Margate was one vast 'Lodgings to let,' and the arrival of the 'boats' – for this was long anterior to railway connection with the metropolis – was looked for with much interest, and the unfortunate Cockneys – I don't use the term disparagingly, but as the vernacular of the period – who arrived were pounced upon, swooped upon, set upon – or any term which signifies actual appropriation – by the 'touters,' and their belongings taken violent possession of by 'the ticket porter,' and as the human was generally dragged away to the Fort, some of his or her family smuggled off down the Dane, and the chattel property of the family carefully deposited at Buenos Ayres, it was probably about midnight before a satisfactory reunion of the scattered entities was effected…

…The Droit Office is not the old building, without clock tower, in the front of which we boys used to play, and probably few will remember the original lighthouse, a little octagon-shaped wooden erection which always suggested to my childish fancy a bottle washing jack. An incident of the new Droit Office presents itself to my mind. On the first occasion of lighting the illuminated clock in the tower, the old man (name forgotten) who was deputed to do so, incautiously allowed the gas to escape, and on his going up with a light the four clock faces were sent to the cardinal compass points they severally faced, and the custodian was picked up somewhat astonished, as were Messrs. S. S. Chancellor and Draper, the then Pier officers…

…I hear during the morning hours, the bellman Philpott – reverently, but not necessarily baptismally, Toby – who rings a large bell and cries some lost property, the various entertainments for the evening, and informs the visitors that every accommodation is provided for them at the tea gardens at Shallows at 1s per head, 8d if you bring your own tea and sugar, half-price for children, ending with a sonorous 'God save the King!' followed by the general addition by some juvenile humorist, 'And hang the Crier,' and so he takes his yellow selvaged three-cornered hat and official coat off the scene.

The bellman Philpot sounding his bell

Billy Stokes, a gaunt lanthorn jawed vendor of lollipops, with a tin tray, scales, &c., slung before him, comes on, and in a shrill treble pipes out, looking most simple and lackadaisical, doggerel, something to this effect:

My ciniment and pepiment and sugar so nice,
Ony vun penny, ony vun penny; Ony vun penny,
so low is the price,
That if you buy vunce you'll buy twice in a trice
Ony vun penny.

Another tinkling bell heralds the approach of a very cross-jack-eyed street merchant, named Waghorn, who in a loud blustering voice inquires whether there are purchasers for 'a plum or seed cake...'

...Coming back to the sea margin, old associations are strong, and I, living down by the sea, was a beach boy; my very nose wakes up its memories, and I sniff on boiling-down days at Old Salter's Soap and Candle Works on Bankside, going up to Pump-Lane stiff, but combined with the aroma of decaying marine vegetation, and the harbour mud was not much behind Cologne. No doubt, however, that sanitary regulations have improved Old Salter and his vats off the face of Bankside...

A donkey ride

…A fellow feeling makes one wondrous kind, and I must not forget the donkeys; they were the delight of the Londoners, and male and female, young and old, went for donkey riding generally in groups of two or three with a youth following up the pace by leathering away at any laggards; the number of ladies – well females – who took asinine exercise gave rise to the following by some poetaster of the time, this may not be the actual text, but it is something like this:

When Balaam swore his wicked vow,
An Angel barred the way,
But donkeys pass through Thanet now
With Angels every day…

…There may be in the few memorial incidents which I send you, something to interest your readers. One of my earliest recollections is of an institution long enough discontinued to be forgotten, save an old fogey like myself, for I believe the custom has not been observed since 1824-5. It was the practice about Christmas time – either Christmas Eve or Twelfth Night – for a band of young fellows to go a 'hoodening.' That is, each being somewhat disguised, and bearing a long staff or broomstick, they brought round one of their party, whose head was enveloped in rude imitation of a horse's head, with a mechanical lower jaw, and painted with large goggle eyes, red lips, and big teeth, which was enough in its entirety of ugliness to afford a good basis for a general nightmare. The party, as I have described it, formed a semi-circle round a door, the 'horse' being in the centre; they then chanted some rude jargon (which my memory fails to furnish, if it was ever intelligible), stamping their staves in tune; on the door being opened and 'largess' demanded, the 'horse' was wont to gnash his teeth in a very dreadful nature, much to the fright of the servant and the children of the family, who clung to her, and peeped round her skirts at the appalling spectacle. The proceeds of this blackmailing, I assume, went in refreshments for the 'hoodeners'… …The custom itself – one more honoured now in the breach than the observance – was suppressed about the date above named, in consequence of a woman I think at St Lawrence, being thereby frightened to death[66]…

…There was a pub at that period that rejoiced in the name of 'The Margate Hoy,' on Bankside, and probably the gallant old ship which was the origin of the sign has long ere fulfilled the law of change, and gone up in smoke to make food for other trees, to build other ships, &c. She was a round-about serving mallet of a vessel, and, like her commander – one Malpas – was about as broad as she was long; a vessel from which the passenger would threaten to 'get out and push behind.' Yet this was the craft in which many hundreds of cocknies voyaged in – certainly justifying Froissart's idea that 'we English take our pleasure sadly' – during their summerings at Margate. She however was, about 1822-3, run off the road as a passenger boat by the steam-boats Eclipse, Dart, Albion, and Magnet, later by the Royal George, William, and Adelaide, then the Herne, &c. up to the fine boats of the present, which are described to me. The Jetty – Jarvis's landing place – then became a necessity, and was the prototype of the present structure. Engineering talent had not developed to the extent it has in later years, and the old construction 'dipped' in the middle, so that unobservant persons – notably foolish young 'spoons,' who thought of nothing but of each other, whose 'two hearts, which beat as one,' – were often 'nipped' on the jetty-head, and the gallant swain had to take up a lovely burden and wade through, amidst the laughter of the more thoughtful, or to hire a boat to reach terra firma…

…Memory takes me wandering down towards the Dane, and I see an old forge nearly opposite Cobb's Bank in which – the forge of course – the incandescent sparks seemed always to have been flying off the anvil. They are gone now; I suppose to make room for a more imposing edifice of some kind. Then there was an allsorts shop – Mrs Arnsell, I think, was the presiding deity – where everything that boyhood loves, or

[66] This incident took place in 1828.

loved, were sold – tinsel for illuminating theatrical characters, cakes, bulls-eyes, a fearful preparation of boiled sugar made tastier with peppermint, fruits of various kinds, and, above all, as it presents itself to my memory's palate, 'scorched peas.' I have since then sat at good men's feasts, have eaten of the delicacies of almost every portion of the globe, but still all depraved as the taste may be, give me ye gods but one small tin measure – a halfpenny the price, I fancy – of Mrs Arnsell's 'scorched peas,' and leave me nothing to desire…

…The Theatre, too, as it seems to be common to all Theatres, stood in the queerest of all queer localities on the high road to nowhere. I have a remembrance of a day light visit to the interior by virtue of a fellowship with the boys of the purveyor of 'apples, oranges, biscuits, or a bill of the play;' it presents itself as dirtier and dingier amongst the scenes than some I have visited in later years. Here the Savilles and Vinings were wont to 'strut their hour,' and some artistes who subsequently obtained eminence in the profession made early appearances; here poor old Sibbald, I think, was the primo in the orchestra. His was an imposing presence – especially looking down at the back of a very bald, shiny, ostrich-egg looking head – and as the war correspondents say, 'drew down the fire of the enemy,' for a very improper young scapegrace named Crow, with a well-directed shot with crab apple (taken in, I fear, purposely for this nefarious purpose), landed bang on the maestro's head and ricocheted across the stage. Youth will be youth, you know, but it was very improper. Bob Crow was full of fun, that's a fact…

…Smuggling was carried on largely at that period thanks to the heavy differential duties imposed; the devices of the contraband traders were many, and ingenious were the schemes to 'run' either cargoes or small consignments, but I always entertained a belief that a judicious application of 'golden ointment' was the best, easiest, and most popular mode. The preventative service, however, kept a good 'look-out' from the cliff, and every load of seaweed (brought up for manure) was duly prodded with a long iron piercer for concealed seekers of spirits, parcels of tobacco, or other dutiable goods; but somehow, in spite of the coast douaniers, a large quantity of goods did escape and come into consumption, and so used were the people to smuggled productions that I have in my memory persons who would have no liquor in the house unless smuggled...

...Of local celebrities, I pay a tribute of respect to one who showed me kindness, Mr John Boys, the solicitor, who, good man (a friend of my father's), gave me a position in his office with the kindly intent of making a lawyer of me. The four walls of an office were, however, too limited a sphere for me, and my exuberance of animal spirits, which, as Mr B said, 'made a bear garden of the office,' rendered it necessary that we should part; but I am glad of the opportunity to pay what is due to his memory. His son, Mr Harvey Boys, I also remember with pleasure and grateful feeling. Of the medicos of the period – Dr Jarvis, a mighty, pompous, white-headed, gold-capped cane gentlemen, too too utter for ordinary mortals to come near; Dr Waddington (his nephew I believe), a keen, shrewd practitioner, who understood the Londoner 'off the chain' exactly, and administered the corrective colocynth and calomel freely and generally with success; then there was dear old Dr Price, whose bland happy manner rendered physic – however nauseous – pleasant to take if ordered by him. There were other doctors Hoffman, Hunter, and others, but I only knew them by name and remember no peculiarity...

...I note with much interest the report of your Regatta, it brings to my mind a very early, I think the first, Regatta, about 1828. Of course there was about the same character of boat sailing and rowing competition, a duck hunt, and a blind wheel-barrow race in the harbour at low water – immense fun. Amongst the names of competitors, I note numbers that are memorially familiar, Emptage, Epps, Sandwell, Doughty, Harman, Crump and others...

...I see an old family residence at the end of Cranbourne Alley, opposite what was then Mr Lewis's Academy. The dwelling presents itself to me as an old Queen Anne house, with two stone steps and pilasters at the sides of the front door; anyway this same domicile had the pleasant reputation of being 'haunted.' The explanatory legend of how a man therein killed his father, grandmother, or what not, does not remain with me; but I know the boys used to go in bands of half a dozen, towards the evening shades – not by dark, oh no; not if they knew it – to wait expectantly for the appearance of his ghostship, only to scatter and run for dear life when some youth, more imaginative than the rest, would cry out, 'there he is! Don't you see it?' I believe the solution of the thing is that some eccentric recluse resides there, and only showed himself occasionally at the windows...

...Margate boys of that period, I think, had a special penchant for ghosts – a relish for the supernatural. There was a traditional ghost too at Albert Square, a little grass plot up behind the Custom House, near Solly's and Gore's boat building shops, but I never saw that spirit. There was some other spots in the neighbourhood where we would not venture after dark, and walked quickly through even in daylight; Pump-Lane, and a mysterious alley leading from thence to the Fort, were of this character, and somewhere 'down the Dane' was believed to be the very stronghold of the spirits.

Apropos of spirits, there was a very fair stroke of contrabandista carried on in those fine old protection times, anterior to the five Bs – 'Bett's British Brandy, Blessed Bad' – or Hodges's cordial, and there was no end of schemes for landing undutied, unexcised liquor over which 'the gauger's stick had never passed,' and 'tubs' or 'half-ankers' (small two gallon kegs) were 'streamed' and anchored at sea, to be picked up when an opportunity occurred for 'running' or landing them. These would be painted a sea-water colour, so as not to attract general attention, the smuggler finding them easily by their bearings; others were painted sand colour, black, or white, as they were to be 'planted' on sand, weedy rocks, or chalk, so as not to be noticeable. These were picked up by carters going under the cliff ostensibly to look for sand, seaweed, or chalk; and the blockade, or preventative service man, rigorously examined even a donkey cart, prodding the load with a long iron searcher for kegs of liquor, or packages of tobacco, or other contraband goods. Still cargoes were 'run' with impunity. It has been said, but then the world is censorious, and the tongue of detraction would undo a saint – and it was a damaging rumour against the 'Joey' (preventative man) – that he was not proof against a saccharine course of treatment. However, there might not have been any real grounds for the suspicion. A London lady sitting up late at her lodgings on the Marine Terrace was held spellbound one night to see a boat enter the harbour, cross over to the sea wall, and simultaneously a body of men make their appearance from the roadway leading up to the back of High Street and seize the cargo, and away in a 'brace of shakes'. Whether it was merely a nightmare, the outcome of an indigestible supper, I know not, and I never heard of any corroboration; but I do remember the seizure of a large galley, 60 feet in length, evidently built expressly for a 'run.' She was loaded with a large cargo, tubs, &c., in the bottom, and on the thwarts alongside each rower was a bale of tobacco or snuff. The boat had evidently been abandoned by her crew on their finding themselves as it were encompassed by the enemy, the revenue cutter outside and the coastguard-men on the land. She shared the fate of all boats similarly seized, and was sawn into three lengths and sold…

…I remember an old oddity of that time, one Solly, a poor old man who presented the singular anomaly, while he was hale enough, of always taking a walk to the Jetty head at low water; his mind was so perfectly a blank, that the sight of a young girl lying in the water drowning, having fallen over the Jetty, and the excited appeals of her companion (myself), a mere child, for help, had no effect upon him whatsoever, and the poor girl would doubtlessly have lost her life had not some boatmen, seeing the casualty which had occurred, rushed the boat down, and she was picked up by one Jethro Sandwell – a fine Newfoundland dog, which had got hold of her first, disputing possession. Poor old Solly kept his walk mechanically, and knew nothing of what was passing…

…of fashionable drinks of that time, there was the warmed beer of Cobb. Sometimes the warming was affected by the aid of a conical shaped pot, but oftener by being stirred with a red-hot poker up to the required temperature; the former generally imparted a tone of smoke, whilst the latter operation gave it a strong chalybeate or warm flat-irony taste. The poker of the tap-room was generally in demand on cold, outside-comfortless days, at houses which the hoveller frequented, such as the 'Hoy' or 'Foy Boat'...

The Parade, Margate

The White Hart Inn is on the left of the picture and the slipway that Viney mentions can just be seen on the bottom right.

...In the cold severe winter weather, when any game which did not involve physical exertion and sequentially warmth of body would not have been popular, the trundling of hoops was the favourite amusement for the winter evenings when 'the stormy winds did blow;' and with a natural association our hoops were named and made to represent the various steamboats running between London and Margate. We did competitive 'spins,' or (what was, I think, the more popular form), each assumed the character of one of the well-known luggers of the period. The area lying between the Jetty end, Bankside, The White Hart, and the slipway and Little Beach was ideally mapped out as the North Sea with its sands. One boy had to accept the rôle of 'a ship on shore' on such and such a sand, and after a little simulated dramatic action of a man on the look-out, a report of 'a ship on shore,' minute guns, &c., off went the lugger 'Victory,' the 'Albion,' the 'Friendship,' or what not, to her assistance, and the difficulties and hazardous character of the service were, as I recollect, rendered with an attention to details which would put to shame by comparison many a representation of this kind of thing in our theatres.

The Droit House and entrance to Jarvis's Jetty

This is the 'Jetty end' or the entrance to Jarvis's Jetty in the 1820s. Notice also the clock tower of the Droit house of which Viney said 'the four clock faces were sent to the cardinal compass points they severally faced.'

Of course there were unheard of difficulties in beating up to the stranded ship, superhuman exertions in getting out anchors, heaving her off, keeping her afloat, and towing her into harbour.

At other times we saw signals of distress flying somewhere away by the first lamp post on the parade wall, and away helter skelter went a fleet of luggers (hoops) in the heaviest of weather, shipping tremendous seas all the way, and the first aboard getting the 'hovel' to bring off an anchor of fabulous weight and chain to match, and as I remember it, all this was gone through with a gravity and affected reality which made it quite exciting. In the matter of an anchor being required, there was no hitch in our 'make-believe.' We had Mr Cobb's office, where we got an order for the required anchor, &c., and the whole thing was gone through in its entirety. How few, probably, of that little crowd continue to trundle the hoops of real life!

...My mind goes back then to the time, as chronological datum, before the building of the present lighthouse on the pier, and, by a natural association to the local shipping of the period and the trade of the port. Some of the early humorists and song-wrights, or writers, have immortalised 'The Margate Hoy,' in descriptions of the incidental fun and discomforts of the early voyagers from Cockaigne to the abode of Hygeia, the Isle of Thanet. I have before me mentally the last remnant of that 'line of packets' which were run off the roads (Margate Roads) by the advent of the steamboat. I see a stout-built round-sterned obese kind of ark, with carved rudder head and ancient tiller, the White Horse and 'Invicta' prominent thereon. This is the Hoy 'Thanet,' of which Captain Malpas, a portly weather-beaten man, is present commander; she once brought down the *élite* of Margate's visitors, now she is a mere carrier of goods and merchandise. Coeval with the 'Thanet,' I see a smarter class of sloop, 'The Countess of Elgin,' sailed by John Stranach, one of a long family of Margate mariners; 'The Lord Hawkesbury,' Mr Blain master; 'The Fox,' owned and sailed by the Fox family. These crafts for some years connected the coast of Flanders and England, carting over horses, butter, cheese, eggs, rabbit, walnuts, fowls, &c., while a smaller craft, 'The British System,' made bolder stretches, under the command of one Solly, to the Channel Islands, and returned with apples in bulk. I don't think there was a boy in St John's Parish but was fully acquainted with the little sloop and her arrival, and for a few days after her

213

making fast to the pier there was a very 'carnival' in the direction of specked apples; explanatorily, 'specked' apples were those bruised or damaged in the passage, and sold at reduced rates. Youth is accredited with a cast-iron stomach, and all the 'specked' fruit went off rapidly. Later on, I may say interpolatively, it was my privilege to lie in the Hooghly (Calcutta), near a smart little barque, bearing the name of a well-known brewer, Thomas Spence, from memory (he had a brewery in the Dane), and hailing from Margate. Going back to the earlier date, when steam began to assert itself as a marine motor, I see, *inter alia*, the Albion, Dart, Magnet, Harlequin, and Columbine, podgy little vessels with overgrown paddle-boxes and very little comfort. They gradually gave place to a better class of packets, Royal George, William, and Adelaide; these, again, were beaten off by improved craft, Red Rover, Herne, and others…

The Harlequin Steamboat at Margate

This picture from the 1820s shows the steam boat Harlequin at the end of Margate pier, along with what appears to be one of the old Hoys.

...Still there was much fun – always provided it was fine weather – in voyaging from the Custom House Wharf to Margate Pier or Jetty; and what, between liquid refreshments, mild flirtations, and an untiring 'band' – that harp, that cornopean, and 'the same fiddle' – the seven or eight hours voyage was worried through agreeably enough. For a time a regular passenger service by steam was maintained between Margate and the Netherlands by the steamboat 'Enderneming,' Captain Cowham, and for a period the mails from the continent were brought to Margate by two steamboats, respectively 'The Fury' and 'The Spit-fire,' but eventually influence shifted the route to Dover. Of the sailing traders to the Netherlands, there was a considerable flood of art, resultant in the production by a Dutch sailor – Nepos, by name – of 'false presentments' of the several vessels above-named. These hardly came strictly within the canons of true art; were, perhaps, somewhat wanting in perspective, and – well, we had not then seen Higgins's and other artists in marine subjects, and with a big burgee flying the name of the ship, and a detailed legend at foot further telling you it was intended for the Countess of Elgin, Ostend, bearing S.E. by E. 1/3 E., and a windmill in the distance to help the imagination. He must be a carping critic who would find fault with minor details. Perhaps some of these triumphs of pictorial art are still extant. I would walk a few miles to renew my acquaintance with them...

("Turner's Margate Through Contemporary Eyes," The Viney Letters, 2009, Stephen Channing)

215

The picture painted here of the Preventive Men along the cliffs of Buenos Ayres is a sad one. Not only were they mainly men from a sea faring background who would probably have preferred to be at sea, many were heroic veterans of the Napoleonic wars. Preventive Men generally had to be recruited from distant areas because of the risk of them being too familiar with the locals. They were not allowed to mingle with or befriend locals and, being a long way from family and friends, they would appear to have had a very lonesome existence.

The Blockade [Preventive] Men

Maturin in his fearful romance of Melmoth[67], has well exemplified the change of character and frequent subversion of intellect occasioned by untoward circumstances. The human mind, like a woody fibre, when submitted to the action of a petrifying stream, gradually assimilates the qualities of its associates. This truth is strikingly verified in the persons of the men on our blockade stations, for the prevention of smuggling. They are a numerous race and inhabit little fortalices on the coasts of our sea-girt isle, which to an imaginative mind would give it the appearance of a beleaguered citadel. The powerful, but still ineffective means resorted to by government for the suppression of illicit traffic, sadly demonstrates the degeneracy of our nature, and may be seen in full operation on the coast between Margate, Dover, and Hastings. For this purpose, the stranger on his arrival at Margate, must take the path leading to the cliffs, eastward of the town, and after walking a little way with the sea on his left hand, he will pass, at intervals, certain neat, though gloomy looking cottages, chiefly remarkable for an odd, military aspect, strongly reminding one of a red jacket turned up with white. These, perched like the eagle's eyrie on the very edge and summit of those crested heights that 'breast the billows foam,' are the Preventive Stations, inhabited by the dumb and isolated members of the blockade. These men will now be seen for the rest of the journey, mounted on the jutting crags, straining their weary eyes over the monotonous expanse of waters which for ever splash beneath them – a sullen accompaniment to their gloomy avocations.

On a first sight of these men, you are ready to exclaim with Mercutio[68], 'Oh, flesh! How art thou fishified;' and begin to think that Shakespeare might have

---

[67] Melmoth the Wanderer is a gothic novel published in 1820, written by Charles Robert Maturin (1782-1824).

[68] Mercutio is a character in Shakespeare's famous tragedy, Romeo and Juliet.

had a living original for his horrid Caliban[69]: for they are mostly selected from amongst fishermen, on account of their excellent knowledge of the coast, and most perfectly retain their amphibious characteristics. The good humoured Dutch looking face is, however, wanting; they have a savage angularity of feature, the effect of their antisocial trade; one feels a sort of creeping horror on approaching a fellow creature, armed at all points, in a lone and solemn place, the haunts of desperate men, and on whose tongue an embargo is laid to speak to no one, pacing the surly rocks, his hands on his arms, ready to deal forth death on the first legal opportunity. Beings such as these an amiable and delicate mind shudders to contemplate, and always finds it difficult to conceive; yet, such are the preventive men who line our coast – melancholy examples of the truth stated at the outset of this paper. Occasionally, however, the good traveller will, much to his joy, meet with an exception to this sad rule, in the person of an old tar, whom necessity has pressed into the service, and who from long acquaintance with the pleasures of traversing the mighty ocean, feels little pleasure in staring at it like an inactive land-lubber, a character which he holds in hearty contempt; besides, to fire at a fellow Briton is against his nature; thief or no thief it crosses his grain, and he looks at his pistols and hates himself. His situation is miserable; he is truly a fish out of water; he loves motion, but is obliged to stand still; his glory is a social 'bit of jaw,' but he dares not speak; he rolls his disconsolate quid over his silent tongue, and is as wretched as a caged monkey. Poor fellow! How happy would a companion make you, to whom you could relate your battles, bouts, and courtships; but mum is the order, and Jack is used to an implicit abeyance of head-quarter orders. The sight of an outward bound vessel drives him mad.

On the appearance of a suspicious sail, the blockader, all vigilance (Jack excepted) awaits in silence the running of the devoted cargo, when suddenly discharging one of his pistols, the air in a moment rocks with a hundred reports, answered successively by his companions. This arouses those in the cottages off duty; the cliffs instantly teem with life; all hurry to the beach, by slanting passages cut in the rocks for that purpose, and a scene of blood and death ensues too horrible for description. Thus are sent prematurely to their graves, many poor fellows, who, had brandy been a trifle cheaper, might have lived bright ornaments of a world they never knew.

After leaving Dover, the scene changes very materially in its appearance; the regimental cottages have vanished, and in their places are found strong brick towers, placed at short distances from each other, containing each a little garrison, over which a lieutenant presides; from the abundance of these towers, and their proximity to each other, the men are numerously scattered

---

[69] Caliban is one of the primary antagonists in Shakespeare's play The Tempest

217

over the bleak sands, and living more together, are a social set of creatures, compared with those westward of Dover. The towers very much resemble the Peel Houses which, 'lang syne,' bristled on the Scottish border, and like them, are built to watch and annoy an enemy from; they are about twenty feet in height, of a circular form, and have a concealed gallery at top with loopholes, for observation. The preventive men have a costume peculiar to them: white trousers, blue jacket, and white hat; a pair of pistols, a cutlass, and a sort of carbine. A well painted picture of them, when surrounding their little castles, a fresh breeze stirring the sea into a rage, and a horizontal sun gilding their rugged features, would fairly rival Salvator Rosa's[70] brigands in the Abruzzi Mountains.

("The Mirror of Literature, Amusement, and Instruction," Volume 14, No. 384, August 8, 1829)

Curious sun-dial

Mr John Abram, of Canterbury, teacher of the Mathematics, and author of the Kentish Tide Tables, has constructed a curious sun-dial, which is to be fixed in the front of the Droit-house, Margate, below the transparent clock. The following are the curious properties of this dial. On the upper part is the hour circle, to show the true solar time. Below the hour circle is the Torrid Zone on a large scale, with the parallels of the sun's declination (hyperbolic curves), corresponding to every half hour of the sun's rising and setting. These half hours are again subdivided into quarters of an hour. The time of the sun's rising and setting for the day is indicated by the extreme point of the shadow of the gnomen traversing the corresponding parallel of declination, which by its diurnal progress over the surface of the dial, also shows, at any given instant, the true bearing of the sun by the compass, indicated by vertical straight lines, marked with different points of the compass. There are, likewise, other parallels of declination, corresponding to the entrance of the sun into each sign of the Zodiac. In short, the dial points out the hour of the day, the sun's place in the Ecliptic, the time of the sun's rising and setting, the length of the natural day and night, and the sun's true azimuth or bearing by the compass.

("The Register of Arts and Journal of patent inventions," Luke Herbert, Vol. 3, 1829, p. 272)

---

[70] Salvator Rosa (1615-1673) was an Italian Baroque painter, poet and printmaker, active in Naples, Rome and Florence.

It appears that by the 1830s Margate was a real fun place – a place to let your hair down, albeit under a different name! One cannot but wonder whether the abundance of Smiths, Hobsons or whatever other adopted pseudonym was used, ever told their 'other halves' the real reasons for being out of town for a while. The following writer appears to imply that certain folk did not want people to know what they were really up to during their visits to Margate! The artist J M W Turner used the pseudonym Mr Booth when visiting Margate for his alleged clandestine affair with a local landlady – but he did come to paint as well!

Watering Places

We are on board the steam-vessel – we are at Margate; of all places of amusement in England none are like unto Margate. Here the commercial character loses its characteristics – the trader no longer thinks of pence and shillings – he gives himself up lavishly to the good things in life – he calleth for hock with a lusty voice – he inquireth tenderly touching the John Dories[71], and, in his soul, he damneth the cost. There too all are equals; the absence of the chilling sneer of the great allows the young apprentice to relax from his stiffness, and to assume the man of ton without the dread of being likened to the original. Sea baths in the morning prepare the appetite for shrimps and eggs; from shrimps and eggs then passes to billiards, to pony-back, or to the reading-rooms. Then, too, to each of the baths, that, bright and newly painted, stretch seaward in a glistening row, is its own pianoforte! – Some damsel gratuitously musical waken its dulcet notes: and such pretty gay-dressed lasses escaped from Aldgate, or from the long street of Oxford, glance, giggle, laugh, and coquet around, that if thou art amorous thou mayest find here the English Cadiz.

Many a Jewish dark eye looks arch at thee under its flowery and feathered bonnet, for Jewesses abound at Margate. The tribes of Solomon and Levi pour forth in abundance down the sultry streets. Here, if thy name be one of gentle note, sink it, and become a Hobson or a Smith; affect no superiority; flirt and dance and laugh thy fill, and never wilt thou find thou time less heavily employed. Here what motley affluence of character, what vast miscellany of humours, greet thy observing but quiet gaze! Here mayest thou find materials, ay, and adventure too, for fifty novels and five hundred plays! Whose vein shall the critics justly declare to be exhausted while Margate opens her arms

---

[71] A species of fish

to all the varieties of the most variegated classes? And beautiful is it to the philanthropist, as well as the gallant or the observer, to behold trade thus throwing off its cares, and the reserve of the mercantile respectability blowing merrily about in the gay breezes of the pier.

Some of my school days were spent in the neighbourhood of this Omphalon Gaiae[72]; and well do I remember the portly president of its pleasures, that most important of all important personages – the Master of the Ceremonies! He was a character. In those good old times, ere the feudal government began to cede to the federal, Margate, Broadstairs, and Ramsgate, the triple Geryon[73] of the coast, were united under one lordly sway; now each community claimeth its own separate Master of the Ceremonies – the union of three kingdoms has been repealed. Thou, O illustrious C----! Wert then supreme – defender of the faith, from the Margate assembly-room of Cecil Square to the Broadstairs library of Nuckell, and the Ramsgate ball-room of the Albion Hotel! Captain C---- was a character! He valued himself on being the living picture of George IV. Fair was he in complexion – comely in stomach – taper of leg; and his bow – it was George the Fourth's to a hair! It is said that when the good monarch visited those regions you could not tell Captain C---- from the king – alike the dignity – alike the condescension. The visitors of Margate were prodigiously proud of the resemblance. – 'Have you seen our Mr C?' was the common inquiry to strangers; 'a perfect gentleman – the very moral of his Majesty!'

Broadstairs is the exclusive circle of Thanet – stiffly cheerful, and superciliously gay are its inhabitants; much do they value themselves on being thoroughly genteel; great is their horror of Margate – great their veneration for the aristocratic tenants of the ten-guinea per week lodging-houses. No changeful and evanescent visitors are they; yearly come down the spinster and dowager habitués intimate are they at the library – sedately settled in their pursuits – fond are they of whist, and moderate are the stakes thereat. Nor is there in the wide world a more charming place for those who think it vulgar to be merry. Ramsgate is the golden medium between the two; it shuns the exuberant mirth of Margate and the sobered monotony of Broadstairs. As at Broadstairs you are asked to tea, so at Ramsgate you are asked to dinner.

("New Monthly Magazine," Watering Places, 1833, PP. 444-445)

---

[72] Omphalos – in Greek Mythology – the centre of the world. Gaiae or gaia, meaning mother or grandmother earth.

[73] In Greek mythology, Geryon was a fearsome giant described variously as having one body and three heads, three bodies, six hands and six feet and as being winged.

Margate Pier and Lighthouse

Leyland, who was here in the reign of Henry VIII, says there was then a pier for ships at this place, but 'sorely decayed.' In the preceding reign it was maintained by certain rates paid for corn and other merchandise landed on it; which rates were confirmed by orders of the Lord Warden in 1615. By an act of parliament passed in 1724, the payment of these duties was enforced, and the pier maintained until 1787, when it was rebuilt of stone, and extended so as to enlarge the harbour and afford competent security for shipping. In 1812, the inhabitants of Margate obtained the sanction of the legislature for an augmentation of the Droits and Pierage, in order to pay the interests of the large sums which were required for the improvements and re-erections which had taken place, or were then anticipated; and a new pier has since been constructed under the direction of the celebrated John Rennie, at an expense of £90,000. It is nine hundred feet in length, and sixty feet wide; and at its termination is a small light-house. Some idea may be formed of the immense traffic carried on between London and Margate during the season, from the fact that 98,128 persons landed here in 1830, from the London steam-vessels.

Here are some other statistics of Margate's increase in visitors over the years:

Edinburgh Gazetteer[74]	42,120	visitors	1819
Mocket's Journal[75]	76,763		1825
Picturesque views of Great Britain[76]	98,128		1830
M'Culloch's Universal Gazetteer[77]	90,000		1844

("The Picturesque Views of Great Britain," Thomas Allen, 1833, p. 23)

---

[74] Edinburgh Gazetteer, Vol. 4, 1822, p. 159.

[75] Mocket's Journal, 1836.

[76] The Picturesque views of Great Britain," Thomas Allen, 1833, p. 23

[77] M'Culloch's Gazetteer, Vol. 2, 1844, p. 309.

Gleanings along the shore

When people go to Margate, they go there, one would presume, with firm intent to frame their minds to mirth and merriment, which bars a thousand harms and lengthens life; and, in the main, it is a pretty good place for the purpose; but if a man be at all given to the penseroso[78] temperament, let him not think to get rid of it at Margate. It is true, that the "proper authorities," with a laudable anxiety to keep people as merry as possible, have locked up the church-yard; so that no man can mope there, without special permission from the sexton; but what signifies locking up the church-yard, when a memento mori[79] stares you in the face at every turning? In one street, an undertaker, having a bed-room to let, and being desirous to make the announcement thereof as conspicuous as may be, sticks it upon the lid of a coffin, in his shop-window, and there the coffin stands, bolt upright, and as large as life, ticketed – 'An apartment for a single gentleman!' In another street, a dipper of second-hand silks writes up over his door, – 'Dying on the shortest notice!' and another – 'A. B begs the ladies of Margate to take notice that he dyes for them upon easy terms!' indeed there is scarcely a street, lane, or alley, in which one or more of these dying dippers is not to be found; and however easy the terms may be upon which they dye, the thing has a very dismal look. Then, in the main thoroughfare, there is the memento mori miniature-painter, reminding you that you must die, and therefore urging you to give him your last shilling, or, as he says, your 'odd shilling,' in exchange for 'your family likeness (in dead black) to be left as a memento when death has taken you from your future progeny!' But all these are but minor motives to melancholy compared with being doomed to see 'some fellow of infinite jest,' whose 'songs and flashes of merriment were wont to set, not the table only, but crowded theatres, in a roar,' wandering about in gloomy abstraction, among the careless herd. Such men are always to be met with in Margate. There was Michael Kelly[80], who, though perhaps he never succeeded in exciting any great degree of merriment in others, was himself as merry as the day was long; and when he could be merry no longer, he came to Margate to pass the remnant of his days, stretched in his couch upon the wild sea beach, gazing upon the wave as it came dancing towards him with its white crest

---

[78] From Milton's 'Penseroso,' one who relishes the mind-wanderings that nocturnal wakefulness brings.

[79] A reminder of one's mortality

[80] Michael Kelly (1762-1826) was an Irish actor, singer (tenor), composer and theatrical manager. He died at Margate in 1824 aged 64.

glittering in the sun, and sighing as it sunk away at his feet to make room for its successor.

("My Daughter's Book," by the Editor of the "Young Gentleman's Book", 1834, P. 373)

The following article, written in 1834, presents a scathing attack, by many disgruntled working people, over the way that the Poor Laws allowed able bodied people in Margate to choose not to work, being better off living on charity handouts:

English Charity

...How can we possibly conceive that the lower orders of this country will stand against the storm, how can we expect that they will be foolish enough, mad enough, to gain their bread by the sweat of their brow, so long as we publicly notify to them, that there is roast-beef and plum pudding, bacon and beans, green peas and mackerel, strong beer, fresh herrings and warm wigs, for those who will cowardly fly from their work. What authority can a parochial officer, the assistant-overseer, have in their eyes, when they find that he is ordered to mix their soup, and to take special care that the Scotch barley, the leeks, the beef, and the onions, are duly congregated!

It happened that when we visited the Poor House of Canterbury, which is conducted under a proclamation very similar to that we have just quoted, we witnessed a scene worth relating. The city is composed of fourteen united parishes, each of which furnishes two citizen-guardians. The government of the poor belongs also to the mayor and corporations, who are, generally speaking, liberal, well-educated men, but as the citizen-guardians out-vote them, they have long agreed to absent themselves from the Workhouse Court. The fitting pride of this court is to stuff the pauper at the expense of the lean ratepayer; and on the day of our visiting their workhouse we found that little puddle in a storm. The contractor had happened to furnish a batch of bread, nutritive, wholesome, and to any hungry man most excellent, but a shade darker than was deemed fit for a pauper. We will not say how very many degrees whiter it was than the bread we have eaten with the Russian and Prussian armies – we will merely observe, it was considerably whiter than the 'brown tommy' of our own soldiers, or than that species of luxury known in our fashionable world by the enticing appellation of brown bread. The Canterbury guardians, however, had declared it to be unfit for the paupers, and the governor had consequently been obliged to furnish them with white bread from one of the bakers of the town. The Assistant-Commissioner not only greedily ate of this bread, but respectfully forwarded a loaf of it to the Poor Law Board, who probably requested Mr Chadwick to digest it and report thereon. The contractor, however, having the whole batch on his hands, and from pride not choosing publicly to dispose of it, ordered it to be given to his pigs. On proceeding to the styes we found these sensible animals literally gorged with it. All but one were lying on their sides in their straw, grunting in dreams of plethoric ecstasy – a large hungry pie-bald hog had just received his share, and as, looking at the Poor-Law Commissioner, he stood crunching and munching this nice bread, there was something so irresistibly comic in his eye, something so sarcastic and satirical, something in its twinkle, that seemed to say – De gustibus non est disputandum[81]! – 'Citizen-guardians for ever and down with the poor-law amendment act!' – That the contractor himself was seen to smile.

And the devil he smiled, for it put him in mind of England's commercial prosperity! The general effect produced by this system may be sufficiently explained by a very few instances. Mr Curling, the governor of Margate workhouse, declared in our hearing – "I am an eye-witness that, by over-feeding the pauper, we have made the labouring classes discontented." He added – "During the fashionable season at Margate, the donkey-drivers, the fly-drivers, and hundreds who are employed by the London ladies, generally receive 24s a week, but it is all spent in beer – there is no prudence, nothing saved, for the cant phrase among them is, 'We have always the Mansion-house to go to.'

We may observe that the cost of 204 indoor paupers at Margate has amounted to about £2,000 a year. An overseer near Canterbury told us that a young man had for nearly a year been receiving 1s. 6d a week from the parish, every Friday – that he always spent this money in hiring a gun to shoot with on Sunday – and that, whenever he received his money, he returned laughing with it in his hand to his fellow workmen, saying, with much less elegance than truth, "What a set of d----d fools they are!" Mr John Davies the overseer of St Peter's, at Sandwich, said:

> "They only wants to thrust themselves into the work'us, to get a belly full of good victuals and do nothing, but I won't let 'em."

---

[81] De gustibus non est disputandum – 'There is no arguing about taste'

It will sound incredible, that the overseers themselves, as well as the governors of the workhouses, are perfectly sensible of the vice of this shocking system – but that such is the case the following extracts from certificates, addressed to the Assistant Commissioner by several of the most respectable of the governors, &c, on the 9th of February last, will clearly show:

"Having been governor of the poor-house of this parish, and also clerk to the guardians, for fourteen years, I have had an opportunity of witnessing that the paupers in this house live a great deal better than many who are trades people, and who help to support them; and I am certain of the fact, that many of the independent labourers do not get meat once a week. The boatmen of this place, at present are in a very distressed situation; and I think it is very often the case that they have no meat in the course of the week. (Signed) A. B."

"I have been guardian of this parish for seven years, and I am quite sure the paupers in the workhouse live better than one-third of the rate-payers of this parish: and 1 have very frequently said to parishioners, the people of our house live much too well, and that they are better off than half the inhabitants; but the reply was, 'That is no business of yours.' (Signed) C. D."

"Having filled the situation of governor these fourteen years past, as also superintendent of the unemployed poor, I am sure, from the experience that I have had of witnessing much the distress of the industrious rate-payer, that he cannot in any decree live equal, nor have those comforts the poor moor workhouse have; which I have frequently stated to our board of officers, but the reply has been, 'If the parishioners are satisfied, what need you trouble yourself about it.' (Signed) E. F."

"I think that not one half of the rate-payers of our parish live as well as the poor in the house; and none of our out-poor live so well as the in-poor. I have often expressed this opinion in committee. (Signed) G. H."

"I really believe that many of the poor rate-payers do not live better, or have meat so often in their family, as the people in the poor-house, as I have been frequently given to understand by different collectors of the poor rates; and am sure, that, out of the five hundred boatmen, none of them live so well as the people in our workhouse, and very few of the boatmen get meat at all. (Signed) K.L."

But if these letters do not, the Kentish fires throw quite light enough on the effects of this system. In no region it has been our fortune to visit have we ever seen a peasantry so completely disorganized. In no enemy's country that we have seen have we ever encountered the churlish demeanour which these men, as one meets them in their lanes, now assume. Perfectly uneducated – neither mechanics, manufacturers, nor artisans – in point of intellect little better than the horses they drive, they govern in a manner which is not very creditable to their superiors. Their system of robbing corn for their horses has, they believe, been almost sanctioned by custom into law; and as, with something like justice, they conceive they are entitled to be higher fed than the scale established for the pauper, nothing they can honestly gain can possibly be sufficient to make them contented. And yet the countenances of these country clods are strangely contrasted with their conduct. We would trust them with our life – in no country in the world are there to be seen infants, boys, and lads of more prepossessing appearance – honesty, simplicity, and courage adorn them; proving that they are the descendants of those who were once complimented by the remark that they were 'Non Angli sed Angeli.'[82] Their women, like their hops, have ten thousand clinging, clasping, blooming, undulating beauties; and there seems to be no reason why, of their lovely native county, it should not still be said, 'Ex his, qui Cantium incolunt longe sunt beatissimi.'[83] But it is not of their materials we complain, it is only of our own workmanship – our poor-laws have ruined them! ...

("The London Quarterly Review," Issues 103-106, Aug 1st 1834, PP. 256-7)

This appears to be an objective view of Margate in 1834. This tourist, who was apparently one of about 100,000 that came to Margate that season, knew what to expect but didn't really care as long as he or she had plenty of fun.

---

[82] Non Angli, sed Angeli – "They are not Angles, but angels" (Gregory the Great)

[83] "Of all these, by far the most blessed are they who dwell in Kent" (Caesar)

Amusements at Margate

Margate, as a bathing-place, might be imagined a retired spot, to which invalids resorted for the benefit of their health, and therefore conclude it presented one vast hospital or receptacle of human misery, far otherwise. There are persons who admire the salubrity of the air, and the kindness of the towns-people. There are also many who think bathing may prove serviceable to them – many who delight in opportunity for care-killing – many whose happiness consists in escaping from a chrysalis state in London, to flutter a butterfly at Margate. To these is the place indebted for the visits of nearly 100,000 persons in the course of a season. There was, in time past, a superior class of visitors; but as their heels were touched by the toes of others considered inferior, the strawberry leaved and the balled coronetted took offence, and vanished. There are, however, three descriptions of persons who retain partialities for Margate. The first consists of families, respectable in every sense of the term; they have houses or lodgings in the squares, or best parts of the town; their amusements and their domestic comforts are united with judgment, and can only be alluded to, as examples to others; they are the affluent merchants and tradesmen of the metropolis, being, *par excellence,* vulgarly denominated carriage company. Another description of persons rent houses, or lodgings, less expensive, and regulate their establishments on principles of economy and respectability, regularly dealing with those most worthy their commands. These are select in their intimacies, enjoying all the amusements of the place unostentatiously, and in many respects approximating to the carriage class, but not of it – therefore may be called the horse and gig company. A third description, for the purposes of distinction only, may be called the foot company, composed of persons who, knowing the few holidays that can be snatched from their occupations ought to be agreeably spent, rush down to Margate with a determination to be happy. A boarding-house is their place of rendezvous. Among these may be found many highly cultivated persons.

Ladies ever form a considerable part of boarding house society; and as they are induced to appear in their best visiting amiability, they produce a corresponding attention to decorum on the part of the gentlemen, which provokes in either the ambition to appear to more than the greatest advantage. Of course every young gentleman is well bred, wealthy, intimate with those who move in the upper circles, frequents the opera and other superior amusements in London. He is therefore prepared to indulge in all the vanities of Margate. Yet, however hyperbole may operate, geese are not swans, nor will conceit or falsehood transform a magpie into a bird of paradise. It is certain that persons cannot make themselves beautiful, if their features be ordinary, nor change a malformation into the first order of fine forms; but they might be candid, and perhaps become intelligent: these are practicable, but unfortunately not fashionable. Therefore, when Jessamy and Flippet meet, a scene of flattery and delusion commences, which, as if by mutual agreement, they determine never to check, or detect, until their marriage has taken place. Then they appear like two celebrated pedestrians who agreed to go a great distance in company. A toll-bridge lay in their road, each believing the other had cash; but neither being provided, they were brought to a stand-still, and the match was off. But to the boarding-house inmates: the meals are announced by jingling a large bell in the passage or hall. At these meetings parties are made. The precious souls, agog to dash through thick and thin, propose a ride to Ferry Grove – a trip to Pegwell-bay – a sail to the Reculvers – a stroll on the Parade – a walk on the Pier, or on the Jetty. Yes; this is most inviting.

The Pier is a stone building with a lighthouse at the extremity, projecting in a slight curve 900 feet into the sea, forming a shelter to vessels within the harbour, which is dry at low water. On an elevated part of the Pier there is a pleasant promenade, for the enjoyment of the sea-breeze and the prospects, in perfect security. A little to the east is the Jetty, a platform constructed of oak, projecting in a straight line 1120 feet out to sea. There are openings between each plank to lessen the action of the rising tides, as at high water the whole is covered. At the extremity is a circular part, a little elevated, the delight of the lovers of mischief. On this, when the tide is rising, large parties assemble; the attention of the ladies is directed to distant objects, or to any thing by which they may be detained till the tide has flowed up to the lower portion of the open planking of the platform; the initiated steal away; the others feel they must hasten over these openings, through which, if the water be the least agitated, a direction of the spray upwards occasions some unpleasant sensations, besides proving that silk stockings are not fishermen's boots. All this the spectators vociferously enjoy. The more timid are often carried over these jet d'eaux by the gentlemen, at which the laugh is not lessened, while the most alarmed are fetched from their situation of increasing danger by the boatmen, whose charge for rescuing such damsels in distress is sixpence each. All this cannot be otherwise than exceedingly amusing, since the same ladies have endured it several times, affording proof positive that whatever is, is right – that all is charming and delectable at enchanting Margate.

Then comes the jaunt to Ramsgate. A string of open carriages waits. After due bedizening with streamers long and gay off they whirl. The sun – despite of parasol – scorching them, and the dust from the chalky roads suffocating them. Refreshment becomes necessary as air to breath. After partaking sumptuously, finding the heat allayed, and the thirst relieved, the party walk on the Pier, where the refracted heat of a summer's sun is so oppressive as often to occasion languor and fainting. But true heart ne'er tires: they enjoy all that can be enjoyed, and return enraptured with the excursion. After such exertions, who would not enjoy a refreshing sleep? – Sleep that seems to cast into oblivion every recollection, save those the most agreeable; for day after day succeeds, in which similar extravaganzas are enacted. Then come the concerts! They must be attended for the sake of harmony and love of melody. Thus evenings are occupied in listening while a singer endeavours to recover a few lost notes. Occasionally they parade up and down the concert room to martial music – the steps of the marchers and the time in the orchestra being now and then together. Yet all is charming. They can see and be seen – no heart aches unless the little urchin Cupid may have been practising his archery. Then there are the libraries! It is impossible not to be a subscriber, although a book be never opened, because it confers a right to squeeze in to hear Mr and Miss Somebody hoot and squeak, if permitted by the rafflers with their dice-boxes and loud announcements of the numbers required to be filled – 'Only three and two and five – five, three and two – five – five!' This is reiterated so frequently and so loud, that it is advisable to be provided with cotton to preserve the drum of the ear. The proper number of names having been written against the numbers of the raffle for one shilling each the parties will then in turn throw with the dice. The highest in three throws being declared the winner, a ticket is presented to the fortunate individual. All this hallooing and rattling is repeated again and again at two or three places in the room, forming a part of the entertainment more astonishing than delighting.

A sing-song at Bettison's library

Mr and Miss somebody 'hooting and squeaking'

Playing dice at Bettison's library

Let it not be forgotten, that at Bettison's library the performer at the grand piano-forte executes, with great taste and expression, some of the best modern music, without being attended to as it deserves, amid the uproar of mountebank trickery. Yet all this is delightful and highly entertaining. Some of the fortunates at the dice-box will become possessed of a great number of tickets, for which, at their departure, the amount may be received in trinketry or trumpery. Nevertheless, all is beautiful and excellent. Criticism at Margate would be considered a fish out of his element. Every lure is set every trap is baited, to catch the contents of the Cockney's purse. Step into the bazaars, they appear as if the Boulevards of Paris had emptied all their fiddle-faddles, sweet scents, and nonsense, to attract. Oh, how pretty! Something must be purchased, or some chances in the lottery must be taken. One of the prizes, an elegant workbox, worth – it is invaluable! It may be gained.

The wheel of fortune turns – a blank! No matter – all is right, all is cheerful. It is a dull heart that never rejoices. The next attempt may be successful. Then there are the gardens – once Shady Grove, then Tivoli, now anything – plenty of fever-cooling refreshments – plenty of charges – plenty of foolery and fire-works, rivalling the giant fool at Vauxhall. Yet how rural, how enchanting! How sweet to walk home by moonlight, and to hear the soft whisperings during that walk. How ecstatic! Mortals hardly ever know the joys that await them. All is most delicious. Then there is the public breakfast at St Peter's. Oh the lovely spot! – The concentration of all that is captivating. Who can refrain? All must go, unless they chance to be eaten up by hypochondria. How shall they go! Oh, dear variety! – Ever stimulating charm! On donkeys to be sure. What can be so entertaining? – So full of pleasurable ideas, the climax of all that is frolicsome. Away goes the porter to collect all the donkeys possible, not less than a dozen. Here they are, and the ladies are ready. How exhilarating!

There is a spring, an elasticity of heart that would persuade the party they were not of earthly mould. The ladies mount their long-eared palfreys, decorated with saddle-cloths of sixpenny cotton and two-penny fringe. The gentlemen, like knights at a tournament, kiss their hands and are greeted with smiles and laughter at each other till they can hardly retain their seats. The ladies have but half a page each – the whole page's business is to trot in the rear of two ladies, chanting, 'Come up, Neddy,' with a chorus of whacks on the crupper. The accompanying knights having permitted their chargers to walk between their legs drop into their seats heroically. Off they all go in chivalry taste, save that regularity of cavalcade is entirely neglected, some preferring the slowest pace, as best adapted to the retention of seat – others choosing the utmost speed, as best calculated to display skill in the ménage. Crossing the fields, they are irresistibly comical in their widely scattered groups, and in their shouts of laughter and screams of mirth at one or more of the party measuring their lengths on the ground. Not having far to fall, renders a recurrence less terrible, however disagreeable, since every one may not fall like Julius Caesar.

They arrive at St Peter's, all save one fair damsel, whose palfrey preferred grazing on the blooming clover to forming any part of the array, which determination the fair rider had no power to oppose. Where is she – where is her page? Oh! He came with Miss Thingame, and there he goes for the other lady. See where she sits like patience on a monument. How cruel to have left her thus! Why did not her Neddy come up? But see where she comes to bless us, blushing like a peony – every eye fixed on her strange movement, caused by the velocity with which the page urged her palfrey. Fortunately no bottles were in her pockets. She dismounts, weary of being a heroine. Tea is ordered, with all the etcetera of a sumptuous breakfast, during which it is resolved not to return by the same means.

They had no idea of encountering the gaze, and being subjected to the animal versions of so many; therefore the pages must be sent home to direct that carriages for the party may be sent from Margate by such a time. The stirring bands of music invite us to the covered dancing-place. They must walk and quadrille a little, although it is so warm. They do so – the little goes on till it assumes the evidences of being much, and they retire exhausted, like so many red lions, to some of the alcoves to recover themselves; during which, the gentlemen will not have taken more than three jellies each, although the practice is so exceedingly fashionable. The carriages come; the excitement being over, they return to dress for dinner.

The recollections of the outrageous publicity of their excursion, with the evidences of their fatigue, produce only simpers, and an endeavour to affix the most ridiculous occurrences on each other. Much of mimicry, burlesque, and hyperbole, is ventured in good humour, and mirthfully retaliated. Amid the conviviality, additional bottles of wine make their appearance, which, like Charles of Spain's shoes, were not prime but such as might be used. All goes on well – the ladies retire – the gentlemen take another glass or two – talk politics, and, in their superior knowledge of legislation, jurisprudence, and political economy, prove beyond contradiction that the Chancellor of the Exchequer is a noodle, and the Premier a doodle. After this, the well-informed disputants are advised to walk under the cliffs, where they splash each other to their heart's content. Some go to smoke half-a-dozen cigars, only because it is fashionable; thence to quiz the girls on the Jetty; others look in at the billiard-table, where there are, or soon will be, players who can always make a hard game of it till the stake is worthy notice, and then – 'It don't signify.' Then there is the Theatre Royal, where Melpomene and Thalia[84] exchange the powers over which they should preside, and, except when a star from one of the metropolitan hemispheres appears, there is darkness visible, serving only to discover sights too insipid to give pleasure, or not contemptible enough to provoke laughter. Yet even here there is novelty.

The strumming and scraping of three persons in the orchestra of an empty theatre, produces a strange effect on the ear, which cannot be described. After a few slapping of box doors, very loud yawning in the pit, and whistling in the gallery, the curtain rises and the strutting and fretting proceeds. Friends in the dress circle shake hands with each other across the pit, and the act is over. The ladies agitate, and peep through their fans – Charming! Every particular of Mrs and Miss' decorations can be scrutinised and descanted upon Urling's lace! Mina nova and paste! Birmingham jewellery! Good gracious, what sagacity to be enabled to point this out! What talent to compare things with those of which they are only the representative! It produces such an enthusiastic delirium, that the play is forgotten in revelry of impatience, and they do not stay to witness the farce! In such a round of folly do some, at other times thinking persons, beguile hours, weeks, and months, till a whisper from home, weariness, or exhausted funds, like a gun in a field covered with birds, puts them on the wing by hundreds, and the principal of the boarding-house is left to preside at a deserted table.

---

[84] From the Greek – tragedy and comedy

To persons of sedentary habits, or whose years place them out of the pale of boarding-house follies, Margate presents much that is satisfactory. The walk along the cliffs to Kingsgate – to Birchington – to many villages in the vicinity, in sight of the ocean – any of the before-mentioned attractions may be enjoyed, free of frivolity and treble expense, by the prudent. There are many bathing machines, tepid and vapour baths, properly constructed and attended to. Sea bathing is good under particular circumstances, taken by the advice of medical experience; but ducking is no panacea. The proprietors of the bathing places have discovered to their cost that persons do not come to Margate to play Tritons and Mermaids, as they did a few years since. The charges for board and lodging, where both are good, are about two guineas per week – wine, spirits, or ale, exclusive. There are stage-coaches to Canterbury, Ramsgate, and Dover, daily. There is no doubt that the Londoners will long retain a partiality for Margate.

("Chambers' Edinburgh Journal," Vol. 2, 1834, pp.155-156)

The pleasures of being on board a boat bound for Margate!

Steaming it to Margate

'Steward, bring me a glass of brandy as quick as you can.' Since the invention of steam, thousands have been tempted to inhale the saline salubrity of the sea air that would never have been induced to try, and be tried, by the experiment of a trip. Like hams for the market, every body is now regularly salted and smoked. The process, too, is so cheap! The accommodations are so elegant, and the sailors so smart! None of the rolling roughness of quid-chewing Jack-tars. Jack-tars! pshaw! they are regular smoke jacks on board a steamer! The Steward ('waiter' by half the cockneys called) is so ready and obliging; and then the provisions is excellent. Who would not take a trip to Margate? There's only one thing that rather adulterates the felicity – a drop of gall in the cup of mead! – And that is the horrid sea-sickness! Learnedly called nostalgia; but call it by any name you please, like a stray dog, it is pretty sure to come.

The cold perspiration – the internal commotion – the brain's giddiness – the utter prostration of strength – the Oh! I never shall forget the death-like feel! – Fat men rolling on the deck, like fresh caught porpoises; little children floundering about; and white muslins and parasols vanishing below! The smoking-hot dinner sends up its fumes, and makes the sick more sick. Soda-water corks are popping and flying about in every direction, like a miniature battery pointed against the assaults of the horrid enemy!

"Steward!" faintly cries a fat bilious man, "bring me a glass of brandy as quick as you can." But alas! He, who can thus readily summon spirits from the vast deep, has no power over the rolling sea, or its reaches "O! My poor pa!" exclaims the interesting Wilhelmina; and is so overcome, that she, sweet sympathizer! Is soon below pa in the ladies' cabin. In fact, the greater part of the pleasure-seekers are taken – at full length. Even young ladies from boarding-school, who are thinking of husbands, declare loudly against maritime delight! While all the single young men appear double.

The pier at last appears – and the cargo of drooping souls hail it with delight, and with as grateful a reverence as if they were received by the greatest peer of the realm! They hurry from the boat as if 'twere Charon's, and they were about stepping into the fields of Elysium!

A change comes o'er the spirit of their dream – their nerves are braced; and so soon are mortal troubles obliterated from the mind, that in a few days they are ready again to tempt the terrors of sea-sickness in a voyage homewards – notwithstanding many of them, in their extremity, had vowed that they never would return by water, if they outlived the present infliction; considering, naturally enough, that it was 'all up' with them!

("Steaming to Margate," The Sketches of Seymore, Robert Seymore, 1836)

A common scene below deck at dinner time

By the look of this lot they are going to need Margate's health giving attributes!

During the 1830s at Margate gambling was a popular pastime. This tale paints a picture of the sort of person frequenting the town at this time. Margate's seafront is still rife with casinos, bingo halls and arcades with machines bent on taking your last penny.

Steam boats and stage coaches

We are decided advocates of steam-boats, provided they run within limited distances – say, for example, as far as Gravesend. We would, also, be numbered among the patrons of those which ply as far as Scotland, or to any part of the North of England; but let us not be reckoned among those who would patronise steam-boats to Margate, and Ramsgate – the former 76, the latter 86 miles from London. We have tried them tame ad nauseam, in every sense of the word. Our friends will ask, 'Why do you speak ill of what you are daily in the habit of using?' We will explain. In the first place, the expense of a journey to Ramsgate is only four shillings by steam; by coach, twelve – certainly a matter of some consideration in these 'hard times;' especially when one is in the habit of going to and fro twice, or oftener, in the course of the week. In the next place, you may depend on the certainty of reaching your place of destination in nine hours at the furthest, escaping dust, extortion, and other annoyances on the road; besides which, there is the benefit of a fine fresh breeze – of itself, a great inducement to patronise steam. What then can be the drawbacks?

Owing to their low fares, the vessels are usually crowded by 'people of all nations, tongues, and languages.' Turks, Jews, Infidels, and Christians are mingled together in delightful variety; the respectable being separated from the questionable, by only a few planks – which planks may be crossed by paying an extra shilling, thus placing all on an equal. The clock strikes nine, or ten, as it may be – the swell mob, who always haunt these boats, watch their opportunity, and away goes the steamer. People now begin to move about, and make their observations; some 'fortifying' their insides by a go of the 'crater' others securing a seat as near the middle of the boat as may be, to secure them from sickness. Mrs Tadleum soon grows great with Mrs Capsicomb and family matters are freely discussed. Mr James Smith, too, soon familiarises himself with Mr John Jones and the little Joneses, and the joke goes round.

The sun comes out, behold it is the signal for a wise remark, – "What a beautiful morning it is, Miss Peterkin!" "Delightful, indeed, Mrs Harricot!"

The clouds now gather blackness, and the rain descends in torrents; it is indeed misery that can be felt; still, it must be talked about. "I say, Zfartichoke, it is a very wet morning." "Yes," groans out Mr Marrowfat, "and I'm afraid I shan't be able to tuck into our beefsteak pudding, for we shall be sure to 'catch it' off the Nore – shan't us, Sal. Here, child, give us the bottle." By and bye, you reach Gravesend and here, if not long before, you are sure to be entertained with a number of 'Gratuitous Treatises on Sea-sickness,' which the publishers foretell will 'come out' at, or below, the Nore – thus creating a nice appetite for a good dinner. When their prophecies are fulfilled, these gentry will not fail to remind you of it. This goes on more or less till you reach Margate, and then you may depend upon a 'full and particular account' of the North Foreland, its history, and properties; all very interesting to a person of weak constitution. This be it observed, occurs, at this season of the year, at least once in every 24 hours.

But the worst part of this steam voyage is yet to be described. A gentleman of a tolerably good constitution – of whom there are many – generally finds his appetite pretty keen before he reaches Gravesend, and, if uninitiated, goes down into the cabin determined on making a hearty meal. The first thing that presents itself, (even when the water is 'confluent as a mirror,') is a lady, or rather a number of ladies, with the whites of their eyes turned up, and their legs en rest reclining on the very cushions set apart for the use of those who wish to take refreshment! Beside them, are smelling-bottles – fans – soda-powders – biscuits – water (very profitable to the steward!), and Eau de Cologne; the room smelling more like the cage of a Civet cat, than a dining-room. We waited, passive spectators of this ludicrous scene, full half an hour on Monday last, before we could induce one of these 'fairest of God's creation' to resign her seat (or rather seats, for she occupied the room of four), and then what a frown we got! – *l'emporte,* it did not take away our appetite.

Again, a lady, or a gentleman, feeling qualmish, walks instinctively to the head of the vessel, where there is most air and least motion. The first thing that presents itself here is either a smoke-dried London dandy, in the shape of a dapper young linen draper's apprentice, or a shop-boy out for a holiday. These you will always find inhaling and exhaling the fumes of a poisonous cheroot, which they will impudently shoot out, so as to ascend to the top of your nostrils! Remonstrate, and they will point significantly and with an air of insolent triumph, to the painted notice, 'No smoking allowed abaft the funnel'; and then dare you to interfere. What is the consequence? You must either submit to the filthy nuisance, or return to the respectable end of the vessel and suffer sickness. These are only one or two drawbacks on the Isle of Thanet and Herne Bay Steam Vessels, but they will suffice for our purpose. We will say nothing about the scenes of sickness on board. Under existing

236

circumstances, we would advise, where time and money are no object that ladies, at all events, should travel by coach. It is certainly more respectable, and more comfortable; securing the traveller, at once, from the impertinencies of beardless shop boys and members of the swell-mob, and from the ridiculous, maudlin affectation of boarding-school misses.

("The Idler, and Breakfast-table Companion," Volume 1, No. 17, 1837, pp. 125-126)

The following extracts are from a book called 'Margate Scandals', which should be read in full to appreciate the real story behind the grievances. Basically, there was a dispute between a member of the powerful Cobb family and his followers and a well known Doctor called J Waddington and his followers. There arose a very bitter public argument concerning some large 'misplaced funds'. This dispute created huge public interest because many citizens were concerned about the power that the Cobb family had over Margate and the welfare of its inhabitants. Below are some of the reactions from various sectors of the community:

Extracts from Margate Scandals

The purport of the letters and communications which appeared in the Canterbury Journal, from October 22nd 1836, to June 17th 1837, relating to the Margate Pier and Harbour Company, was to expose the errors and omissions in their accounts laid before Parliament, with a view to obtain an investigation of the Sinking Fund, in which the public is so deeply interested.

The important nature of the contents of these letters, and the extraordinary demand for the Journal in which they appear, induced the Committee of the Margate Municipal Reform Association, to offer a selection to the notice of the public, but more particularly of persons interested in the welfare of the town of Margate; its ultimate prosperity being materially dependent upon the arrival of the Sinking Fund at its maximum, viz. £20,000, and which event, so anxiously desired by the holders of property in that town, is retarded by the practices detailed in these letters.

237

The committee request attention to the curious information they contain, respecting the Management of this Company, and they ask, whether they do not furnish proofs of large sums of money being received before their annual accounts were made up and sent to Parliament, which sums were not included therein; but were kept back, until after the said accounts were closed, to the prejudice of the Sinking Fund, and contrary to the 66th and 77th sections of their Act.

The Directors having thought proper to publish Mr Sterland's charges against them in the report of the Special Meeting, only those letters which have reference to that report have been selected, and without any attention to the order of dates or their connexion with each other.

The Committee, to speak in the mildest terms, consider it most extraordinary that the Directors should object to have their accounts examined, and that they should refuse to correct errors which they do not deny, unless compelled by the interference of the Court of Queen's Bench, or the House of Commons; a mode of adjustment at once tedious and expensive, and not more satisfactory than the one proposed, in the first instance, by Mr Sterland, viz. – by a Barrister, 'or by a committee wholly unconnected with the Margate Pier and Harbour Company – wholly unconnected with all the parties mixed up in this transaction – wholly beyond the reach or influence from either side, &c.'

The Committee offer no apology to the individuals whose names are freely mentioned in this publication, for, had those persons consented to the conciliatory and honourable mode of setting the matter at rest above alluded to, these letters would never have been written, nor this pamphlet made its appearance.

J S Marsh, Hon. Sec.

To the Margate Municipal Reform Association.

Committee Room, Margate, July 19th, 1837.

Directors of the Margate Pier and Harbour Company

The Blue Bottle Fly

An excellent new song; as licensed to be sung at all Margate Meetings, under the permission of His Worship the Deputy. 'Good Master Cob-web, if I cut my finger, I shall make bold with you.' (Midsummer Nights Dream)

There was once a Spider long and lank,
Spinning a Cob-web on a Bank;
It's body was thin, its colour was brown,
And this Spider was hatched in Margate Town.

With a jointed tail and bloated head,
It spun in the dark a subtle thread;
One line of the web you could easily trace,
From the central Bank to the Market Place.

A second thread shewed quite as clear,
To Jarvis's Jetty and the pier.
Where over the coals 'twas so thickly spun,
That their price was rais'd Four Shillings a Ton!

239

A third was wove in the Spider's loom,
Reaching to the Commissioners' Room;
And a fourth, as foul as a witch's spell,
Was drawn around the Royal Hotel.

It shut up the windows, it closed the door,
Till the sound of pleasure was heard no more;
It darkened the organ, it covered the tables,
(We must not say How) with a widower's sables.

It stopped the dance, it silenced the glee,
Till the ball was closed sans ceremonie;
And towards the Theatre, sullen and sly,
From the Cob-web was cast an ominous eye.

This Spider was piously set against folly,
At Levy-ty scoffed, and all that was jolly;
So it thought of stretching a thread as far,
As from the Bank would reach the Bazaar.

Quoth the Spider – "Now my Cobweb is strong,
Each thread is woven fine and long;
And if Margate dares to stir, I can spancel[85] her –
I, and my Cobs, and S S Chancellor."

"For the Margate flies are poor and small,
And my Cob-web surely will catch them all."
So he spun out his threads still wider and wider;
Till many were caught by this sly Old Spider

But one fine day came fluttering by,
Careless and free, a Blue Bottle Fly;
"Oh, oh" – says the Spider – "Master Blue,
I should like to make a breakfast on you!"

---

[85] Tie with rope, hobble

The Blue Bottle rattled blithely on,
Till he chanced to pass where the web was spun;
"Oh, oh" – says the Blue Bottle – "here's a job!"
"you shall see how I'll settle this dirty Cob,"

So he dashed the nuisance through and through;
While the Spider was knocked about by the Blue;
"Somewhere else" – says he – "your web may be spun,
But you don't lodge here, Mister Ferguson."

Now the Margate flies may bless the day,
When the Spider's snare was brushed away;
For the Cob-web will in vain be spun,
To catch her Blue-Bottle Waddington.

("Margate Scandals", 1817-37)

Margate Pier and Harbour Company

To the editor of the Canterbury Journal

Sir,

I beg leave to communicate of the most extraordinary dullness
in auditing public accounts, ever heard of. On the 2nd April 1832
the directors erroneously reserved £1,968.9s.3d, which they
ought to have invested in the *Sinking Fund* according to the 66th
section of our Pier Act and whereby, the Treasurer who was
also a Director, was a gainer. The Auditors, who were
themselves Directors, and whose duty it was to audit the
Treasurer's account, were appointed to that office by the
Directors. The money was then in possession of their Chairman,
the late Dr Jarvis, and the Directors appointed that gentleman
one of the auditors. The Auditors, after all their labour, where
unable to discover that any error had been committed, or that
any money had been reserved by the Directors; neither could
they, with all their united talent, find out that it was then in
possession of one of themselves!! The Treasurer's account of
money received and paid to April 2nd, 1832, inclusive, was, I
believe, verified by the signatures of the Auditors, April 13th,

and the annual account was presented to both House of Parliament, August 2nd, 1832, but the above sum of £1,968. 9s. 3d was not included.

I trust, Sir, that you see the absolute necessity of the *Sinking Fund* in which the public is so deeply interested, being investigated, as I have proposed, viz., by a Barrister, or by a committee that is fully competent.

I am, Sir, yours, &c.

J STERLAND

Margate, Sept. 7th, 1837.

("Margate Scandals" page 1)

Margate Grievances and their Remedies

To the Editor of the Canterbury Journal

Sir, – I desire to call your attention to the depreciated value of property, and to the impoverished condition of the inhabitants of this place – no longer called 'Old Margate,' but, 'Cobb-Town,' or more properly, 'Cripplegate.' In proof of my position, I need only refer to the late sales of houses, (one in Hawley Square, valued at £500, fetched £260; another in Union Crescent, with law offices attached, valued at £1,000, realised £420!) to the late numerous and heavy failures; and, to the universal stagnation of trade.

My object is to suggest a remedy; in doing which, I am aware I shall displease more than one of the 'family party,' but this will not deter me. Truth shall be my guide; let them disprove that which I state, if they can. In the first place, however, I must go back to the period when the late Dr Jarvis, as chairman, aided by his toadies and sycophants, ruled the 'Pier and Harbour Company', – and frequently the town – with a rod of iron; he was, indeed, obeyed, although 'more from fear, than from love.'

The Treasurer of the Company, and Deputy of town, at that time (the late Mr F Cobb, commonly called 'King Cobb'), was a quiet, inoffensive man; in truth, little fitted for the endless worry and strife of public business, which induced him to leave much for Dr Jarvis to arrange. The latter (a vain, ambitious character), it is said, heartily disliked the 'Royal Family,' but, occasionally consulted his own views and interests, by giving the Treasurer and Deputy, a large 'sop in the pan.' Thus, the time of paying the dividends of the pier and Harbour Company, was notoriously altered from the 6th April, solely for the purpose of pleasing 'His Majesty,' by increasing his already enormous profits.

The next very improper scheme, of keeping a 'reserved fund' in hand, of more than £1,000, to insure a dividend of 10 per cent to the Proprietors, originated with Dr Jarvis; but remember, 'King Cobb,' together with his eldest son, (the present Deputy), acquiesced in this cunning measure, and as in the former instance, reaped the whole benefit. Moreover, I am told, it did not displease Mr Osborn, nor his son, Mr L Osborn, both Directors of the Pier, whose cheques for 'Lastage and Poundage,' were, I have heard, 'bottled up,' or laid by, for twelve months, although the nearsighted farmers, no doubt, paid the said heavy Pier dues every week.

On the 13th August, 1831, our late Deputy departed this life, when the present F W Cobb, became first in the firm of 'Cobb and Son, Treasurer of the Pier and Harbour Company.' Did he object to the before-mentioned arrangements? Certainly not.

Thus matters stood until the spring of 1832, when the declining health of Dr Jarvis warned him to look for some person whose talents and industry would supply his place. That gentleman – a perfect God-send, – he found in the person of a Mr Sterland, of whom Dr Jarvis spoke in the highest terms, ending (so say his nephew, Mr Waddington), with the following remarkable words; – "Mr Osborn has introduced me to his friend, Sterland; a very clever fellow; he must be made a Director of the Pier, and when I am gone, he will put you all to rights!"

I am, &c.

Humphrey Search.

Margate, 25th Feb. 1838.

("Margate Scandals," page 18)

243

...Dr Jarvis died on or about the 18th of March, 1833, having repeatedly said, during his last illness, as recorded in print by his nephew, Mr Waddington, "If ever Mr F W Cobb attempts to take the reins of the town of Margate, or of the Pier and Harbour Company, remember my words, Over You All Go!"

How truly these remarkable words are about to be verified, I must reserve for my next letter, wherein I shall call your attention to the 'Pier-bag' of money, or 'reserved fund,' said to contain 'more than one thousand pounds,' and which Mr Waddington has publicly declared 'he gave, after his uncle's decease, to Mr S S Chancellor, to carry to Mr F W Cobb, the Treasurer of the Company.'

I am, Sir, yours, &c.

Humphrey Search.

Margate, 1st March, 1838.

("Margate Scandals," page 19)

Editor's Remarks (Kentish Observer)

Many of our readers must have observed, and regretted, the distracted state of Margate, without perhaps, having very carefully inquired into, or reflected upon, the causes, remote and immediate, of that distraction. The two factions of the Guelphs and Ghibelines (if we may compare great things with small), did not rage more furiously in Italy during the fourteenth century, than the Cobbites and Waddingtonians now rage in Margate. The war of words, and the war of squibs, in verse and prose, is carried on most ferociously. If Lord Durham had not actually sailed for Canada, we should have strongly recommended his being appointed to compose the ruffled spirits of this place, before he entered upon his office of pacificator on the other side of the Atlantic.

How the growing strife is to be allayed, we know not, but this we know, that every inhabitant of Margate has a personal interest in its suppression...

("Margate Scandals," page 22)

Grand Conundrum

Answer me this – and answer me true – Why is Margate like an old shoe?

1.   Because that poor unfortunate town
Is shamefully trodden and trampled down.
Pretty well guessed – but it will not do
Why is Margate like an old shoe?

2.   Because both her upper and under decays,
Being used in so many dirty ways.
Rather better – but 'twill not do
Why is old Margate like an old shoe?

3.   Because with defaming, disturbing, disputing,
Her credit has got on a very bad footing.
Better still – but it will not do
Why is Margate like an old shoe?

4.   Because, by some folks' scandalous dealing,
Her state is in desperate want of healing.
Another good guess – but it will not do
Why is Margate like an old shoe?

5.   Because her tyrants so hard are grown,
She no longer can call her sole her own.
Best of all – but it will not do
Why is Margate like an old shoe?

6.   Can anybody answer? – You, Sir? – You?
I give it up – 'tis in vain to try,
I cannot guess it, nor I, nor I
Listen to me and I'll tell you why.

7.   When next you are asked for the reason true,
Why Poor Margate is like an old shoe?
Let this be your answer plumply said
'Because Poor Margate is Cobb-led'

Simon Squib.

("Margate Scandals," page 24)

The following list of local people, and their various occupations, gives us a rare early insight into who was doing what in and around Margate at the time. Perhaps an ancestor of yours is mentioned here?

Some Early Data of the People of Margate

Adams W	Plumber
Adams W	Tap to the club house
Adams G	Plumber
Adams, miss	Schoolmistress
Atkinson G	Linen draper
Austen W	Journeyman
Baker, miss	
Baker, Mrs	
Baker A O	Not known
Barrow F	Minister of Trinity Chapel
Bassett G	
Bassett, miss	Lodging house
Bassett, Mrs	Lodging house
Baylay W F	Vicar, non resident
Bell, Mrs	Lodging house
Bentley D	Cooper
Bettison S	Library
Bettison W G	Secretary to the club
Bishop T. Jun.	Farmer
Blakeney J	Tailor
Boswell J T	
Boys J, Hengrove,	Chairman of the club
Brasier R	Confectioner
Brasier R	Journeyman
Brizley S	Journeyman
Brice J	Shoemaker
Bristow J	Constable
Brooke, Robt.	Wingham Green
Brooke W	Mr Cobb's solicitor
Brooke H	Mr Cobb's solicitor
Brooke S	Apprentice to Messrs Hoffman
Brooke J H	
Brooke H	Wine vaults
Brooman James	

Brown Mrs M A	Hair dresser
Brown J	Organist
Brown Mrs A T	
Brown H	Constable
Burton Sir R, knight.	Director, St Peter's
Davis R	Journeyman
Dennison R B	M D
Dering Mrs	
Dixon C	
Dixon J	Pastry cook
Dixon G	Parish clerk
Dixon C	Printer
Dixon W	
Dixon J	Sailor
Dorson, miss	
Dove H	
Dowsett miss	Lodging house
Dowson T	Constable
Draper J E	Pier collector
Dunn T	Constable
Dunkin C D	Sexton
Dwyer Robt	R N
Dye J	Journeyman
Eastland W	Jolly Farmers
Eastland R	Mr Munns' Gardener
Edmunds W	Surveyor to the pier
Edwards W	Porter
Ellis Mrs	Lodging house
Euden J	Storehouseman
Evans Mrs	
Eysham J C	
Fagg J	Watchmaker
Fassam Mrs	Lodging house
Feakins W	Gardener
Finnis G	
Fishlock R	Green grocer
Flint T R	Ironmonger
Foat R	Butcher
Foreman J	Labourer
Forster Mrs	
Forster C F	Undertaker

Forster T	Beer-shop
Fox Mrs	
Francklin T	Baker
Freebody J	Baker
French Mrs	
Frith W	
Friend J	
Hobbs J	Tailor
Hoffman G H	Mr Cobb's surgeon
Hoffman G H, Jun.	Mr Cobb's surgeon
Hoile Mrs	Lodging house
Holmans S	Coach master
Hollams J	Undertaker
Hopkins R	Painter
Howe F	
Howe F T	Club house
Howland E	Servant to Mr Cobb
Howland F	Servant to Mr Cobb
Hubbard W	Sailor
Hubbard W	Porter
Hudson W	Foy Boat [pub]
Hunter G Y	Surgeon to Messrs Cobb
Hunter Mrs	
Hurst J	Coal merchant
Jacobs D	Sailor
Jarman J	Waggoner to the mills
Jenkins J	Director
Jenkins R	Brother to the director
Jones T	Chemist
Keble T H	Printer
Keene W C L	Dent-de-Lion
Kelsey J	Carpenter
Kennett S	Servant to Mr Price, surgeon
Kennard J D	Hatter
Kidman Mrs	Jolly Sailor [pub]
Killick miss E	Boarding house
Knight G	Beer shop
Knowler J	Constable
Knowler H	Cooper
Knott J, sen.	Shoemaker
Ladson W B	Gilder

Ladd G	Sailor
Ladd T	Cinque Port Arms
Lansell W	
Lansell T	
Lawrence R	Director
Lawrence R	Son of director
Lemon W	Fisherman
Leslie Mrs	
Lewis S	Mr Cobb's clerk
Radford J	Pawnbroker
Ralph J	Customs
Rammell G	Farmer
Righton J B	Farmer
Robinson W	China shop
Rogers G	Grocer
Rogers C	Shoemaker
Rooff W	Blacksmith
Rolfe J S	Journeyman
Rood F	Wheatsheaf [pub]
Rowe A	Shoemaker
Rowe Hills	Farmer
Rowe T S	Director
Rowe G	Brother of director
Rybot R	
Sackett Mrs A	
Sackett H	Farmer
Sadler T	Dissenting minister
Sayer J	Star Inn [pub]
Scott E T	Chemist
Selby T J	Solicitor
Shaw J	Clerk, not known
Sinnock H	Broker
Sinnock W	
Sisley J	Carpenter
Slater J	
Smithe H Mrs	
Smithe Mr	Farmer
Soper W	Builder
Soper J	Carpenter
Soper W	Master of the infant school
Sowell T	

Staner G, Jun.	Baker
Stead miss	Milliner
Streatfield J	Curate
Stride R H	
Surflen Mrs	Boarding house
Sutton W	Deputy to under sheriff
Swinford J	Hoyman
Swinford J, Jun.	
Symonds J	Clerk to Mr Cobb
Tadhunter Mrs	Lodging house
Thunder T	Journeyman

This very clever and funny account of a stay at Margate in 1838 gives us an idea of the type of character that gave Margate its vibrancy.

Aquatics

The shady side of Cheapside had become a luxury, and footmen in red plush breeches objects of real commiseration, when Mr Jorrocks, tired of the heat and ungrateful hurry of the town, resolved upon undertaking an aquatic excursion. He was sitting, as is his custom always in the afternoon, in the arbour at the farther end of his gravel walk, which he dignifies by the name of 'garden,' and had just finished a rough mental calculation, as to whether he could eat more bread spread with jam or honey, when the idea of the jaunt entered his imagination. Being a man of great decision, he speedily winnowed the project over in his mind, and producing a five-pound note from the fob of his small clothes, passed it in review between his fingers, rubbed out the creases, held it up to the light, refolded and restored it to his fob. "Batsay," cried he, "bring my castor – the white one as hangs next the blue cloak;" and forthwith a rough-napped, unshorn-looking, white hat was transferred from the peg to Mr Jorrocks's head. This done, he proceeded to the 'Piazza,' where he found the Yorkshireman exercising himself up and down the spacious coffee-room, and, grasping his hand with the firmness of a vice, he forthwith began unburthening himself of the object of his mission.

" 'Ow are you?" said he, shaking his arm like the handle of a pump. " 'Ow are you, I say? – I'm so delighted to see you, ye carn't think – isn't this charming weather! It makes me feel like a butterfly – really think the 'air is sprouting under my vig." Here he took off his wig and rubbed his hand over his bald head, as though he were feeling for the shoots.

"Now to business – Mrs Jorrocks is away at Tooting, as you perhaps knows, and I'm all alone in Great Coram Street, with the key of the cellar, larder, and all that sort of thing, and I've a werry great mind to be off on a jaunt – what say you?" "Not the slightest objection," replied the Yorkshireman, "on the old principle of you finding cash, and me finding company." "Why, now I'll tell you, werry honestly, that I should greatly prefer your paying your own shot; but, however, if you've a mind to do as I do, I'll let you stand in the half of a five-pound note and whatever silver I have in my pocket," pulling out a great handful as he spoke, and counting up thirty-two and sixpence. "Very good," replied the Yorkshireman when he had finished, "I'm your man; – and not to be behind hand in point of liberality, I've got threepence that I received in change at the cigar divan just now, which I will add to the common stock, so that we shall have six pounds twelve and ninepence between us." "Between us!" exclaimed Mr Jorrocks, "now that's so like a Yorkshireman. I declare you Northerns seem to think all the world are asleep except yourselves; – howsomever, I von't quarrel with you – you're a goodish sort of chap in your way, and so long as I keep the swag, we carn't get far wrong. Well, then, tomorrow at two we'll start for Margate – the most delightful place in all the world, where we will have a rare jollification, and can stay just as long as the money holds out. So now good-bye – I'm off home again to see about wittles for the woyage."

It were almost superfluous to mention that the following day was a Saturday – for no discreet citizen would think of leaving town on any other. It dawned with uncommon splendour, and the cocks of Coram Street and adjacent parts seemed to hail the morn with more than their wonted energy. Never, save on a hunting morning, did Mr Jorrocks tumble about in bed with such restless anxiety as cock after cock took up the crowin every gradation of noise from the shrill note of the free street-scouring chanticleer[86] before the door, to the faint response of the cooped and imprisoned victims of the neighbouring poulterer's, their efforts being aided by the flutterings and impertinent chirruping of swarms of town-bred sparrows. At length the boy, Binjimin, tapped at his master's door, and, depositing his can of shaving-water on his dressing-table, took away his coat and waistcoat, under pretence of brushing them, but in reality to feel if he had left any pence in the pockets. With pleasure Mr Jorrocks threw aside the bed-clothes, and bounded upon the floor with a bump that shook his own and adjoining houses.

---

[86] Chanticleer: A cock, so called from the clearness or loudness of his voice in crowing.

On this day a few extra minutes were devoted to his toilet, one or two of which were expended in adjusting a gold fox head pin in a conspicuous part of his white tie, and in drawing on a pair of new dark blue stocking-net pantaloons, made so excessively tight, that at starting, any of his Newmarket friends would have laid three to two against his ever getting into them at all. However, they fully enveloped the substantial proportions of his well-rounded limbs, while his large tasselled Hessians showed that the boot maker had been instructed to make a pair for a 'great calf.' A blue coat, with metal buttons, ample laps, and pockets outside, with a handsome buff kerseymere waistcoat, formed his costume on this occasion. Breakfast being over, he repaired to St Botolph Lane, there to see his letters and look after his commercial affairs; in which the reader not being interested, we will allow the Yorkshireman to figure a little. About half-past one this enterprising young man placed himself in Tommy Sly's wherry at the foot of the Savoy stairs, and not agreeing in opinion with Mr Jorrocks that it is of 'no use keeping a dog and barking oneself,' he took an oar and helped to row himself down to London Bridge.

At the wharf below the bridge there lay a magnificent steamer, painted pea-green and white, with flags flying from her masts, and the deck swarming with smart bonnets and bodices. Her name was the Royal Adelaide, from which the sagacious reader will infer that this excursion was made during the late reign. The Yorkshireman and Tommy Sly having wormed their way among the boats, were at length brought up within one of the vessels, and after lying on their oars a few seconds, they were attracted by, 'Now, sir, are you going to sleep there?' addressed to a rival nautical whose boat obstructed the way, and on looking up on deck what a sight burst upon the Yorkshireman's astonished vision! – Mr Jorrocks, with his coat off, and a fine green velvet cap or turban, with a broad gold band and tassel, on his head, hoisting a great hamper out of the wherry, rejecting all offers of assistance, and treating the laughter and jeers of the porters and bystanders with ineffable contempt. At length he placed the load to his liking and putting on his coat, adjusted his hunting telescope, and advanced to the side, as the Yorkshireman mounted the step-ladder and came upon deck. "Werry near being over late," said he, pulling out his watch, just at which moment the last bell rang, and a few strokes of the paddles sent the vessel away from the quay. "A miss is as good as a mile," replied the Yorkshireman; "but pray what have you got in the hamper?" "In the 'amper! Why, wittles to be sure. You seem to forget we are going a woyage, and 'ow keen the sea hair is. I've brought a knuckle of weal, half a ham, beef, sarsingers, chickens, sherry white, and all that sort of thing, and werry acceptable they'll be by the time we get to the Nore, or may be before."

"Ease her! Stop her!" cried the captain through his trumpet, just as the vessel was getting into her stride in mid-stream, and, with true curiosity, the passengers flocked to the side, to see who was coming, though they could not possibly have examined half they had on board. Mr Jorrocks, of course, was not behindhand in inquisitiveness, and proceeded to adjust his telescope. A wherry was seen rowing among the craft, containing the boatman, and a gentleman in a woolly white hat, with a bright pea-green coat, and a basket on his knee. "By jingo, here's Jemmy Green!" exclaimed Mr Jorrocks, taking his telescope from his eye, and giving his thigh a hearty slap. "How unkimmon lucky! The werry man of all others I should most like to see. You know James Green, don't you?" addressing the Yorkshireman – "young James Green, junior, of Tooley Street – everybody knows him – most agreeable young man in Christendom – fine warbler – beautiful dancer – everything that a young man should be."

"How are you James?" cried Jorrocks, seizing him by the hand as his friend stepped upon deck; but whether it was the nervousness occasioned by the rocking of the wherry, or the shaking of the step-ladder up the side of the steamer, or Mr Jorrocks's new turban cap, but Mr Green, with an old-maidish reserve, drew back from the proffered embrace of his friend. "You have the adwantage of me, sir," said he, fidgeting back as he spoke, and eyeing Mr Jorrocks with unmeasured surprise – "Yet stay – if I'm not deceived it's Mr Jorrocks – so it is!" and thereupon they joined hands most cordially, amid exclamations of, " 'Ow are you, J----?" " 'Ow are you, G---- ?" " 'Ow are you, J----?" "So glad to see you, J----" "So glad to see you, G----" "So glad to see you, J----" "And pray what may you have in your basket?" inquired Mr Jorrocks, putting his hand to the bottom of a neat little green-and-white willow woman's basket, apparently for the purpose of ascertaining its weight. "Only my clothes and a little prowision for the woyage. A baked pigeon, some cold maccaroni, and a few pectoral lozenges. At the bottom are my Margate shoes, with a comb in one, and a razor in t'other; then comes the prog, and at the top, I've a dickey and a clean front for to-morrow, I abominates travelling with much luggage. Where, I ax, is the use of carrying nightcaps, when the innkeepers always prowide them, without extra charge? The same with regard to soap. Shave, I say, with what you find in your tray. A wet towel makes an excellent tooth-brush, and a pen-knife both cuts and cleans your nails. Perhaps you'll present your friend to me," added he in the same breath, with a glance at the Yorkshireman, upon whose arm Mr Jorrocks was resting his telescope hand. "Much pleasure," replied Mr Jorrocks, with his usual urbanity. "Allow me to introduce Mr Stubbs, Mr Green, Mr Green, Mr Stubbs: now pray shake hands," added he, "for I'm sure you'll be werry fond of each other;" and thereupon Jemmy, in the most patronising manner, extended his two forefingers to the Yorkshireman, who presented him with one in return.

For the information of such of our readers as may never have seen Mr James Green, senior junior, either in Tooley Street, Southwark, where the patronymic name abounds, or at Messrs Tattersall's, where he generally exhibits on a Monday afternoon, we may premise, that though a little man in stature, he is a great man in mind and a great swell in costume. On the present occasion, as already stated, he had on a woolly white hat, his usual pea-green coat, with a fine, false, four-frilled front to his shirt, embroidered, plaited, and puckered, like a lady's habit-shirt. Down the front were three or four different sorts of studs, and a butterfly brooch, made of various coloured glasses, sat in the centre. His cravat was of a yellow silk with a flowered border, confining gills sharp and pointed that looked up his nostrils; his double-breasted waistcoat was of red and yellow tartan with blue glass post-boy buttons; and his trousers, which were very wide and cut out over the foot of rusty-black chamois-leather opera-boots, were of a broad blue stripe upon a white ground. A curly, bushy, sandy-coloured wig protruded from the sides of his woolly white hat, and shaded a vacant countenance, which formed the frontispiece of a great chucklehead. Sky-blue gloves and a stout cane, with large tassels, completed the rigging of this borough dandy. Altogether he was as fine as any peacock, and as vain as the proudest.

"And 'ow is Mrs J----?" inquired Green with the utmost affability – "I hopes she's uncommon well – pray is she of your party?" looking round. "Why, no," replied Mr Jorrocks, "she's off at Tooting at her mother's and I'm just away, on the sly, to stay a five-pound at Margate this delightful weather. 'Ow long do you remain?" "Oh, only till Monday morning – I goes every Saturday; in fact," added he in an undertone, "I've a season ticket, so I may just as well use it as stay poking in Tooley Street with the old folks, who really are so uncommon glumpy, that it's quite refreshing to get away from them." "That's a pity," replied Mr Jorrocks, with one of his benevolent looks. "But 'ow comes it, James, you are not married? You are not a boy now, and should be looking out for a home of your own." "True, my dear J----, true," replied Mr Green; "and I'll tell you wot, our principal book-keeper and I have made many calculations on the subject, and being a man of literature like yourself, he gave it as his opinion the last time we talked the matter over, that it would only be avoiding silly and running into crab-beds; which I presume means Quod or the Bench. Unless he can have a wife 'made to order,' he says he'll never wed. Besides, the women are such a bothersome encroaching set. I declare I'm so pestered with them that I don't know vich vay to turn. They are always tormenting of me. Only last week one sent me a specification of what she'd marry me for, and I declare her dress, alone, came to more than I have to find myself in clothes, ball-and-concert-tickets, keep an 'oss, go to theatres, buy lozenges, letter-paper, and everything else with. There were bumbazeens, and challies, and merinos, and crape, and gauze, and dimity, and caps, bonnets, stockings, shoes, boots, rigids, stays, ringlets; and, would you believe it, she had the unspeakable audacity to include a bustle! It was the most monstrous specification and proposal ever read, and I returned it by the twopenny post, axing her if she hadn't forgotten to include a set of false teeth. Still, I confess, I'm tired of Tooley Street. I feel that I have a soul above hemp, and was intended for a brighter sphere; but vot can one do, cooped up at home without men of henergy for companions?"

"No prospect of improvement either; for I left our old gentleman alarmingly well just now, pulling about the flax and tow, as though his dinner depended upon his exertions. I think if the women would let me alone, I might have some chance, but it worries a man of sensibility and refinement to have them always tormenting of one. – I've no objection to be led, but, dash my buttons, I von't be driven." "Certainly not," replied Mr Jorrocks, with great gravity, jingling the silver in his breeches-pocket. "It's an old saying, James, and times proves it true, that you may take an 'oss to the water but you carn't make him drink – and talking of 'osses, pray, how are you off in that line?" "Oh, werry well – uncommon, I may say – a thoroughbred, bang tail down to the hocks, by Phantom, out of Baron Munchausen's dam – gave a hatful of money for him at Tatts'. – five fives – a deal of tin as times go. But he's a perfect 'oss, I assure you – bright bay with four black legs, and never a white hair upon him. He's touched in the vind, but that's nothing – I'm not a fox-hunter, you know, Mr Jorrocks; besides, I find the music he makes werry useful in the streets, as a warning to the old happle women to get out of the way."

"Pray, sir," turning to the Yorkshireman with a jerk, "do you dance?" – As the boat band, consisting of a harp, a flute, a lute, a long horn, and short horn, struck up a quadrille, – and, without waiting for a reply, our hero sidled past, and glided among the crowd that covered the deck. "A fine young man, James," observed Mr Jorrocks, eyeing Jemmy as he elbowed his way down the boat – "fine young man – wants a little of his father's ballast, but there's no putting old heads on young shoulders. He's a beautiful dancer," added Mr Jorrocks, putting his arm through the Yorkshireman's, "let's go and see him foot it."

Having worked their way down, they at length got near the dancers, and mounting a ballast box had a fine view of the quadrille. There were eight or ten couples at work, and Jemmy had chosen a fat, dumpy, red-faced girl, in a bright orange-coloured muslin gown, with black velvet Vandyked flounces, and green boots – a sort of walking sunflower, with whom he was pointing his toe, kicking out behind, and pirouetting with great energy and agility. His male vis-à-vis was a waistcoatless young Daniel Lambert, in white ducks, and a blue dress-coat, with a carnation in his mouth, who, with a damsel in ten colours, reeled to and fro in humble imitation.

"Green for ever!" cried Mr Jorrocks, taking off his velvet cap and waving it encouragingly over his head: "Green for ever! Go it Green!" and, accordingly, Green went it with redoubled vigour. "Wiggins for ever!" responded a female voice opposite, "I say, Wiggins!" which was followed by a loud clapping of hands, as the fat gentleman made an astonishing step. Each had his admiring applauders, though Wiggins had the call among the ladies – the opposition voice that put him in nomination proceeding from the mother of his partner, who, like her daughter, was a sort of walking pattern book. The spirit of emulation lasted throughout the quadrille, after which, sunflower in hand, Green traversed the deck to receive the compliments of the company. "You must be 'ungry," observed Mr Jorrocks, with great politeness to the lady, "after all your exertions," as the latter stood mopping herself with a coarse linen handkerchief – "pray, James, bring your partner to our 'amper, and let me offer her some refreshment," which was one word for the Sunflower and two for himself, the sea breeze having made Mr Jorrocks what he called unkimmon peckish.

The hamper was speedily opened, the knuckle of veal, the half ham, the aitch bone of beef, the Dorking sausages (made in Drury Lane), the chickens, and some dozen or two of plovers' eggs were exhibited, while Green, with disinterested generosity, added his baked pigeon and cold maccaroni to the common stock. A vigorous attack was speedily commenced, and was kept up, with occasional interruptions by Green running away to dance, until they hove in sight of Herne Bay, which caused an interruption to a very interesting lecture on wines, that Mr Jorrocks was in the act of delivering, which went to prove that port and sherry were the parents of all wines, port the father, and sherry the mother; and that Bluecellas, hock, Burgundy, claret, Tenerife, Madeira, were made by the addition of water, vinegar, and a few chemical ingredients, and that of all 'humbugs,' pale sherry was the greatest, being neither more nor less than brown sherry watered.

Mr Jorrocks then set to work to pack up the leavings in the hamper, observing as he proceeded, that wilful waste brought woeful want, and that 'waste not, want not,' had ever been the motto of the Jorrocks family. It was nearly eight o'clock ere the Royal Adelaide touched the point of the far-famed Margate Jetty, a fact that was announced as well by the usual bump, and scuttle to the side to get out first, as by the band striking up God save the King and the mate demanding the tickets of the passengers. The sun had just dropped beneath the horizon and the gas-lights of the town had been considerately lighted to show him to bed, for the day was yet in the full vigour of life and light. Two or three other cargoes of cockneys having arrived before, the whole place was in commotion and the beach swarmed with spectators as anxious to watch this last disembarkation as they had been to see the first. By a salutary regulation of the sages who watch over the interests of the town, all manner of persons are prohibited from walking upon the jetty during this ceremony, but the platform of which it is composed being very low, those who stand on the beach outside the rails, are just about on a right level to shoot their impudence cleverly into the ears of the new-comers who are paraded along two lines of gaping, quizzing, laughing, joking, jeering citizens, who fire volleys of wit and satire upon them as they pass.

Arrival at Margate by steamboat

"There's leetle Jemmy Green again!" exclaimed a nursery-maid with two fat ruddy children in her arms, "he's a beauty without paint! Hallo, Jorrocks, my hearty! Lend us your hand," cried a brother member of the Surrey Hunt. Then there was a pointing of fingers and cries of "That's Jorrocks! That's Green!" "That's Green! That's Jorrocks!" and a murmuring titter and exclamations of "There's Simpkins! How pretty he is! "But there's Wiggins who's much nicer." "My eye, what a cauliflower hat Mrs Thompson's got!" "What a buck

257

young Snooks is!" "What gummy legs that girl in green has!" "Miss Trotter's bustle's on crooked!" from the young ladies at Miss Trimmer's seminary who were drawn up to show the numerical strength of the academy and act the part of walking advertisements. These observations were speedily drowned by the lusty lungs of a flyman bellowing out, as Green passed, "Hallo! My young brockley-sprout, are you here again? – now then for the tizzy you owe me, – I have been waiting here for it ever since last Monday morning." This salute produced an irate look and a shake of his cane from Green, with a mutter of something about 'imperance,' and a wish that he had his big fighting foreman there to thrash him.

When they got to the gate at the end, the tide of fashion became obstructed by the kissings of husbands and wives, the greetings of fathers and sons, the officiousness of porters, the cries of flymen, the importunities of innkeepers, the cards of bathing-women, the salutations of donkey drivers, the programmes of librarians and the rush and push of the inquisitive; and the waters of 'comers' and 'stayers' mingled in one common flood of indescribable confusion. Mr Jorrocks, who, hamper in hand, had elbowed his way with persevering resignation, here found himself so beset with friends all anxious to wring his digits, that, fearful of losing either his bed or his friends, he besought Green to step on to the 'White Hart' and see about accommodation. Accordingly Green ran his fingers through the bushy sides of his yellow wig, jerked up his gills, and with a neglige air strutted up to that inn, which, as all frequenters of Margate know, stands near the landing-place, and commands a fine view of the harbour.

Mr Creed, the landlord, was airing himself at the door, or, as Shakespeare has it, 'taking his ease at his inn,' and knowing Green of old to be a most unprofitable customer, he did not trouble to move his position farther than just to draw up one leg so as not wholly to obstruct the passage and looked at him as much as to say "I prefer your room to your company. Quite full here sir," said he, anticipating Green's question. "Full, indeed?" replied Jemmy, pulling up his gills – "that's werry awkward, Mr Jorrocks has come down with myself and a friend, and we want accommodation." "Mr Jorrocks, indeed!" replied Mr Creed, altering his tone and manner; "I'm sure I shall be delighted to receive Mr Jorrocks – he's one of the oldest customers I have – and one of the best – none of your 'glass of water and toothpick' gentleman – real downright, black-strap man, likes it hot and strong from the wood – always pays like a gentleman – never fights about threepences, like some people I know," looking at Jemmy. "Pray, what rooms may you require?" "Vy, there's myself, Mr Jorrocks, and Mr Jorrocks's other friend – three in all, and we shall want three good, hairy bedrooms." "Well, I don't know," replied Mr Creed, laughing, "about their hairiness, but I can rub them with bear's grease for you."

Jemmy pulled up his gills and was about to reply when Mr Jorrocks's appearance interrupted the dialogue. Mr Creed advanced to receive him, blowing up his porters for not having been down to carry up the hamper which he took himself and bore to the coffee-room amid protestations of his delight at seeing his worthy visitor. Having talked over the changes of Margate, of those that were there, those that were not, and those that were coming and adverted to the important topic of supper, Mr Jorrocks took out his yellow and white spotted handkerchief and proceeded to flop his Hessian boots, while Mr Creed, with his own hands, rubbed him over with a long billiard-table brush. Green, too, put himself in form by the aid of the looking-glass, and these preliminaries being adjusted, the trio sallied forth arm-in-arm, Mr Jorrocks occupying the centre.

It was a fine, balmy summer evening, the beetles and moths still buzzed and flickered in the air and the sea rippled against the shingly shore with a low indistinct murmur that scarcely sounded among the busy hum of men. The shades of night were drawing on – a slight mist hung about the hills and a silvery moon shed a broad brilliant ray upon the quivering waters of the dark blue sea and an equal light over the wide expanse of the troubled town. How strange that man should leave the quiet scenes of nature to mix in myriads of those they profess to quit cities to avoid! One turn to the shore and the gas-lights of the town drew back the party like moths to the streets, which were literally swarming with the population. 'Cheapside, at three o'clock in the afternoon,' as Mr Jorrocks observed, 'was never fuller than Margate streets that evening.' All was lighted up – all brilliant and all gay – care seemed banished from every countenance, and pretty faces and smart gowns reigned in its stead.

Mr Jorrocks met with friends and acquaintances at every turn, most of whom asked 'when he came?' and 'when he was going away?' Having perambulated the streets, the sound of music attracted Jemmy Green's attention and our party turned into a long, crowded and brilliantly lighted bazaar, just as the last notes of a barrel-organ at the far end faded away and a young woman in a hat and feathers, with a swan's-down muff and tippet, was handed by a very smart young man in dirty white Berlin gloves and an equally soiled white waistcoat, into a sort of orchestra above where, after the plaudits of the company had subsided, she struck-up: 'If I had a donkey vot vouldn't go.' At the conclusion of the song and before the company had time to disperse, the same smart young gentleman, – having re-handed the young lady from the orchestra and pocketed his gloves, – ran his fingers through his hair and announced from that eminence, that the spirited proprietors of the Bazaar were then going to offer for public competition in the enterprising shape of a raffle, in tickets, at one shilling each, a most magnificently genteel, rosewood, general perfume box fitted up with cedar and lined with red silk velvet, adorned with cut-steel clasps at the sides and a solid, massive, silver name-plate at the top, with a best patent Bramah lock and six chaste and beautifully rich cut-glass bottles and a plate-glass mirror at the top – a box so splendidly perfect, so beautifully unique, as alike to defy the powers of praise and the critiques of the envious; and thereupon he produced a flashy sort of thing that might be worth three and sixpence, for which he modestly required ten subscribers, at a shilling each, adding, 'that even with that number the proprietors would incur a werry heavy loss, for which nothing but a boundless sense of gratitude for favours past could possibly recompense them.'

The youth's eloquence and the glitter of the box reflecting, as it did at every turn, the gas-lights both in its steel and glass had the desired effect – shillings went down and tickets went off rapidly until only three remained. "Four, five, and ten, are the only numbers now remaining," observed the youth, running his eye up the list and wetting his pencil in his mouth. "Four, five and ten! Ten, four, five! five, four, ten! are the only numbers now vacant for this werry genteel and magnificent rosewood perfume-box, lined with red velvet, cut-steel clasps, a silver plate for the name, best patent Bramah lock, and six beautiful rich cut-glass bottles, with a plate glass mirror in the lid – and only four, five, and ten now vacant!" "I'll take ten," said Green, laying down a shilling. "Thank you, sir – only four and five now wanting, ladies and gentlemen – pray, be in time – pray, be in time! This is without exception the most brilliant prize ever offered for public competition. There were only two of these werry elegant boxes made, – the unfortunate mechanic who executed them being carried off by that terrible malady, the cholera morbus, – and the other is now in the possession of his most Christian Majesty the King of the French. Only four and five wanting to commence throwing for this really perfect specimen of human ingenuity – only four and five!" "I'll take them," cried Green, throwing down two shillings more – and then the table was cleared – the dice box produced, and the crowd drew round.

"Number one! – who holds number one?" inquired the keeper, arranging the paper and sucking the end of his pencil. A young gentleman in a blue jacket and white trousers owned the lot, and, accordingly, led off the game. The lottery-keeper handed the box and put in the dice – rattle, rattle, rattle, rattle, rattle, rattle, plop and lift up – "seven and four are eleven – now again, if you please, sir," putting the dice into the box – rattle, rattle, rattle, rattle, rattle, rattle, plop and lift up – a loud laugh – "one and two make three" – the youth bit his lips; – rattle, rattle, rattle, rattle, rattle, rattle, rattle, plop – a pause –

and lift up – "threes! – six, three, and eleven, are twenty. Now who holds number two? – what lady or gentleman holds number two? Pray, step forward!" The Sunflower drew near – Green looked confused – she fixed her eye upon him, half in fear, half in entreaty – would he offer to throw for her? No, by Jove, Green was not so green as all that came to and he let her shake herself. She threw twenty-two, thereby putting an extinguisher on the boy and raising Jemmy's chance considerably. Three was held by a youngster in nankeen petticoats, who would throw for himself and shook the box violently enough to be heard at Broadstairs. He scored nineteen, and, beginning to cry immediately was taken home. Green was next, and all eyes turned upon him, for he was a noted hand. He advanced to the table with great sangfroid, and, turning back the wrists of his coat, exhibited his beautiful sparkling paste shirt buttons and the elegant turn of his taper hand, the middle finger of which was covered with massive rings. He took the box in a neglige manner and without condescending to shake it, slid the dice out upon the table by a gentle sideway motion – "sixes!" cried all and down the marker put twelve. At the second throw he adopted another mode. As soon as the dice were in he just chucked them up in the air like as many halfpence and down they came five and six – "eleven," said the marker. With a look of triumph Green held the box for the third time which he just turned upside down and lo, on uncovering, there stood two – "ones!"A loud laugh burst forth, and Green looked confused.

"I'm so glad!" whispered a young lady, who had made an unsuccessful 'set' at Jemmy the previous season in a tone loud enough for him to hear. "I hope he'll lose," rejoined a female friend rather louder. "That Jemmy Green is my absolute abhorrence," observed a third. " 'Orrible man with his nasty vie," observed the mamma of the first speaker – "shouldn't have my darter not at no price." Green, however, headed the poll, having beat the Sunflower, and had still two lots in reserve. For number five, he threw twenty-five, and was immediately outstripped, amid much laughter and clapping of hands from the ladies, by number six, who in his turn fell a prey to number seven. Between eight and nine there was a very interesting contest who should be lowest and hopes and fears were at their altitude, when Jemmy Green again turned back his coat-wrist to throw for number ten. His confidence had forsaken him a little, as indicated by a slight quivering of the under-lip, but he managed to conceal it from all except the ladies, who kept too scrutinising an eye upon him. His first throw brought sixes, which raised his spirits amazingly; but on their appearance a second time, he could scarcely contain himself, backed as he was by the plaudits of his friend Mr Jorrocks. Then came the deciding throw – every eye was fixed on Jemmy, he shook the box, turned it down, and lo! there came seven. "Mr James Green is the fortunate winner of this magnificent prize!" exclaimed the youth holding up the box in mid-air and thereupon all the ladies crowded round Green, some to congratulate him,

261

others to compliment him on his looks, while one or two of the least knowing tried to coax him out of his box. Jemmy, however, was too old a stager and pocketed the box and other compliments at the same time.

Another grind of the organ, and another song followed from the same young lady, during which operation Green sent for the manager, and, after a little beating about the bush, proposed singing a song or two, if he would give him lottery-tickets gratis. He asked three shilling-tickets for each song and finally closed for five tickets for two songs, on the understanding that he was to be announced as a distinguished amateur, who had come forward by most particular desire. Accordingly the manager – a roundabout, red-faced, consequential little cockney – mounted the rostrum and begged to announce to the company that that 'celebrated vocalist, Mr James Green, so well known as a distinguished amateur and convivialist, both at Bagnigge Wells, and Vite Conduit House, London, had werry kindly consented, in order to promote the hilarity of the evening, to favour the company with a song immediately after the drawing of the next lottery,' and after a few high-flown compliments, which elicited a laugh from those who were up to Jemmy's mode of doing business, he concluded by offering a papier-mâché tea-caddy for public competition, in shilling lots as before.

As soon as the drawing was over, they gave the organ a grind and Jemmy popped up with a hop, step, and a jump, with his woolly white hat under his arm and presented himself with a scrape and a bow to the company. After a few preparatory 'hems and haws,' he pulled up his gills and spoke as follows: "Ladies and gentlemen! hem" – another pull at his gills – "ladies and gentlemen – my walued friend, Mr Kitey Graves, has announced that I will entertain the company with a song; though nothing, I assure you – hem – could be farther from my idea – hem – when my excellent friend asked me," – "Hookey Walker!" exclaimed someone who had heard Jemmy declare the same thing half a dozen times – "and, indeed, ladies and gentlemen – hem – nothing but the werry great regard I have for Mr Kitey Graves, who I have known and loved ever since he was the height of sixpennorth of coppers" a loud laugh followed this allusion, seeing that eighteen penny-worth would almost measure out the speaker. On giving another 'hem,' and again pulling up his gills, an old Kentish farmer, in a brown coat and mahogany-coloured tops, hollowed out, "I say, sir! I'm afeared you'll be catching cold!" "I 'opes not," replied Jemmy in a fluster, "is it raining? I've no umbrella and my werry best coat on!" "No! Raining, no!" replied the farmer, "only you've pulled at your shirt so long that I think you must be bare behind! Haw! haw! haw!" at which all the males roared with laughter and the females hid their faces in their handkerchiefs and tittered and giggled and tried to be shocked. "ORDER! ORDER!" cried Mr Jorrocks, in a loud and sonorous voice, which

262

had the effect of quelling the riot and drawing all eyes upon himself. "Ladies and gentlemen," said he, taking off his cap with great gravity and extending his right arm, "immodest words admit of no defence, for want of decency is want of sense;" a couplet so apropos and so well delivered, as to have the immediate effect of restoring order and making the farmer look foolish.

Encouraged by the voice of his great patron, Green once more essayed to finish his speech, which he did by a fresh assurance of the surprise by which he had been taken by the request of his friend Kitey Graves and an exhortation for the company to make allowance for any deficiency of 'woice,' inasmuch as how as labouring under 'a wiolent 'orseness,' for which he had long been taking pectoral lozenges. He then gave his gills another pull, felt if they were even, and struck up: 'Bid me discourse,' in notes compared to which the screaming of a peacock would be perfect melody. Mr Jorrocks having taken a conspicuous position, applauded long, loudly, and warmly, at every pause – approbation the more deserved and disinterested, inasmuch as the worthy gentleman suffers considerably from music and only knows two tunes, one of which, he says, 'is God save the King, and the other isn't.'

Having seen his protégé fairly under way, Mr Jorrocks gave him a hint that he would return to the 'White Hart' and have supper ready by the time he was done; accordingly the Yorkshireman and he withdrew along an avenue politely formed by the separation of the company who applauded as they passed. An imperial quart and a half of Mr Creed's stoutest draft port, with the orthodox proportion of lemon, cloves, sugar and cinnamon, had almost boiled itself to perfection under the skilful superintendence of Mr Jorrocks, and the coffee-room fire and a table had been handsomely decorated with shrimps, lobsters, broiled bones, fried ham, poached eggs, when just as the clock had finished striking eleven, the coffee-room door opened with a rush and in tripped Jemmy Green with his hands crammed full of packages and his trousers' pockets sticking out like a Dutch burgomaster's.

"Vell, I've done 'em brown to-night, I think," said he, depositing his hat and half a dozen packages on the sideboard and running his fingers through his curls to make them stand-up. "I've won nine lotteries and left one undrawn when I came away, because it did not seem likely to fill. Let me see," said he, emptying his pockets, – "there is the beautiful rosewood box that I won ven you was there; the next was a set of crimping-irons, vich I von also; the third was a jockey-vip, which I did not want and only stood one ticket for and lost; the fourth was this elegant box, with a view of Margate on the lid; then came these six sherry labels with silver rims; a snuff-box with an inwisible mouse; a coral rattle with silver bells; a silk yard measure in a walnut-shell; a couple of West India beetles; a humming-bird in a glass case, which I lost; and then these dozen bodkins with silver eyes – so that altogether I have made a pretty good night's work of it. Kitey Graves wasn't in great force, so after I had sung, Bid Me Discourse, and I'd Be A Butterfly, I cut my stick and went to the hopposition shop, where they used me much more genteelly; giving me three tickets for a song and introducing me in more flattering terms to the company – don't like being considered one of the nasty 'reglars,' and they should make a point of explaining that one isn't. Besides, what business had Kitey to say anything about Bagnigge Vells? a hass! – Now, perhaps, you'll favour me with some supper." "Certainly," replied Mr Jorrocks patting Jemmy approvingly on the head – "you deserve some. It's only no song, no supper, and you've been singing like a nightingale;" thereupon they set to with vigorous determination.

A bright Sunday dawned, and the beach at an early hour was crowded with men in dressing-gowns of every shape, hue and material with buff slippers – the 'regulation Margate shoeing,' both for men and women. As the hour of eleven approached and the church bells began to ring, the town seemed to awaken suddenly from a trance and bonnets the most superb and dresses the most extravagant, poured forth from lodgings the most miserable. Having shaved and dressed himself with more than ordinary care and attention, Mr Jorrocks walked his friends off to church, assuring them that no one need hope to prosper throughout the week who did not attend it on the Sunday and he marked his own devotion throughout the service by drowning the clerk's voice with his responses. After this spiritual ablution Mr Jorrocks bethought himself of having a bodily one in the sea; and the day being excessively hot and the tide about the proper mark, he pocketed a couple of towels out of his bedroom and went away to bathe, leaving Green and the Yorkshireman to amuse themselves at the 'White Hart.' This house, as we have already stated, faces the harbour and is a corner one running a considerable way up the next street, with a side door communicating as well as the front one with the coffee-room. This room differs from the generality of coffee-rooms, inasmuch as the windows range the whole length of the room and being very low they afford every facility for the children and passers-by to inspect the interior. Whether this is done to show the Turkey carpet, the pea-green cornices, the bright mahogany slips of tables, the gay trellised geranium-papered room, or the aristocratic visitors who frequent it is immaterial – the description is as accurate as if George Robins had drawn it himself.

In this room then, as the Yorkshireman and Green were lying dozing on three chairs apiece, each having fallen asleep to avoid the trouble of talking to the other, they were suddenly roused by loud yells and hootings at the side door and the bursting into the coffee-room of what at first brush they thought must be a bull. The Yorkshireman jumped up, rubbed his eyes and lo! before him stood Mr Jorrocks, puffing like a stranded grampus with a bunch of sea-weed under his arm and the dress in which he had started, with the exception of the dark bluestocking-net pantaloons, the place of which were supplied by a flowing white linen kilt, commonly called a shirt, in the four corners of which were knotted a few small pebbles – producing, with the Hessian boots and one thing and another, the most laughable figure imaginable. The blood of the Jorrockses was up, however, and throwing his hands in the air, he thus delivered himself. "Oh gentlemen! gentlemen! – here's a lamentable occurrence – a terrible disaster – oh dear! oh dear! – I never thought I should come to this. You know, James Green," appealing to Jemmy, "that I never was the man to raise a blush on the cheek of modesty; I have always said that 'want of decency is want of sense,' and see how I am rewarded! Oh dear! oh dear! that I should ever have trusted my pantaloons out of my sight."

While all this, which was the work of a moment, was going forward, the mob, which had been shut out at the side door on Jorrocks's entry, had got round to the coffee-room window and were all wedging their faces in to have a sight of him. It was principally composed of children, who kept up the most discordant yells, mingled with shouts of 'there's old cutty shirt!' – 'who's got your breeches, old cock?' – 'make a scramble!' – 'turn him out for another hunt!' – 'turn him again!' – until, fearing for the respectability of his house, the landlord persuaded Mr Jorrocks to retire into the bar to state his grievances.

It then appeared that having travelled along the coast as far as the first preventive station house on the Ramsgate side of Margate, the grocer had thought it a convenient place for performing his intended ablutions, and, accordingly, proceeded to do what all people of either sex agree upon in such cases – namely to divest himself of his garments; but before he completed the ceremony, observing some females on the cliffs above and not being (as he said) a man 'to raise a blush on the cheek of modesty,' he advanced to the water's edge in his aforesaid unmentionables and forgetting that it was not yet high tide, he left them there, when they were speedily covered and the pockets being full of silver and copper, of course they were 'swamped.' After dabbling about in the water and amusing himself with picking up sea-weed for about ten minutes, Mr Jorrocks was horrified, on returning to the spot where he thought he had left his stocking-net pantaloons, to find that they had disappeared; and after a long fruitless search the unfortunate gentleman was compelled to abandon the pursuit and render himself an object of chase to all the little boys and girls who chose to follow him into Margate on his return without them.

265

Jorrocks, as might be expected, was very bad about his loss and could not get over it – it stuck in his gizzard, he said – and there it seemed likely to remain. In vain Mr Creed offered him a pair of trousers – he never had worn a pair. In vain he asked for the loan of a pair of white cords and top-boots, or even drab shorts and continuations. Mr Creed was no sportsman and did not keep any. The bellman could not cry the lost unmentionables because it was Sunday and even if they should be found on the ebbing of the tide, they would take no end of time to dry. Mr Jorrocks declared his pleasure at an end and forthwith began making inquiries as to the best mode of getting home. The coaches were all gone, steamboats there were none, save for every place but London and posting, he said, was 'cruelly expensive.' In the midst of his dilemma, 'Boots,' who is always the most intelligent man about an inn, popped in his curly head and informed Mr Jorrocks that the 'Unity' Hoy, a most commodious vessel, neat, trim and water-tight, manned by his own maternal uncle, was going to cut away to London at three o'clock and would land him before he could say 'Jack Robinson.' Mr Jorrocks jumped at the offer and forthwith attiring himself in a pair of Mr Creed's loose inexpressibles, over which he drew his Hessian boots, he tucked the hamper containing the knuckle of veal and other etceteras under one arm and the bunch of sea-weed he had been busy collecting instead of watching his clothes under the other, and, followed by his friends, made direct for the vessel.

Everybody knows, or ought to know, what a Hoy is – it is a large sailing-boat, sometimes with one deck, sometimes with none; and the 'Unity', trading in bulky goods, was of the latter description, though there was a sort of dog-hole at the stern which the master dignified by the name of a 'state cabin,' into which he purposed putting Mr Jorrocks if the weather should turn cold before they arrived. The wind, however, he said, was so favourable and his cargo – 'timber and fruit,' as he described it, that is to say, broomsticks and potatoes – so light, that he warranted landing him at Blackwall at least by ten o'clock where he could either sleep or get a short stage or an omnibus on to Leadenhall Street. The vessel looked anything but tempting, neither was the captain's appearance prepossessing, still Mr Jorrocks, all things considered, thought he would chance it; and depositing his hamper and sea-weed and giving special instructions about having his pantaloons cried [by the bell-man] in the morning – recounting that besides the silver and eighteen-pence in copper, there was a steel pencil-case with 'J.J' on the seal at the top, an anonymous letter and two keys – he took an affectionate leave of his friends and stepped on board, the vessel was shoved off and stood out to sea.

Monday morning drew the cockneys from their roosts betimes, to take their farewell splash and dive in the sea. As the day advanced, the bustle and confusion on the shore and in the town increased and everyone seemed on the move. The ladies paid their last visits to the bazaars and shell shops and children extracted the last ounce of exertion from the exhausted leg-weary donkeys. Meanwhile the lords of the creation strutted about, some in dressing-gowns, others, 'fullpuff,' with bags and boxes under their arms – while sturdy porters were wheeling barrows full of luggage to the jetty. The bell-man went round dressed in a blue and red cloak with a gold hatband. Ring-a-ding, ring-a-ding, ring-a-ding, dong, went the bell and the gaping cockneys congregated around. He commenced – "To be sold in the market-place a quantity of fresh ling." Ring-a-ding, ring-a-ding, dong: "The Royal Adelaide, fast and splendid steam-packet, Capt. Whittingham, will leave the pier this morning at nine o'clock precisely and land the passengers at London Bridge Steam-packet Wharf – fore cabin fares and children four shillings – saloon five shillings." Ring-a-ding, ring-a-ding, dong: "The superb and splendid steam-packet, the Magnet, will leave the pier this morning at nine o'clock precisely, and land the passengers at the St Catherine Docks – fore-cabin fares and children four shillings – saloon five shillings." Ring-a-ding, ring-a-ding, dong: "Lost at the back of James Street – a lady's black silk – black lace wale – whoever has found the same and will bring it to the crier, shall receive one shilling reward." Ring-a-ding, ring-a-ding, dong: "Lost, last night, between the jetty and the York Hotel, a little boy, as answers to the name of Spot, whoever has found the same and will bring him to the crier, shall receive a reward of half-a-crown." Ring-a-ding, ring-a-ding, dong: "Lost, stolen, or strayed, or otherwise conveyed, a brown-and-white King Charles's setter as answers to the name of Jacob Jones. Whoever has found the same, or will give such information as shall lead to the detection and conversion of the offender or offenders shall be handsomely rewarded." Ring-a-ding, ring-a-ding, dong: "Lost below the prewentive sarvice station by a gentleman of great respectability – a pair of blue knit pantaloons containing eighteen penny-worth of copper – a steel pencil-case – a werry anonymous letter and two keys. Whoever will bring the same to the crier shall receive a reward. – God save the King!"

Then, as the hour of nine approached, what a concourse appeared! There were fat and lean, short and tall and middling going away, and fat and lean, short and tall and middling waiting to see them off and Green, as usual, making himself conspicuous and canvassing everyone he could lay hold of for the Magnet steamer. At the end of the jetty, on each side, lay the Royal Adelaide and the Magnet, with as fierce a contest for patronage as ever was witnessed. Both decks were crowded with anxious faces – for the Monday's steamboat race is as great an event as a Derby and a cockney would as leave lay on an outside horse as patronise a boat that was likely to let another pass her. Nay, so high is the enthusiasm carried, that books are regularly made on the occasion and there is as much clamour for bets as in the ring at Epsom or

Newmarket. "Tomkins, I'll lay you a dinner – for three – Royal Adelaide against the Magnet," bawled Jenkins from the former boat. "Done," cries Tomkins. "The Magnet for a bottle of port," bawled out another. "A whitebait dinner for two, the Magnet reaches Greenwich first." "What should you know about the Magnet?" inquires the mate of the Royal Adelaide. "Vy, I think I should know something about nauticals too, for Lord St Wincent was my godfather." "I'll bet five shillings on the Royal Adelaide." "I'll take you," says another. "I'll bet a bottom of brandy on the Magnet," roars out the mate. "Two goes of Hollands" the Magnet's off Herne Bay before the Royal Adelaide." "I'll lay a pair of crimping-irons against five shillings the Magnet beats the Royal Adelaide," bellowed out Green, who having come onboard had mounted the paddle-box. "I say, Green, I'll lay you an even five if you like." "Well, five pounds," cries Green. "No, shillings," says his friend. "Never bet in shillings," replies Green, pulling up his shirt collar. "I'll bet fifty pounds," he adds, getting valiant. "I'll bet a hundred ponds – a thousand pounds – a million pounds – half the National Debt, if you like."

Precisely as the jetty clock finishes striking nine the ropes are slipped and the rival steamers stand out to sea with beautiful precision amid the crying, the kissing of hands, the raising of hats, the waving of handkerchiefs, from those who are left for the week, while the passengers are cheered by adverse tunes from the respective bands onboard. The Magnet, having the outside gets the breeze first hand, but the Royal Adelaide keeps well alongside and both firemen being deeply interested in the event, they boil up a tremendous gallop without either being able to claim the slightest advantage for upwards of an hour and a half, when the Royal Adelaide manages to shoot ahead for a few minutes, amid the cheers and exclamations of her crew. The Magnet's fireman, however, is on the alert and a few extra pokes of the fire presently bring the boats together again, in which state they continue nose and nose, until the stiller water of the side of the Thames favours the Magnet and she shoots ahead amid the cheers and vociferations of her party and is not neared again during the voyage. This excitement over the respective crews sink into a sort of melancholy sedateness and Green, in vain, endeavours to kick up a quadrille.

The men were exhausted and the women dispirited and altogether they were a very different set of beings to what they were on the Saturday. Dull faces and dirty-white ducks were the order of the day. The only incident of the voyage was, that on approaching the mouth of the Medway, the Royal Adelaide was hailed by a vessel and the Yorkshireman, on looking overboard, was shocked to behold Mr Jorrocks sitting in the stern of his Hoy in the identical position he had taken up the previous day, with his bunch of sea-weed under his elbow and the remains of the knuckle of veal, ham and chicken spread on the hamper before him. "Stop her?" cried the Yorkshireman and then hailing Mr Jorrocks he hollowed out, "In the name of the prophet, Figs, what are you doing there?" "Oh, gentlemen! gentlemen!" exclaimed Mr Jorrocks, brightening up as he recognised the boat, "take compassion on a most misfortunate indiwidual – here have I been in this 'orrid 'oy, ever since three o'clock yesterday afternoon and here I seem likely to end my days – for blow me tight if I couldn't swim as fast as it goes." "Look sharp, then," cried the mate of the steamer, "and chuck us up your luggage." Up went the sea-weed, the hamper and Mr Jorrocks; and before the Hoy man awoke out of a nap, into which he had composed himself on resigning the rudder to his lad, our worthy citizen was steaming away a mile before his vessel, bilking him of his fare. Who does not recognise in this last disaster, the truth of the old adage? 'Most haste, least speed.'

("Aquatics, Mr Jorrocks at Margate," Surtees, Robert Smith, 1838)

Mr Poole's description of Margate during the winter months is quite telling. Also, his disclosure of where all the apparently French souvenir items are really manufactured would have infuriated many a visitor who had been duped into believing they had brought home something special. Apparently cologne and 'French' pomatum (used for hair styling) were made locally. 'French' watches, clocks, jewels and trinkets were from Birmingham and Sheffield, 'French' work boxes, dressing cases and toys were from Tonbridge, and Worcester supplied Margate with all its 'French' porcelain – especially the best specimens, purporting to come from the Sèvres manufactory!

Mr John Poole's description of Margate

Margate is a town, supposed by the more cultivated among cockneys to be still on the Kentish coast; and this is nearly the only fact relating to its whereabouts which can be asserted with any degree of certainty. The changes which the last twenty years have effected in relations of time and space, have created a confusion in the geographical notions of the citizens, touching this their paradise, out of which they have not yet had time to emerge into anything like a clear and definite conception of its bearing and distance from Capel Court. Twenty years ago, the distance of Margate from London by land was about seventy-two miles – what it actually is very few people know – what it may be twenty years hence nobody can possibly tell. The accuracy of the past distance which I have attributed to the place, could have been attested by ninety-nine out of every hundred travellers who then visited it, – their own evidence being corroborated by that of six dozen of as respectable mile-stones as any in all England, each and all of unimpeachable veracity.

Of its present distance, it is impossible to speak with the decision befitting the importance of the subject; since, upon the most minute, as well as extensive researches, which I have been enabled to make, I have not heard of one person, in his or her right senses, who has lately made an over-land trip to Margate. Such an event, indeed, is not within the memory of the oldest pot-house on the road; and, although I have been told that the driver and guard of the Royal Mail (the only two individuals who are even suspected of going that way), might say something to the point, it is still far from improbable that they perform part of their journey by the Great Western, or the London and Birmingham, or some other of the numerous railways – all of which profess to carry you, by the shortest cut, to anywhere, and everywhere, you may desire to be carried to.

For the future distance of the place, still less can be said even than for its present; that is a secret which is concealed within the bosoms of time and the railroad projectors and reduced by the patriotic rivalry of the latter, it may, in the course of next summer, be only fifty miles – or thirty – or ten – or, in short (such are the wonderful feats which the joint powers of iron and hot water are capable of performing), no distance at all! By water (Cocknice sea) the distance, both past and present, from London to Margate may be calculated with a nearer approach towards accuracy.

Let us take for the basis of our calculations the chart, which gives us eighty miles – taking for granted at the same time, eighty miles to have been the old distance; and since, according to the travelling interpretation of the term 'distance,' it is taken to mean 'time' and the average difference of time consumed upon the voyage by the old system of canvas and the new system of scalding water, being as about four to one, Margate may now be said to count no more than twenty miles from the metropolis!

My own first sea trip to the place in question, which was performed in a thing called a Hoy (a sort of Billingsgate slaver licensed to carry as many as its inhuman commander might choose to cram into it), endured for seven-and-thirty mortal hours; and, but for some lucky change in the wind was expected to last through seven-and-thirty more – my last, in a steamer, was accomplished in about six hours and a half! "We are late today," said someone to the captain as we touched the jetty. "Why sir," replied the captain in a tone of exculpation, "you know the wind and tide were dead against us for the greater part of the way." I thought of my Billingsgate slave ship and wished the unconscionable complainant – did I wish him worse than he deserved? – On board of her for seven-and-thirty hours.

The manufactures of Margate consist chiefly of Eau de Cologne, French Pomatums and French perfumery in general. French artificial flowers and the lighter articles of French millinery from Paris are also made here in great abundance. But Margate does not aspire to the making of French watches and clocks or of French jewels and trinkets; these are the produce of Birmingham and Sheffield. Its French work-boxes, dressing cases and toys, again, it derives from Tunbridge; whilst Worcester has the honour of supplying it with all its French porcelain, especially the best specimens from the Sevres manufactory. Neither, I believe, are the real Havannah cigars made in the town, – at least there are no large plantations of cabbages within a convenient distance of it. All these articles are purchased in great quantities by the visitors from the Metropolis and if they can but be procured 'duty free,' at the depot, authorised by the commissioners of Her Majesty's customs to sell smuggled goods, seized and confiscated, they are carried off with an avidity which is truly astonishing.

The commerce of Margate is comprised under the preceding head; and I am not aware that the place is remarkable for its natural productions – if we except shrimps, cockle shells, bathing women and a few other marine curiosities. Of the population of Margate it is difficult, if not impossible, to form any idea. My own settled opinion is that, of population, properly so called – that is to say, a number of persons who dwell in a given place from year's end to year's end – it has none at all! It is true that if you visited Margate ten years ago, or five – last year or this – you may always have read certain names over certain doors; as, for instance, – Snackett and Shackett, Shummery and Dummery, Twitchener and Switchener, Munns and Hunns, and others; which would seem to give a sort of local identity to their possessors. This, however, proves nothing in favour of a settled and established population, and I make this assertion advisedly.

It happened to me a few years ago on Christmas day, to be shipwrecked at Ramsgate. The next day, prompted by curiosity to see how Margate looked in the winter, I paid the place a visit. Did you ever chance to go through Tunbridge Wells at the same season? The one old woman you may have seen creeping along the Pantiles, every one of its shops being shut; the one man ringing the bell at the closed doors of the 'Sussex,' which, after a delay of five minutes, are opened to him by a waiter grown fat from compulsory idleness; the other one man pacing up and down outside the 'Kent,' waiting for the arrival of the coach which passes through now only twice a week, – these are a crowd, a crush – this is gaiety running even into riot compared with what

Margate presented. All was closed! Not a living creature was to be seen! Not a sound was to be heard, save the melancholy echo of my own footsteps as I paced the desolate streets. Had I chosen to run away with the town – pier and all – I might have done so; for not even a town keeper was left in charge of it to say me nay. Yet there were the same names, – the Dummerys and the Shummerys, the Shacketts and Snacketts, – but no apparent proprietors of them. What then could have been done with them? I lately took the liberty of putting that question to one of the natives; but the answer I received from him convinced me that it is a sore subject with them. All he replied was – 'stuff, sir!' Being thus driven to my own resources for a solution of the difficulty, I will state it as my belief that at the termination of one season the resident population are all packed up and carefully put away somewhere till the commencement of another.

But the accidental population of Margate (the visitors), at the height of the season, must be utterly incalculable. This opinion is grounded upon the fact that of children alone, of which about one-third are babies in arms, it would require, if not defy, the power's of Babbage's[87] calculating machine to state the number. Oh, Herod! – It may be doubted whether so many are to be seen together on any other spot of the whole habitable globe. Then add to these the requisite allowance of wet-nurses and dry-nurses in charge of such as can and such as cannot walk for themselves; the due proportion (allowing nine little children to a family), of fathers, mothers, elder brothers and sisters, uncles and aunts, to say nothing of independent spinsters and bachelor visitors – again, I assert, the number of the temporary population of Margate is incalculable!

The salubrity of the place is unquestionable; yet I have heard doubts expressed concerning it from the very circumstances of the parents, who are blessed with more children they know well what to do with, bringing or sending them there. The loss, however, of those 'future men and women,' (as they have been interestingly called), is small; for, including those that have accidentally dropped over the pier, fallen from the cliffs, or been lost out of bathing machines, it seldom exceeds, I am told, six hundred in a season.

Margate is the classical resort of the citizens of London – the baiae[88] of Cockney land; and badinage[89] apart, a very pleasant retreat from the close

---

[87] Charles Babbage, (1791 – 1871) – an English mathematician, philosopher, inventor and mechanical engineer who originated the concept of a programmable computer.

[88] Baiae – a Roman seaside resort on the Bay of Naples.

alleys and crowded thoroughfares of the vast sleepless city it is. For drives, rides and walks as beautiful almost as are anywhere to be found, for breezes which infuse health into the frame and impart elasticity to the spirits, for the temporary oblivion, which the very genius of the place seems to compel, of the cares and annoyances by which all are, more or less, beset; above all these, for the pleasure of contemplating a greater sense of human enjoyment, manifested by a larger number of happy, laughing faces than any other place can, at any other time, exhibit, they, I say, who would enjoy all this, must, once in its season, pay a visit to Margate.

("The Mirror, Of Literature, Amusement, and Instruction," No. 926, Supplementary Number, Spirit of the Annuals for 1839, Mr John Poole's description of Margate)

This story, detailing an incident that happened around 1844, sums up the feelings of local people, both rich and poor, towards the smugglers, who were not believed to be necessarily bad people, but who were considered to be risking their lives to satisfy the demand for cheap goods. I wonder whether any of Dick Churchman's descendants are still living locally? The 'Tartar Frigate' public house in Broadstairs still exists today (2011)

Modern folk ballads

In former days almost every event that attracted popular attention was versified in rude fashion by some rustic poet, and the ballad was the common song of the lower classes. These quaint old effusions have now become nearly obsolete; and you hear instead snatches of Negro melodies, or songs from farces or comic entertainments, wherever you go, but rarely anything like the old 'folk poetry.'

A short time ago, taking a long run out to sea with some of the boatmen from Ramsgate – who I should say, par parenthese, are generally very civil and intelligent men – several of the usual tales about smuggling were narrated to me. Among the rest was the story I venture to relate below. I was also told a ballad had been written on the subject by some of the fishermen which was often sung by them; and a very touching song it is, my informant said. With some difficulty a copy was procured; and as it is probably very nearly the last of the class of poetry it is enclosed exactly as given to me.

---

[89] badinage – jesting

The story is this. About twenty years ago, an attempt was made to 'run' some tea at a 'gap,' or opening cut through the cliff down to the beach not far southward of Margate. The preventive men got scent of the matter and opposed the landing; and at last one of them fired on the smugglers and wounded one of them in the thigh a little above the knee. This man was a fine strong fellow called Dick Churchman: a first rate seaman and a great favourite all along the coast. So slight did the wound seem to him that he took no notice of it at all but kept on rowing and after six hours they landed at Broadstairs and went into a public-house there called 'The Tartar Frigate.' Whether they had succeeded in 'running their goods' or not, I was not told. However, shortly after they entered the house, Churchman for the first time complained of feeling 'a little faint' and asked for some beer, which he drank and then slipped gently off his seat and fell on the floor stone dead. It was found a small artery had been divided and the man had literally bled to death without any one of his mates having the slightest idea that he had received a serious hurt.

A report soon spread that the preventive man had cut his bullets into quarters when he loaded his piece, for the better chance of hitting the men; and in the horrible hope that the wounds inflicted by the ragged lead might be more deadly. As might have been expected, there was a tremendous burst of popular indignation and the authorities were obliged to remove the preventive man to some distant part of the country. A sort of public funeral was given to 'poor Dick Churchman' and these are the lines that record his fate. They are at once so simple and genuine; I make no apology for them, rude as they may be. At any rate it was some satisfaction to find that the spirit which had listened to the popular lay of the bard, the glee-man, the minstrel and the ballad-singer, was not wholly extinct in England.

LINES ON THE DEATH OF RICHARD CHURCHMAN

Good people give attention
To what I will unfold,
And, when this song is sung to you,
Twill make your blood run cold:

For Richard Churchman was that man
Was shot upon his post,
By one of those preventive men,
That guard along our coast.

It was two o'clock one morning,
As I've heard many say,
Like a lion bold he took his oar,
For to get under weigh:

For six long hours he laboured,
All in his bleeding gore,
Till at eight o'clock this man did faint –
Alas! He was no more!

And when this bold preventive man
Was forced to run away,
For on the New Gate station
He could no longer stay.

There was hopes they'd bring him back again,
And tie him to a post;
As a warning to all preventive men,
That guard along our coast.

Then they took him to St Lawrence church,
And he lies buried there;
All with a hearse and mourning coach,
And all his friends were there:

And sixty couples of blue-jackets[90],
With tears all in their eyes,
All for the loss of Churchman,
Unto their great surprise.

For he was beloved by all his friends,
Likewise by rich and poor;
Let's hope the men that murdered him
Will never rest no more!

("Notes and Queries" Vol. 5, 3rd S, (115), Mar 12 1864, Page 209)

---

[90] A reference to the Preventive Men

The next few extracts are taken from the widely loved Punch Magazine. One could always rely on Punch to either raise a few eyebrows or cause someone to choke on their morning coffee. Their caricatures were highly amusing – to all but the subject!

Margate at Vauxhall

Margate at Vauxhall

We understand a company has been formed for the purpose of converting Vauxhall Gardens into a bathing place, by bringing the sea-water up to town along a line of railway. The projectors have been already in negotiation with the directors of the South-Eastern for permission to introduce pipe into the sea at Folkestone harbour, and to run a main by the side of the rails to the Bricklayers' Arms, with a continuation as far as Vauxhall, where a resident turncock will be permanently stationed. There will be branch plugs at some of the intermediate stations, and a ball-cock at each terminus.

Vauxhall Gardens will be fitted up to resemble the town of Margate; the fire-work ground being dug out and lined with zinc to represent the sea, while a pair of flats at the back will realise the notion of the Marine Terrace, with Buenos Ayres in the distance, and its romantic little oyster shop nestling under it. The entrance to the gardens will be converted into a facsimile of the jetty, and a pasteboard packet will be in attendance, which will work in a groove, and give the visitors the idea that they have arrived by steamer. A set piece will be arranged on the right hand, showing the Bathing Rooms and Marine Library; to give effect to which persons will be engaged who will shake a dice-box, exclaiming, 'I want but one – only one wanted to complete the sweepstakes!' While others make bows, and observe that the 'sea is in fine order for bathing.' To complete the illusion, Margate slippers and telescopes may be had at the doors; so that the public will have an opportunity of realising, in every particular, the luxury of a trip to that favourite watering-place. The wall of the adjoining Hotel will be whitewashed, to represent the cliffs, and some of the supper-boxes will be converted into chasms on the shore; while cockle-shells will be profusely scattered about in all directions, so that nothing may be wonting to give an air of marine freshness to the locality.

("Punch," Vol. VI, 1844, p. 213)

THE RAFFLE at the LIBRARY.

"Only one wanted Ladies, who'll make one?"

The dice table

277

Margate's first railway station

The above is a picture of Margate's railway station, built in 1846 to link Margate with London. It was soon replaced by a much bigger station (below) to receive the East Kent, London, Chatham and Dover railway line. This new line was also to incorporate the new 'upmarket' Westgate-on-sea railway station.

The new Margate railway station in the 1860s

Margate theatricals

The dramatic prospects of Margate have this season materially brightened, and the theatre has been restored to its legitimate use, after doing duty as a broker's warehouse during the last two or three summers. The fortunes of the building fluctuate with the taste of the visitors and the inhabitants. Sometimes it is an auction room, sometimes a bazaar for painted tea-trays; sometimes it is a literary institution; sometimes it is a wax-work exhibition; sometimes it is a tea and coffee house; but this year it has become the sea-side asylum of the legitimate drama. A bill is now before us in which we find the following announcement:

> "On Thursday a variety of entertainments: being by desire and under the Patronage of the Captains, Officers, and Stewards of the Herne Bay Steam Packets."

We are glad that these gallant fellows are going to patronise the Margate theatre and we have no doubt that Captain Large will become 'larger than ever,' like some gigantic gooseberry tarts we once saw labelled with those words in the window of a cheap pastry cook. We understand that a private box has been taken for the inhabitants of Herne Bay on this occasion and three places in the dress boxes for the visitors, all of whom have promised to attend. By the way, who are the 'Captains, Officers, &c.' of a Herne Bay steam boat? Is the stoker an officer? Or does the grade go no lower than the brave Briton who rushes to the side of the boat with that great thing like a porter's knot, technically called a fender, in the event of a collision? We are given to understand that the 'Captains, Officers and Stewards,' will all attend the theatre in full uniform. Captain Large has ordered four additional epaulettes, intending to wear one on each elbow and two upon his breast, in addition to the ordinary pair upon the shoulders. The man at the wheel has sent up to the Admiralty to inquire what the regulation uniform will be in his case; but the Stewards have determined on adopting the costume of the unattached butlers, with the gold band of the Ancient Order of the Ale and Sandwich.

("Punch," Vol. 11, 1846, p. 122)

279

New bathing costume for 1846

A Great Man

At the opening of the branch line from Ramsgate to Margate on the South-Eastern Railway, which shortens the distance from London by making one hundred and five miles out of seventy-two, the health of Mr Cobb the brewer was proposed as that of a gentleman who 'was born great, had achieved greatness and had had greatness thrust upon him.' It is evident that the brewer is not thought small beer of in his own neighbourhood. We wonder that Margate is capable of holding so great a man with his triple amount of magnitude. To be born great is enough for some people and to achieve greatness is what few attempt to go beyond; but a gentleman who has beyond all this some more greatness thrust upon him, must really have more to bear than he can know well what to do with. Poor Mr Cobb must be as much embarrassed as the prize-bullocks who always have 'greatness thrust upon them at this festive period.'

(Punch, Vol. 11, 1846, p242)

"Can't you see nothing Joseph?" "No – they are all civered in"

Half an hour in the Isle of Thanet

Margate and its telescopes

Taking advantage of the rapidity of steam communication, which enables one to go to Margate and back on the same day, and, landing on the end of the jetty, walk to the top and return in time for the starting of the steamer on its voyage home, we threw our sandwich-box – our only luggage – into the hold and were soon steaming it in the Red Rover, Captain Large – larger than ever, by the bye – past the Bay of old Herne till we arrived at Margate.

The landlords' party must be regarded as being in the ascendant throughout Margate and nearly every one is interested as a landlord either in four stories or two, which are divided into separate holdings, for terms varying from a week, or even a day, to a month or season. The relations between a landlord and his tenant are thus by no means permanent. The whole place may, in fact, be said to derive its entire population from a system of temporary emigration which lasts during a short portion of the year and at its conclusion the landlords are left to their own resources, which are limited in the extreme. Many of the landlord party prefer wintering in a large building called the Union and leave their own domains perfectly uninhabited until the return of their tenants is expected. To tempt this class, a few beds are cultivated but beyond this the native industry of the Margatonians does not extend. These beds are the chief sources from which the landlords raise their means of support.

Beds to let

The anxiety to draw attention to these beds is so excessive, that their existence is notified at every turn to the stranger; and even the buoys in the sea are adorned with announcements of 'Beds,' 'Beds,' 'Beds.' This practice is by no means so ridiculous as it may at first appear, for the buoys are most appropriately used to call attention to those beds which enable the inhabitants to keep themselves above water. A couple of beds form, in fact, a sort of life-buoy for the summer season, preventing the unhappy native from being completely swamped.

From the aspect of Margate in the height of the season it might be imagined that an invasion was expected and that the inhabitants were prepared for the reception of some foreign enemy by making a porthole of every window and defending it with a huge gun. The different directions in which these massive machines appear to be aiming would seem to indicate that Margate was determined to be prepared for invasion at all points. It is only on a very close inspection that the truth can be ascertained that these extraordinary engines, with which Margate seems to bristle in the summer or autumn sun, are not cannons at all but telescopes, through which the inhabitants are keeping a constant look-out to count the passengers on the steam-boats and calculate the amount of bed-letting on which the hungry natives may depend.

Sightseeing at Margate

Sometimes the real nature of the instrument is ascertained in a rather disagreeable manner by a closeness of contact which it is desirable to avoid. The stranger sauntering along the cliff hears a sort of rushing or sliding sound and before he has time to look about him, there issues from a window on the basement floor a huge telescope of ninety spectacle power which in being pushed out to its proper focus, brings an object much nearer than the object itself approves. We must not, however, blame the Margate landlords who rush naturally enough to the most gigantic telescopes, or to anything else, indeed, that may improve their somewhat wretched look-out.

Mind the telescope

It is understood that they use the wrong end of the telescope to look at pieces of butter, remains of cold meat and other articles belonging to their tenants, which articles are of course reduced to mere mouthfuls too insignificant to be accounted for by the peculiar manner in which they are viewed. Thus the telescope serves a double purpose in the hand of the ingenious native of Margate.

(Punch, Vol. XII, 1847, p. 87)

Sketches in Salt and Fresh Water

'Life on the ocean waves'

If watering-places were arranged like the divisions of a theatre, Margate would be the pit and Ramsgate the dress circle. The two places of amusement almost touch one another and yet how wide apart are the people who frequent them in their manners, appearance and notions of enjoyment! A person in the pit – I mean Margate – laughs outright and is quite indifferent about his dress. In fact he would as soon take off his coat and sit in his shirt sleeves as look at you. He generally takes his provisions with him too; and, when he is thirsty, pulls out a stone jug and applies it to his lips in the faces of all the company. Far from being abashed, he passes it to his wife and holds the cork, turning away his head whilst his good lady drinks. He does not mind what people say. He has come out to enjoy himself and he is determined to do it.

How different is the company in the dress circle! I am speaking now of Ramsgate. The ladies are dressed very prettily; the gentlemen have most superior gloves and altogether the coats, gowns, opera and eye-glasses and jewellery are selected with the most fastidious taste. It is impossible for people to be more genteel but gentility, I am afraid, must be dull work. They all seem afraid to enjoy themselves. They smile occasionally and simper with the best grace but appear about as lively as if they were sitting for their portraits. They never laugh – at least heartily. When a good roar wakes them up, they look down with supreme contempt upon the pit below and wonder how people can be so vulgar?

I have now mixed in both circles and have arrived at the following pleasant conclusions: – 1st, That Ramsgate is very genteel; 2nd, That Margate is very vulgar. This means that the latter enjoys itself unreservedly, not caring twopence (which is the amount at which people, it seems, estimate the world's opinion) for what people think and that the former is afraid to appear in public and follow its impulses for fear of being considered vulgar. If the two towns could be made to amalgamate, the junction would probably be one of the pleasantest watering-places in England. The starchiness of the one would soon be taken out of it by the freedom of the other.

As for myself, I would sooner live in Margate than Ramsgate – and for this reason: that I would sooner walk in pattens than strut about on stilts any day; but, mind you, I am not fond of either.

It is a curious fact that no lady is complete at a watering-place without a watch. At Margate the watches grow to a very large size. At Ramsgate, however, the gentility is apparent again on the face of them. They are rarely bigger than fourpenny pieces. They are so small that you imagine they must be sold, like shrimps, by the pint. I should say, thirty Ramsgate watches make one Margate ditto.

Margate is populated with Bazaars. They drive a rattling trade, if I may judge from the dice-boxes. I was passing by one when a gentleman rushed out and exclaimed up and down the street, 'Only one wanted for sixpence.'

This was at noon. As I passed the same Bazaar at ten o'clock at night the same individual was at the door bawling out the same demand for the same amount of money. Good gracious! Could he have been wanting one for ten long hours and that one had not relieved his want yet? One felt ashamed of oneself! I gave him the sixpence and slept that night the sleep of the blessed!

Margate, I am afraid, is a very dissipated place since the raffling begins at twelve o'clock in the day; though the smallness of the stakes may somewhat atone for the continued extravagance. An improvement, however, has been

285

introduced into that exciting game. Ladies' dresses are now put up as some of the prizes. This is better than the old match-cases and card-holders; though, if I had won a bombasine, or a visite, I confess I should have been puzzled rather what to do with it. Gentlemen's clothing should also be admitted into the raffling, or at all events legs of mutton with trimmings, or a barrel of oysters, or a cod's head and shoulders, should occasionally be thrown into the stakes and then there would be something to please all tastes. One of the amusements at Margate is looking through the telescope. The ships in the Downs, far from moving on, like many people, if you stare at them, will stand perfectly still for days; or, if you have another hankering after the beautiful, you may amuse yourself by admiring the opposite coast of 'La Belle France', when you will be surprised how Frenchmen can make revolutions and cut each other's throats in the name of fraternity for so very little.

The touting for baths near the harbour is really as bad as the touting for bonnets used to be, I recollect in Cranbourne Alley before I went to sea. You are pulled in and almost have your clothes pulled off your back and thrown into a shower-bath before you can persuade the touters you did not come to Margate to be shocked all day. Margate must be very full. I saw a placard hanging on a bathing-machine with the tempting inscription, 'One bed to let'

The native produce of Margate is the bellman, who, with his bell, seems to be a perpetual wag and goes down with the visitors as much as Cobb's ale. There are likewise the portraits taken in shells, much better adapted, I should say, to show off the strong points of a Musselman than to delight the cockles of Englishmen. I send you two choice specimens, the best I could pick up. They are faithful likenesses of:

The Queen & Prince Albert

286

The great feature about Margate is the Jetty. The Pier is pleasant to walk on with its two stories – the ground-floor is gratis, the first floor, one penny; but it sinks to nothing by the side of that long wooden gridiron on which innocent visitors are boiled or broiled, according to the weather, at one single turn. Ladies cannot be too careful. It is a perfect trap to catch little ducks with spray feet. As the water dashes up through the open lines, it leaves no other impression on your trousers and your mind than that it must have been built originally to rule the waves. This looks all smooth and easy enough when the broad sheet of the ocean is far away but when the tide brings up the large volume of water, it is soon proved that if the Jetty rules the sea governs. The wind, too, carries hats, bonnets and everything before it and gives many a young man a lift in the world that he little expected to come from such a quarter. It is a continual game between Neptune and Jarvis' Jetty as to who shall have the upper hand. The contest is renewed every day and when one goes down the other comes up, and vice versa.

Riding a storm

It is most amusing to watch the ladies when the packets come in. They draw themselves up on the end of the Jetty opposite to one another as if they were going to dance Sir Roger de Coverley; the passengers pass down the double line, like so many convicts each man is closely surveyed – no disguise can possibly avail him – and as soon as his wife detects him, let him be ever so disfigured by nautical causes, she pounces upon him and carries him off in triumph. This arrangement must have been made for the express gratification of the Mrs Caudles of England and is much more stringent than all the passports on the Continent. Can a gendarme's eye compete in vigilance with a wife's?

Some ladies, however, are sometimes too precipitate. One lady (the shadow of Mrs Armitage) threw her arms around me, crying 'My dearest Charles.' Before she had discovered her mistake, I was nearly smothered. I advise all persons with wooden legs not to land on the Jetty. The reason must be open to the blindest imagination.

Visitors are not aware that the middle of the Jetty is covered with water long before the lower end. From the frequent accident it would seem as if the Jetty was wickedly bent on mischief in order to throw customers into the watermen's boats. The visitor perseveres with his 'Fatal Error,' when all of a sudden he feels his feet rather wet; he looks up from his novel and sees that, like Soyer's Irish soup, he is surrounded with nothing but water. The Jetty is impassable. He cannot swim. What shall he do? He has not made his will! He thinks of the dinner waiting for him at home and the water comes into his mouth. At last a boat nears him. A voice hails him. "Do you want a boat?" Why, of course he does. "What will you give?" He offers half-a-sovereign – no answer; a sovereign – no reply; the water rises higher – anything you like and he is helped off just as a rude wave knocks off his hat. What the price of his ransom was I cannot tell but judging from his person it must have been something heavy.

Never shall I forget the awful position of Mr and Mrs Fydgets when they were surprised in a similar manner. I was in the water at the time and overheard their conversation carried on under the following difficulties:

Getting caught-out by the incoming tide on Jarvis's Jetty
288

Mrs Fydgetts (screaming). "My Child! My Child!"

Mr Fydgetts. "What's the use of making that noise! Can't you be quiet?"

Mrs F. "You are a brute sir"

Mr F. "I wish I were; for then I should be able to swim."

Mrs F. "Mr Fydgetts! Ain't you a-coming to help me?"

Mr F. "No! It serves you right for bringing me down to this stupid place."

Mrs F. "I, indeed, why, I wanted to go to Brighton and you would come to Margate – you said it was cheaper."

Mr F. "It's false; I said no such thing."

Mrs F. "You did, You did!"

Mr F. "O, Woman! Woman! Where do you expect to go?"

Mrs F. "To the bottom; unless you come and help me!"

Mr F. "Help yourself. I'm s-i-n-k-i-n-g"

Mrs F. "My Child! My Child!"

Mr F. (rising from the water). "Be quiet, can't you! Woo-o-m (the rest is inaudible, but the watery pair are saved just in time, and renew their dispute in the boat as soon as they are rescued from their perilous position.

("Punch," volume 14, Mark Lemmon, Henry Mayhew, Tom Taylor, Shirley Brooks, Sir Francis Cowley Burnand, Sir Owen Seaman, 1848, pp. 113-114)

By 1853 some of Margate's famous attractions, like Tivoli, Dandelion and Ranelagh Gardens, frequented by the visiting tourists in their hundreds on a good summer's day, had gradually declined in popularity. Even though the lodging houses were crowded, the attendances at these one time 'hot spots' fell into decline. Margate's seafront appeared to be providing more than enough entertainment to cater for the majority of holiday makers who, therefore, saw no reason for costly travel out of the vicinity.

Margate in 1853

...In the 'Hoy' days there were public gardens and public breakfasts with music and dancing on well-kept lawns at Dandelion; but Dandelion is now a farm-house (though still deserving of a visit on account of the tower and picturesque gatehouse of its ancient manor-house). The Tivoli Gardens have been obscured by the high chalk viaduct of the railway; nevertheless, there are in the season piping and dancing, and fireworks, and other amusements, albeit the support given to the proprietor is but poor. It appears that there has been a general decay of custom and attendance at these places. Ranelagh, at the neighbouring village of St Peter's, though a pretty place and with good exhibitions, and music, and good appliances for dancing, has had but poor seasons of it lately, though Margate and Ramsgate and all the other lodging-places have been crowded. There is also a racecourse. The other places of resort are numerous in the town and the neighbourhood and have they not been sung of in heroic verse by Peter Theophilus Turner, Schoolmaster and Poet Laureate of Margate? There is a Bazaar and there is another Bazaar called (the godfathers of misnomers best know why!) the Boulevard, where ladies in white muslin (and measureless bustles) play upon pianos and gentlemen and ladies try the 'wheel of fortune,' and shake dice-boxes at raffles...

The Clifton Baths mentioned below was where the Lido is today – just past Fort Paragon.

...The Clifton Baths are among the delights and wonders of Margate. They are cut out of the chalk cliff, and are really curious. There are winding passages, subterranean chambers, terraces, newspapers, of course spy-glasses and an organ upon which everybody may play...

...Behind the town, in the part called the 'Dane,' is a curious grotto cut out in the chalk, and prettily and fancifully covered with shells. It has long passed for an antique but it now appears that, although the cave was old, the shell-work was done by an ingenious artisan of Margate, who some years ago went to America...

In this early mention of the Grotto it appears that people then saw it as the work of a local Margate resident, whereas today there is a school of thought which believes it to be the work of ancient peoples. With the introduction of the Grotto, the Clifton Baths and a multitude of other entertainments along Margate's seafront, it is no wonder that places like Tivoli Gardens, Dandelion and Ranelagh – which were 'off the beaten track' – were in decline.

...Such are a few of the lions of the place. But other amusements are not wanting. Italian organ-boys, image-boys, fortune-telling gipsies, bears and monkeys, a camel, hurdigurdies[91], conjurors, tumblers, fish-hawkers, shrimp-sellers, criers of fruit and vegetables, match-vendors, sellers of corn-plaster and the town bellman, keep the Fort – the choicest part of all Margate – alive

---

[91] The hurdigurdies or hurdy-gurdy is a stringed musical instrument that produces sound by a crank-turned wheel rubbing against the strings.

and ringing from eight o'clock in the morning till nine at night. And this busy and noisy tune lasts all through June, July, August and September. We have omitted many of the performers; but of one of those we have enumerated we must say a few words. And this is the Bellman – the famous Margate Bellman – in his blue coat, gilt buttons, red collar, gold lace and gold laced hat – the noble Margate Bellman! Rough and weather-beaten and who always looks tipsy without ever having been known to be so. Many are the years we have known him and his bell and his jokes. A friend, a humorist, a man of wit, who could find fun everywhere and in everything, but who, woe the while! Is gone where there is no more laughing – used to say that were there no other public amusements in Margate the public Bellman would be enough. He is a poet, our Bellman and has often been the cause of poetry in others. He announces tea and cakes, tea-gardens and skittle grounds, in rhyme; he bids you to Tivoli or St Peter's in verse; he has rhymes for auctions and lost pocket-handkerchiefs and a standing rhyming joke for a lady's lost bustle; he tells you of the departures and arrivals of steamers in rhyme and he will sell you, for fourpence, the history of his life and adventures written in verse.

Thomas 'Toby' Philpot the Bellman (1775-1857)

291

Once again we hear of the support that smuggling had, even from civic dignitaries. One can understand why smuggling was so prolific, considering the winter hardship experienced by those whose income from the short summer season was not enough to sustain them throughout the year. The fishing industry and all the other trades that supported it at Margate had gradually deteriorated before, as well as alongside, the rise in Margate's new-found industry, tourism. The following explains why smuggling became one of the alternatives to the workhouse (the Union) when the summer season drew to a close:

...As for the natives they are nearly all lodging-house keepers or letters of lodgings or bedrooms. They work very hard during the season and seem to care about doing very little during the other eight months of the year. About the middle of September the boats and the trains come down almost empty and go back full and this reflux of population to London soon leaves Margate as quiet as a town can be. Then the matrons of the place count their gains and take their ease and pleasure. The husbands – who take things easily during the toils of summer – are not very profitable during the long winter months unless they are sailors, or fishermen, or boatmen – there is not much that others can turn their hand to. Industry is at a low ebb at Margate – manufacturers there are none; only a few ropes are spun and a few fishing nets are made. But even the most steady and industrious of the sailors get but precarious earnings during the winter months. As matters are, the sailors and boatmen have nothing to count upon during so many months but the inshore fishing (often very unproductive), and 'hovelling.' We believe there was formerly a distinction between the various sorts of occupation; but 'hovelling' now means carrying off provisions to a vessel, or aiding any vessel that may need assistance, or carrying off anchors, or looking after the fragments or cargo of such vessels as may be wrecked on the Goodwin Sands, &c.

Many poor fellows are obliged to give up fishing altogether and to depend wholly upon hovelling and their summer savings. They thrive most when the winter is stormy. At times they get good salvage – dividing as much as £50, or £100, or even £150 and more among six, eight, or ten. When extraordinarily fortunate, a man may get as much as £50 for helping to save a ship from wreck. But these gains are very precarious, many are constantly on the look-out for ships and generally the first boat that reaches the distressed ship gets all the prize. A considerable number of the best of these hovellers have lately, however, associated together, upon the principle that whatever is gained by any boat or party of them shall be thrown into a common stock and then divided, share and share alike. This renders the gains of the calling somewhat more steady. The Admiralty Droits, the dues of the Lord Warden of the

Cinque Ports, &c., materially diminish the profits obtained by the recovery of wrecked property.

During the winter and whenever the weather is stormy or threatening, telescopes are employed to much better purpose than by the summer visitants. The pier-head is constantly lined by a few fellows in dreadnought coats looking seaward with their glasses; a sharp look-out is kept from the Fort and from other points: every part of the wide expanse of water – and at Margate you have very nearly the whole arc of the circle – that is constantly swept by glasses; vigilant night watches are kept; and at any sight or sound of distress at sea boats are launched and manned and then away out to sea however rough it may be, or however hard or from whatsoever quarter the wind may blow. Not a winter but these good fellows save some lives. By a strange mis-arrangement there are rewards for saving goods but none for rescuing mariners or passengers from their watery grave. This ought to be altered in the proper quarter; and Foreign Consuls ought to be enabled by their respective governments to act with rather more liberality than they are accustomed to do towards sailors who have risked their lives in saving the lives of strangers.

It may be supposed that the winter amusements of Margate are few enough. The best of them is to be found in a smart walk on the Pier and a long 'yarn' from these mariners and hovellers. They have good tales to tell and some of them can tell them well. Besides shipwrecks and founderings and swampings and drownings close to the beach, their stories and still more their traditions, embrace the adventures and hap-hazards of smuggling. When the Magistrates of the place thought it no disgrace to join in this illicit traffic; when nearly every man in the Isle of Thanet from Reculver to Pegwell Bay and the Richborough mouth of the Stour, would, without scruple, speculate in smuggled goods, or purchase them for his own consumption, the trade was carried on most extensively and without any dishonour. That time is not very remote; but it may be said to have passed. Little, we believe very little, remains of smuggling, except the stories which are told about it.

Of the salubrity of Margate we must speak highly. We think it by far the healthiest place in the Isle of Thanet – we think the Fort one of the healthiest spots in England. Though so much exposed to the wind, it is during the winter some degrees warmer than any place in the neighbourhood of London. In the summer there are some complaints which it may not suit; but, generally speaking, the sick seem to recover their health there in a surprising manner.

About 2 miles from Margate is the North Foreland, a promontory so called to distinguish it from another promontory called the 'South Foreland,' between Deal and Dover. It was well known to the Roman seaman under the name of

Cantium Promontorium. The lighthouse which has long stood on this point is not a very picturesque or striking object; but the dangerous neighbourhood of the Goodwin Sands, which lie off the promontory, renders it one of the most useful of our lighthouses. The sea views along the summit of the North Foreland Cliff are remarkably fine.

("Knight's, Tourist's Companion, through the land we live in," 1853, pp. 8-12)

By the end of this period, 1815 – 1853, the railways had arrived in Margate, heralding a new era for Margate. Huge numbers of day trippers as well as holiday makers descended on Margate via this safer, faster, cleaner and cheaper mode of transport – but this era would need to be the subject of a book of its own!

Other publications from Ōzaru Books

Reflections in an Oval Mirror

Anneli Jones

8th May 1945 — VE Day — was Anneliese Wiemer's twenty-second birthday. Although she did not know it then, it marked the end of her flight to the West, and the start of a new life in England.

These illustrated memoirs, based on a diary kept during the Third Reich and letters rediscovered many decades later, depict the momentous changes occurring in Europe against a backcloth of everyday farm life in East Prussia (now the north-western corner of Russia, sandwiched between Lithuania and Poland).

The political developments of the 1930s (including the Hitler Youth, 'Kristallnacht', political education, labour service, war service, and interrogation) are all the more poignant for being told from the viewpoint of a romantic young girl. In lighter moments she also describes student life in Vienna and Prague, and her friendship with Belgian and Soviet prisoners of war. Finally, however, the approach of the Red Army forces her to abandon her home and flee across the frozen countryside, encountering en route a cross-section of society ranging from a 'lady of the manor', worried about her family silver, to some concentration camp inmates.

ISBN: 978-0-9559219-0-2

Travels in Taiwan

Gary Heath

For many Westerners, Taiwan is either a source of cheap electronics or an ongoing political problem. It is seldom highlighted as a tourist destination, and even those that do visit rarely venture far beyond the well-trod paths of the major cities and resorts.

Yet true to its 16th century Portuguese name, the 'beautiful island' has some of the highest mountains in East Asia, many unique species of flora and fauna, and several distinct indigenous peoples (fourteen at the last count).

On six separate and arduous trips, Gary Heath deliberately headed for the areas neglected by other travel journalists, armed with several notebooks... and a copy of War and Peace for the days when typhoons confined him to his tent. The fascinating land he discovered is revealed here.

ISBN: 978-0-9559219-1-9

Turner's Margate Through Contemporary Eyes
The Viney Letters

Stephen Channing

Margate in the early 19th Century was an exciting town, where smugglers and 'preventive men' fought to outwit each other, while artists such as JMW Turner came to paint the glorious sunsets over the sea. One of the young men growing up in this environment decided to set out for Australia to make his fortune in the Bendigo gold rush.

Half a century later, having become a pillar of the community, he began writing a series of letters and articles for Keble's Gazette, a publication based in his home town. In these, he described Margate with great familiarity (and tremendous powers of recall), while at the same time introducing his English readers to the "latitudinarian democracy" of a new, "young Britain".

Viney's interests covered a huge range of topics, from Thanet folk customs such as Hoodening, through diatribes on the perils of assigning intelligence to dogs, to geological theories including suggestions for the removal of sandbanks off the English coast "in obedience to the sovereign will and intelligence of man".

His writing is clearly that of a well-educated man, albeit with certain Victorian prejudices about the colonies that may make those with modern sensibilities wince a little. Yet above all, it is interesting because of the light it throws on life in a British seaside town some 180 years ago.

This book also contains numerous contemporary illustrations.

ISBN: 978-0-9559219-2-6

Sunflowers
– Le Soleil –

Shimako Murai

A play in one act
Translated from the Japanese by Ben Jones

Hiroshima is synonymous with the first hostile use of an atomic bomb. Many people think of this occurrence as one terrible event in the past, which is studied from history books.

Shimako Murai and other 'Women of Hiroshima' believe otherwise: for them, the bomb had after-effects which affected countless people for decades, effects that were all the more menacing for their unpredictability – and often, invisibility.

This is a tale of two such people: on the surface successful modern women, yet each bearing underneath hidden scars as horrific as the keloids that disfigured Hibakusha on the days following the bomb.

ISBN: 978-0-9559219-3-3

Ichigensan
– The Newcomer –

David Zoppetti

Translated from the Japanese by Takuma Sminkey

Ichigensan is a novel which can be enjoyed on many
levels – as a delicate, sensual love story, as a depiction of
the refined society in Japan's cultural capital Kyoto, and as
an exploration of the themes of alienation and prejudice
common to many environments, regardless of the
boundaries of time and place.

Unusually, it shows Japan from the eyes of both an
outsider and an 'internal' outcast, and even more unusually,
it originally achieved this through sensuous prose carefully
crafted by a non-native speaker of Japanese. The fact that
this best-selling novella then won the Subaru Prize, one of
Japan's top literary awards, and was also nominated for the
Akutagawa Prize is a testament to its unique narrative
power.

The story is by no means chained to Japan, however, and
this new translation by Takuma Sminkey will allow readers
world-wide to enjoy the multitude of sensations engendered
by life and love in an alien culture.

ISBN: 978-0-9559219-4-0

Lightning Source UK Ltd.
Milton Keynes UK

172690UK00002B/6/P